Real Estate Resource Book
Fourth Edition

Bruce Harwood
John Ellis

A Reston Book
Prentice-Hall
Englewood Cliffs, New Jersey 07632

REAL ESTATE RESOURCE BOOK, Fourth Edition

Bruce Harwood/John Ellis

ISBN: 0-8359-6555-4

Copyright 1986, 1983, 1980, 1977 by Prentice-Hall
A Division of Simon & Schuster, Inc.
Englewood Cliffs, New Jersey 07632

A Reston Book
Published by Prentice-Hall
A Division of Simon & Schuster, Inc.
Englewood Cliffs, New Jersey 07632

10   9   8   7   6   4   3

Printed in the United States of America.

Contents

This workbook is designed to accompany both

REAL ESTATE PRINCIPLES, Fourth Edition

and

REAL ESTATE: AN INTRODUCTION TO THE PROFESSION, Fourth Edition.

If you are using the latter book, there are

footnotes in each chapter indicating the

questions you may omit.

ACKNOWLEDGMENT

A special thanks is extended by the authors to the following persons for their help in reviewing this edition of the Real Estate Resource Book. They are: Betty Barrett, Tom Cook, Mary Elliott, Barney Fletcher, Jeffrey Keil, Paul Metzger, Herb Porter and Dennis Tosh.

A NOTE OF EXPLANATION REGARDING THE ANSWER KEYS IN THIS BOOK

The solutions for each chapter's questions and problems are located at the end of that chapter. In addition to the correct letter answer, you will receive an explanation of that answer. Why did your authors place the answers at the end of the chapters rather than at the end of the book, or not in the book at all? The reasons are that we want the Real Estate Resource Book to be a learning tool for you as well as a testing tool, and we want the book to be convenient for you to use.

Your authors recommend that you answer each question and work each problem before looking for its answer. This will be your opportunity to see if you understand what you have read in the textbook. Also, you will gain experience in test taking that you can apply in the classroom and for license examination. After you have worked the question or problem to the best of your ability, then look for the answer and read the explanation. This will tell you if you are correct and the explanation will serve as reinforcement of your study. Do not give in to the temptation of looking in the answer key first, thereby letting the answer key do the job of answering for you. Doing so will give you a false sense of security because in the real world, there is no answer key at the back of each chapter, only the results of your choices.

Nature and Description of Real Estate

Chapter 2

1. The term "real estate" includes
   I.   the right to use land.
   II. anything affixed to land with the intent of being permanent.
   III. rights to the air above the land.
   IV. rights to subsurface minerals.
   A. I only
   B. I, III and IV only
   C. II, III and IV only
   D. I, II, III and IV

2. Determining what is a fixture and what is not is important when
   I.   property taxes are calculated.
   II. real estate is mortgaged.
   III. a tenant attaches an object to a rented building.
   IV. hazard insurance is purchased.
   A. I, II and III only
   B. II, III and IV only
   C. I, III and IV only
   D. I, II, III and IV

3. Benson conveyed land to Rose by means of a deed which described the land
   but made no mention of buildings or improvements. Does this deed convey
   ownership of the buildings and improvements to Rose?
   A. Yes, because once they are permanently installed, buildings and
      improvements cannot be separated from the land.
   B. Yes, because buildings and improvements are considered to be part of
      the land.
   C. No, buildings and improvements are classified as personal property.
   D. No, because buildings and improvements must be conveyed by separate
      bill of sale.

4. Things which the law considers to be permanently attached to the earth are
   called
   A. fixtures.
   B. emblements.
   C. surface rights.
   D. subsurface rights.

Note: If you are reading <u>Real Estate: An Introduction to the Profession</u>
      you may omit the following questions: 46--49.

5. Property which is not considered to be real estate is called
   A. littoral property.   C. riparian property.
   B. personal property.   D. private property.

6. In determining whether an article of personal property has become a
   fixture, which of the following tests would NOT be applied?
   A. The manner of attachment.
   B. The cost of the article.
   C. The adaptation of the article to the land.
   D. The existence of an agreement between the parties.

7. Which of the following would be considered to be fixtures because of the
   manner of their attachment to the property?
       I. A fireplace grate and andirons.
      II. A set of fire tools for a fireplace.
   A. I only   C. Both I and II
   B. II only   D. Neither I nor II

8. In remodeling their home, the Wades put the items described below in the
   home. Once in place all would be fixtures EXCEPT:
   A. an oriental throw rug in the front entry hall.
   B. the built-in kitchen range.
   C. the built-in dishwasher.
   D. custom fitted wall-to-wall carpet installed over plywood sub-
      flooring.

9. Able has rented a commercial building for the operation of a printing
   shop. He has installed shelves which are fastened to the walls, and
   printing equipment which is bolted to the floor. Are these now the
   property of the landlord?
   A. Yes, because they are installed in a permanent manner.
   B. Yes, because their removal will damage the property.
   C. No, because they are not specifically adapted to the property.
   D. No, because trade fixtures remain the property of the tenant if
      removed before expiration of the lease.

10. If a tenant in a rented house installs wall-to-wall carpet for his own
    pleasure and comfort,
        I. it may be removed upon expiration of the lease if the lease
           provides for its removal.
       II. it may be removed prior to the termination of the lease if the
           property is not damaged by its removal.
    A. I only   C. Both I and II
    B. II only   D. Neither I nor II

11. Prior to offering his home for sale, an owner removed the toilets from
    from all the bathrooms. Was he within his rights in doing this?
    A. Yes, because he removed them before offering the property for sale.
    B. Yes, because they were personal property.
    C. No, because they were adapted to the property.
    D. No, because fixtures become a permanent part of the realty.

12. Which of the following are NOT classified as real property?
    A. Fixtures.   C. A shrub planted in the ground.
    B. Emblements.   D. Air rights.

13. Easements, rights-of-way and condominium parking stalls are examples of
    A. emblements.   C. riparian rights.
    B. trade fixtures.   D. appurtenances.

14. The right of an owner to use water from a stream for his own use is called
    A. an emblement right.   C. a littoral right.
    B. a riparian right.   D. a percolating right.

15. Holmes owns a farm which borders on one bank of Dodge Creek. He wants to use water from the creek for irrigation. Is he entitled to do so?
    A. Yes, because Holmes has absolute ownership of the water flowing past his land.
    B. Yes, because he has riparian rights to use water from the creek.
    C. No, because the water belongs to the state and not to any private owner.
    D. No, because his land borders on only one bank of the creek.

16. Underground water which is not confined to a defined underground waterway is called
    A. appropriated water.   C. table water.
    B. percolating water.   D. littoral water.

17. The term "water table" refers to
    A. the level at which water will be located.
    B. the difference between the high and low water marks in a stream.
    C. sea level at high tide.
    D. sea level at low tide.

18. The lease on Ford's rented house identified the property as 645 West Maple Avenue, Grandview, Anystate. Assuming this to be the correct address of the property, is this an adequate means of identifying the property in the lease?
    A. No, because it does not contain a complete legal description of the property.
    B. Yes, it is sufficiently accurate for use in a residential lease contract.
    C. No, because if the street name or number were ever changed, the property could not be identified.
    D. No, because all contracts dealing with real estate must contain a complete legal description by metes and bounds or government rectangular survey.

19. The use of informal reference in land description is usually limited to
    I. instruments placed in the public record.
    II. situations where convenience is more important than precision.
    A. I only   B. II only   C. Both I and II   D. Neither I nor II

20. Which of the following land description methods identifies a parcel of land by specifying its shape and boundaries?
   I.   Metes and bounds.   III. Recorded plat.
   II. Government survey.   IV.   Assessor's parcel number.
   A. I, III and IV only   C. I only
   B. II only   D. I, II, III and IV

21. The major drawbacks of the early land descriptions were
   I.   the possible lack of convenient monuments or boundaries.
   II. the possibility that monuments or boundaries could be moved or might disappear.
   A. I only   B. II only   C. Both I and II   D. Neither I nor II

22. Which of the following have been utilized as monuments to designate the corner of a parcel of land in the metes and bounds description of the land?
   I.   An iron pipe driven in the ground.
   II.   A tree.
   III. A fence corner.
   IV.   A pile of rocks.
   A. I and II only   C. I, II and III only
   B. I and IV only   D. I, II, III and IV

23. The term "point of beginning" refers to
   A. a permanent reference marker.
   B. the first corner of the parcel to be surveyed.
   C. a benchmark.
   D. the intersection of a principal meridian with its base line.

24. 1/60th of 1/60th of 1/360th of a circle is known as a
   I.   degree.
   II.   minute.
   III. second.
   A. I only   B. II only   C. III only   D. Not I, II or III

25. As measured from north, an angular bearing of 135° would be equivalent to which of the following in a surveyor's description of the same angle?
   A. S 45° W   C. N 45° E
   B. N 45° W   D. S 45° E

26. Goodwin, a surveyor, was called upon to make a metes and bounds survey of an irregularly shaped parcel of land. Which of the following statements would be correct?
   I.   Goodwin could travel in either a clockwise or counter-clockwise direction in making the survey.
   II.   Goodwin must always travel in a clockwise direction in making the survey.
   III. The angular bearings of all boundary lines would be measured from north.
   IV.   The corner where the survey was begun would be identified as the point of beginning.
   A. I, III and IV only   C. I and IV only
   B. II, III and IV only   D. II and IV only

27. In the rectangular survey system of land descriptions, which of the following run in a north-south direction?
   I. Principal meridians.   III. Longitude lines.
   II. Guide meridians.   IV. Standard parallels.
   A. I, II, III and IV   C. I, II and III only
   B. I, II and IV only   D. I and II only

28. East-west lines in the government rectangular survey system are known as
   I. base lines.
   II. guide meridians.
   A. I only   B. II only   C. Both I and II   D. Neither I nor II

29. In the U. S. public land survey system, each 24-by-24 mile area created by the guide meridians and correction lines is called a
   I. check.
   II. quadrangle.
   A. I only   B. II only   C. Both I and II   D. Neither I nor II

30. In a diagram of a township, section 10 lies directly south of section
   A. 3   C. 16
   B. 4   D. 15

31. A township is
   A. six miles square.   C. six square miles.
   B. one mile square.   D. one square mile.

32. A line of townships running in a north-south direction in a rectangular survey is known as a
   A. section.   C. base line.
   B. range.   D. township.

33. Forty-three thousand, five hundred and sixty is the number of square feet in
   A. an acre.   C. a township.
   B. a section.   D. a tier.

34. How many square miles are there in a section?
   A. 640   C. 6
   B. 36   D. 1

35. Which of the following is a true statement?
   I. All sections of land contain exactly 640 acres.
   II. All townships are exactly 6 miles square.
   A. I only   B. II only   C. Both I and II   D. Neither I nor II

36. The NW 1/4 of the NW 1/4 of the NW 1/4 of a section of land contains
   A. 80 acres.   C. 20 acres.
   B. 10 acres.   D. 40 acres.

37. Standard equipment of a land survey team includes all of the following EXCEPT:
   A. transit.   C. sight pole.
   B. steel tape.   D. pocket compass.

38. The system of land description which identifies land by reference to a recorded plat may be referred to by any of the following terms EXCEPT:
    A. recorded survey system.   C. recorded map system.
    B. lot-block-tract system.   D. assessor's parcel system.

39. An assessor's parcel number
    I. is the final authority for the legal description of a parcel of land.
    II. is often used as a legal description in a deed.
    A. I only   B. II only   C. Both I and II   D. Neither I nor II

40. A formal land description by reference to documents other than maps can be based on
    I. a recorded deed.
    II. a recorded mortgage.
    III. an assessor's parcel number.
    A. I only   B. II only   C. I and II only   D. I, II and III

41. Several states use a state-sponsored set of intersection survey points based on latitude and longitude that is known as a
    I. grid system.
    II. coordinate system.
    A. I only   B. II only   C. Both I and II   D. Neither I nor II

42. The point, line or surface from which vertical height or depth is measured in a vertical land description is called a
    I. plat.
    II. datum.
    A. I only   B. II only   C. Both I and II   D. Neither I nor II

43. When describing sub-surface mineral rights, the datum chosen can be
    I. a bench mark set by government survey teams.
    II. the surface of the parcel.
    A. I only   B. II only   C. Both I and II   D. Neither I nor II

44. In describing an air lot, the description will include
    I. identification of the parcel of land over which the air lot exists.
    II. the elevation of the air lot over the parcel.
    A. I only   B. II only   C. Both I and II   D. Neither I nor II

45. A contour map shows
    I. topographical features of the land.
    II. hills, valleys, etc.
    A. I only   B. II only   C. Both I and II   D. Neither I nor II

46. Which of the following is NOT a physical characteristic of land?
    A. Immobility.   C. Nonhomogeneity.
    B. Indestructibility.   D. Fungibility.

47. Generally recognized economic characteristics of land include
    I. scarcity.   III. permanence of investment.
    II. modification.   IV. situs.
    A. I, II and III only   C. I, II, III and IV
    B. I, II and IV only   D. I, III and IV only

48. Because one parcel of land cannot be precisely substituted for another, it is said to be
    A. nonfungible.   C. fungible.
    B. immobile.   D. mobile.

49. Area preference in the location of land is described as
    I. fixity.
    II. situs.
    A. I only   B. II only   C. Both I and II   D. Neither I nor II

50. It has been said that the three most important factors when buying real estate are "location, location, and location." To what characteristic of real estate does this statement refer?
    A. Scarcity   C. Indestructibility
    B. Modification   D. Situs

Tests of a Fixture

Indicate whether the following articles would be classified as fixtures or personal property.

1. Mail box, on post in ground
   A. Fixture
   B. Personal property

2. Custom-fitted storm windows
   A. Fixture
   B. Personal property

3. Perennial shrubbery
   A. Fixture
   B. Personal property

4. Dining room chandelier
   A. Fixture
   B. Personal property

5. Kitchen cabinets
   A. Fixture
   B. Personal property

6. Warm air furnace
   A. Fixture
   B. Personal property

7. Table fan, plugged in
   A. Fixture
   B. Personal property

8. Tree
   A. Fixture
   B. Personal property

9. Child's backyard swing set
   A. Fixture
   B. Personal property

10. Barn
    A. Fixture
    B. Personal property

11. Fence around barnyard
    A. Fixture
    B. Personal property

12. Garden tractor
    A. Fixture
    B. Personal property

13. Crops in vegetable garden
    A. Fixture
    B. Personal property

14. TV antenna installed on roof
    A. Fixture
    B. Personal property

15. Kitchen sink
    A. Fixture
    B. Personal property

Lot Types

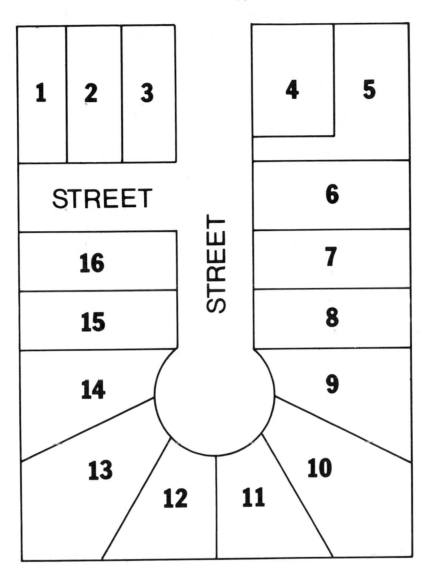

In the above subdivision plat, which lot numbers are

A. cul de sac lots? _____9, 10, 11, 12, 13, 14_____

B. flag lots? _____9, 10, 11, 12, 13, 14_____

C. corner lots? _____3, 4, 6_____

D. inside lots? _____1, 2, 5, 6 7, 8, 15, 16_____

E. key lots? _____

F. T-lots? _____5_____

Subdivision Plat

From the accompanying plat, answer the following 12 questions.

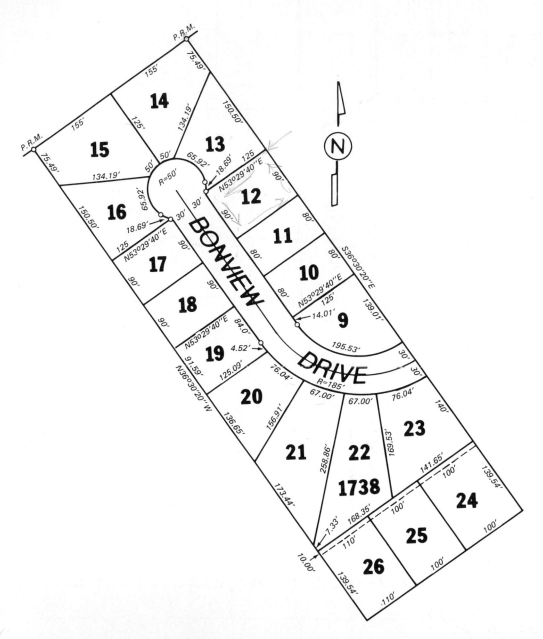

1. From the following metes and bounds description, identify the parcel of land described:
   "Beginning at a permanent reference marker located at the northernmost corner of lot 14, 225.99 feet on course S 36° 30' 20" E to the point of true beginning, thence 125 feet on course S 53° 29' 40" W, thence 90 feet on course S 36° 30' 20" E, thence 125 feet on course N 53° 29' 40" E, thence 90 feet on course N 36° 30' 20" W to the point of true beginning."
   This describes: A. Lot 10   B. Lot 11   C. Lot 12   D. Lot 13

Subdivision Plat (cont'd.)

2. A house built on lot 22, block 1738 would face approximately
    A. north.   C. east.
    B. south.   D. west.

3. Which of the following lots do not contain an equal number of square feet?
    A. 14 and 15   C. 11 and 12
    B. 13 and 16   D. 17 and 18

4. The area of lot 24 is approximately
    A. 1,395 square feet.   C. 19,590 square feet.
    B. 1,959 square feet.   D. 13,950 square feet.

5. Bonview Drive is
    A. 30 feet wide.   C. 60 feet wide.
    B. 50 feet wide.   D. 185 feet wide.

6. The circle at the end of Bonview Drive is
    A. 30 feet in diameter.   C. 60 feet in diameter.
    B. 50 feet in diameter.   D. 100 feet in diameter.

7. The frontage of lot 16 is
    A. 18.69 feet.   C. 84.61 feet.
    B. 65.92 feet.   D. 150.50 feet.

8. Which of the following lots have the same frontage?
        I. Lots 20 and 23.
       II. Lots 21 and 22.
    A. I only   B. II only   C. Both I and II   D. Neither I nor II

9. The angle formed by the lot lines in the northernmost corner of lot 12 is
    A. exactly 45 degrees.   C. exactly 180 degrees.
    B. exactly 90 degrees.   D. can't tell.

10. How many degrees are there between due north and S 36° 30' 20" E?
    (Shortest way around.)
    A. 36° 30' 20"   C. 143° 29' 40"
    B. 126° 30' 20"   D. 216° 30' 20"

11. The plat shows a ten-foot-wide utilities easement running along the
    backyards of
        I. lots 22 and 23.
       II. lots 24, 25 and 26.
    A. I only   B. II only   C. Both I and II   D. Neither I nor II

12. The depth of lot 26 is
    A. 110.0 feet   C. 139.54 feet
    B. 129.54 feet   D. 146.87 feet

Rectangular Survey

Use the following section of land diagram for the next 10 questions.

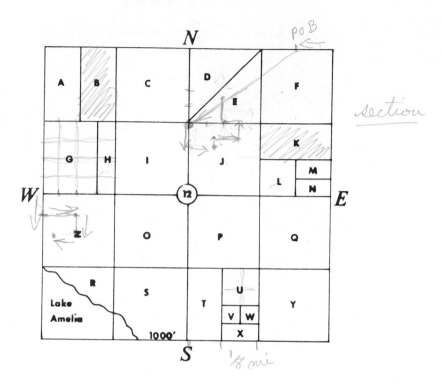

1. The NE 1/4 of the SW 1/4 of the SE 1/4 of Section 12 is identified as parcel
   A. L   C. U
   B. W   D. F

2. How many acres are in parcel H?
   A. 10   C. 30
   B. 20   D. 40

3. The N 1/2 of the SE 1/4 of the NE 1/4 of Section 12 is identified as parcel
   A. L   C. B
   B. K   D. M

4. What are the dimensions of parcel X?
   A. 2640' x 1320'   C. 1320' x 660'
   B.   660' x 330'   D. 1320' x 1320'

5. The total acreage of parcels Q and Y is
   A. 160 acres   C. 20 acres
   B.   40 acres   D. 80 acres

6. Locate and shade in the E 1/2 of the NW 1/4 of the NW 1/4 of Section 12.
   This is identified as parcel
   A. A   C. D
   B. B   D. F

7. Locate and shade in the N 1/2 of the SE 1/4 of the NE 1/4 of Section 12. This is identified as parcel

   A. K   C. M
   B. L   D. N

8. The NW 1/4 of the SE 1/4 of the SW 1/4 of the SE 1/4 of Section 12 is is identified as parcel

   A. U   C. M
   B. W   D. V

9. Identify the parcel of land described as follows:
   Beginning at the NW corner of the SW 1/4 of Section 12, South for a distance of 1320 feet to the point of beginning, thence 2640 feet easterly, thence 1320 feet southerly, thence 1000 feet westerly, thence northwesterly along the shore of Lake Amelia to the point of beginning.

       I. This describes the land in parcels Z, O, R, & S.
      II. This describes land in parcels R & S only.

   A. I only   B. II only   C. Both I and II   D. Neither I nor II

10. Locate and shade in the parcel described as follows:
    Beginning at the NE corner of Section 12, westerly for a distance of 1320 feet, to the point of true beginning, thence on course S 45° W to the NW corner of the SW 1/4 of the NE 1/4, thence southerly for 1320 feet, thence easterly for 1980 feet, thence northerly for 330 feet, thence easterly for 660 feet, thence northerly for 330 feet, thence westerly for 1320 feet, thence northerly for 1980 feet to the point of true beginning.

    Land described in this parcel is located in parcels

    A. F, E, J, L, & M.
    B. D, E, J, K, L, & M.
    C. E, J, L, & N.
    D. E, J, L, & M.

Answers—Chapter 2

Multiple Choice Questions

1. D   The term "real estate" includes rights to use land, air rights, sub-surface rights, and anything permanently attached to the land.

2. D   Determining what is a fixture is important when taxes are calculated, real estate is mortgaged, hazard insurance is purchased, and when a tenant attaches an object to a rented building.

3. B   The deed conveys ownership of the buildings and improvements as well as the land because they are considered to be a part of the land.

4. A   Fixtures are things which the law considers to be permanently attached to the earth.

5. B   Any property which is not considered to be real estate is classified as personal property.

6. B   The cost of the article has no bearing on whether an article has become a fixture; but the manner of attachment, its adaptation to the land, and the existence of an agreement between the parties would be considered.

7. D   Neither a fireplace grate and andirons nor a set of fire tools would be considered a fixture because they are not permanently attached to the property.

8. A   An oriental throw rug would not be a fixture, but built-in appliances and custom-fitted wall-to-wall carpet installed over plywood sub-flooring would be.

9. D   Personal property installed in a rented building by a tenant for the operation of a business is a trade fixture, and remains the property of the tenant if removed before expiration of the lease.

10. C   Tenant-installed fixtures may be removed upon expiration of a lease if the lease provides for their removal, and prior to the termination of the lease if the property is not damaged by their removal. *carpeting*

11. A   Fixtures may be removed prior to the offering of a property for sale. *toilets*

12. B   Emblements are personal property; but fixtures, shrubbery and air rights are classified as real property.

13. D   An appurtenance is a right, privilege, or improvement which belongs to and runs with the land. Easements, rights-of-way and condominium parking stalls meet this test.

14. B   Riparian rights permit an owner to use water from a stream which abuts his land.

15. B   The owner of land which abuts a stream has riparian rights to use water from the stream.

16. B   Percolating water is water which is not confined to a defined underground waterway.

17. A   The level at which water will be located is known as the water table.

18. B   A street address is sufficiently accurate for use in a residential lease contract, but not in most other real estate contracts.

19. B   Informal references are normally used only in situations where convenience is more important than precision.

20. C   A metes and bounds description identifies a parcel of land by specifying its shape and boundaries, but neither a government survey, recorded plat, nor assessor's parcel number do so.

21. C   The possible lack of convenient monuments or boundaries and the possibility that monuments or boundaries could be moved were both drawbacks of the early land descriptions.

22. D   Any permanent identifiable object may be used as a monument in a metes and bounds description.

23. B   The first corner of a parcel of land to be surveyed is known as the point of beginning.

24. C   A second is 1/60th of a minute, which is 1/60th of a degree, which is one 360th of a circle.

25. D   To determine: Add the distance from North to East, 90 degrees, and add one-half the distance from East to South, 45 degrees. Total equals 135 degrees.

26. C   The surveyor may travel in either direction, but will always begin at a corner identified as the point of beginning. The angular bearings are measured from north or south toward east or west. *metes & bounds*

27. C. Principal meridians, guide meridians, and longitude lines run north-south. Standard parallels run east-west.

28. A   Base lines run in an east-west direction. Guide meridians run north-south.

29. C   A check or quadrangle measures 24 by 24 miles and is created by the guide meridians and correction lines.

30. A   Sections are numbered as follows: 6   5   4   3   2   1
                                                                           7   8   9   10   11   12
Section 10 lies directly south of section 3.

31. A   A township consists of 36 sections, is six miles on a side, and contains 36 square miles.

32.   B   Ranges run in a north-south direction, and are identified by counting them east or west of the principal meridian.

33.   A   An acre is any parcel of land, in any shape, which contains exactly 43,560 square feet.

34.   D   A section of land measures 1 mile on a side and contains one square mile (1 x 1 = 1).

35.   D   Because of the convergence of the meridians toward the north pole, correction lines must be made which alter the shape of some sections and townships so that they are not precisely square in shape, and thus do not contain exactly 640 acres.

36.   B   1/4 x 1/4 x 1/4 = 1/64th
            640 x 1/64th = 10 acres.

37.   D   A pocket compass would not be standard equipment of a land survey team, but a transit, steel tape and sight pole would be.

38.   D   The terms "recorded survey system," "lot-block-tract system" and "recorded map system" all refer to identification of land by a recorded plat. The assessor's parcel system has its own reference system.

39.   D   An assessor's parcel system is not the final authority for the legal description of a parcel of land, nor is it to be used as a legal description in a deed.

40.   C   A formal land description may be based on a recorded deed or a recorded mortgage, but not on an assessor's parcel number.

41.   C   A "grid system" or "coordinate system" based on latitude and longitude is used in several states.

42.   B   Datum is the point, line or surface from which vertical height or depth is measured in a vertical land description. A plat is a map showing the boundaries of a parcel of land.

43.   C   Either a benchmark set by a government survey team or the surface of the parcel may be used as the datum to describe subsurface minerals.

44.   C   Both the elevation and identification of the parcel of land over which it exists are used to describe an air lot.

45.   C   Topographical features such as hills, valleys, etc. are shown on a contour map.

46.   D   Fungibility is not a characteristic of land, but immobility, indestructibility, and nonhomogeneity are all charactistics of land (note that fungible means freely substitutable).

47.   C   Scarcity, modification, permanence of investment and situs are all economic characteristics of land.

48. A   One parcel of land cannot be precisely substituted for another, and thus land is nonfungible.

49. B   The term "situs" refers to the preference of people for a given location. Fixity refers to the fact that land requires a long time to pay for itself.

50. D   "Location, location and location" means that people will pay more for certain preferred sites than for other sites.

Tests of a Fixture

1. A	4. A	7. B	10. A	13. B
2. A	5. A	8. A	11. A	14. A
3. A	6. A	9. B	12. B	15. A

Lot Types

A. cul de sac lots: 9, 10, 11, 12, 13, 14
B. flag lots: 5
C. corner lots: 3, 16
D. inside lots: 1, 2, 4, 6, 7, 8, 15
E. key lots: 2, 15
F. T-lots: 6

Subdivision Plat

1. C   This describes lot 12. You begin at the northernmost P.R.M., then travel 225.99 feet in a southeasterly direction to the northern corner of lot 12 and thence around lot 12 in a clockwise direction as instructed in the problem.

2. A   Lot 22 faces north. (The facing side of a lot is the street side.)

3. C   Lot 11 is 80' by 125' and lot 12 is 90' by 125'. All the other pairs are of equal square footage.

4. D   Lot 24 is 100' x 139.54' = 13,954 sqft, which is approximately 13,950 sqft.

5. C   Bonview Drive is 30' from each side to the center, hence a total width of 60'.

6. D   The radius shown for the Bonview circle is R = 50'; hence the diameter is twice that or 100'.

7. C   Lot 16 has frontage of 65.92' plus 18.69', for a total frontage of 84.61'.

8. C   Lot 20 has 76.04' of street frontage, as does lot 23. Lot 21 has 67.00' of street frontage, as does lot 22.

9. B   The northern corner of lot 12 is formed by the intersection of lines N53° 29' 40" E and S 36° 30' 20" E. From S 36° 30' 20" E to due south is 36° 30' 20". Note that N 53° 29' 40" E is the same line as S 53° 29' 40" W. From S 53° 29' 40" W to due south is 53° 29' 40". Adding 53° 29' 40" to 36° 30' 20" gives 90° 00' 00", the total angle of the northern corner of lot 12.

10. C   The fastest way to solve this is to know that from due north to due south is 180° 00' 00". S 36° 30' 20" E is 36° 30' 20" less than 180°, and when subtracted from 180° gives 143° 29' 40". By the way, the long way around is 180° + 36° 30' 20" = 216° 30' 20".

11. B   The easement shown by the dashed line runs along the backyards of lots 24, 25, and 26.

12. C   The depth of a lot is the distance from front to back; in the case of lot 20 that is 139.54 feet.

Rectangular Survey

1. **C** The easiest way to work rectangular survey problems is to read the description backwards. Thus, with the NE 1/4 of the SW 1/4 of the SE 1/4, you first look for the SE 1/4, then within it the SW 1/4, then within that the NE 1/4. This describes parcel U.

2. **A** Parcel H is a half of a half of a quarter of a quarter of a section. That's 1/2 x 1/2 x 1/4 x 1/4 x 640 = 10 acres.

3. **B** Work in reverse, starting in the NE 1/4, then within it the SE 1/4 and then within that the N 1/2. This leads you to parcel K.

4. **B** Parcel X is 1/2 of 1/4 of 1/4 of 1/4 of a section. Lengthwise, it occupies 1/2 of 1/4 of the south side of section 12. That makes it 1/2 x 1/4 x 5,280' = 660'. The width is 1/4 x 1/4 x 5,280' = 330'.

5. **D** Parcel Q is 1/4 x 1/4 x 640 = 40 acres. Parcel Y is the same, so the total is 80 acres.

6. **B** Again, go in reverse starting in the NW 1/4, then within that the NW 1/4, and within that the E 1/2.

7. **A** Again, go in reverse starting in the NE 1/4, then within that the SE 1/4, and within that the N 1/2.

8. **D** Start in the SE 1/4, within that the SW 1/4, within that the SE 1/4 and within that the NW 1/4.

9. **B** Start in the SW 1/4 and locate its northwest corner. Then go south one-quarter mile to the point of beginning. Then go a half-mile east, a quarter-mile south, 1,000 feet west, northwest along Lake Amelia back to the point of beginning. This describes parcels R and S.

10. **D** Same method as in number 9 above. Start at the northeast corner of the section, follow the directions and remember that a section is 5,280 feet on a side.

Rights and Interests in Land

Chapter 3

1. The system under which individuals are given the right to own land is
known as the
   A. feudal system.
   B. allodial system.
   C. chattel system.
   D. fee system.

2. Under the feudal system of land ownership, the responsibility for
providing government services, determining land use, etc. was held by
   A. vassals.
   B. lords.
   C. the king.
   D. parliament.

3. Property taxes are characteristic of the
   I. allodial system of land ownership.
   II. feudal system of land ownership.
   A. I only   B. II only   C. Both I and II   D. Neither I nor II

4. In today's society, real property taxes may be used to provide revenues
for any of the following governments EXCEPT:
   A. state.
   B. city.
   C. federal.
   D. county.

5. By which of the following processes may a government acquire ownership
of privately held land?
   I. Eminent domain.   III. Police power.
   II. Taxation.   IV. Escheat.
   A. I, II, III and IV   C. I only
   B. I, II and IV only   D. I and IV only

6. A government may exercise its power of eminent domain to take private
land for public use, through the process of
   A. condemnation.
   B. appropriation.
   C. assemblage.
   D. allocation.

Note: If you are reading <u>Real Estate: An Introduction to the Profession</u>
you may omit the following questions: 1, 2, 3, 7, 8, 9 and 10.

7. Severance damages are paid
    I. when only a portion of a parcel of land is being taken.
    II. as compensation for damages to the remaining land after a portion has been taken through condemnation.
  A. I only   B. II only (C.) Both I and II   D. Neither I nor II

8. When the value or utility of a parcel of land is diminished as a result of a government taking, the landowner may seek compensation in any of the following forms EXCEPT:
  A. severance damages.   C. consequential damages.
  (B.) adverse damages.   D. inverse condemnation.

9. A private landowner suffered a decrease in the value of his land as a result of a voluntary sale to the city of an adjoining parcel of land to be used as a sanitary landfill. May the owner seek compensation from the city for these damages?
  A. Yes, because this action entitles him to severance damages.
  (B.) Yes, because the action resulted in consequential damages to his property.
  C. No, because the government's action did not involve his property.
  D. No, because his action should be against the previous owner of the property.

10. Mrs. Murphy operates a small restaurant on land which she owns near the borders of the City of Grandview. The city has decided to construct a new sewage treatment plant on land adjacent to the restaurant. Mrs. Murphy feels that the odors emanating from the plant will damage her restaurant business. Under the laws dealing with eminent domain, Mrs. Murphy
    I. might claim and be awarded consequential damages.
    II. might successfully demand that the city purchase her land under inverse condemnation proceedings.
    III. would have no recourse against the city.
  A. III only (B.) I and II only   C. II only   D. I only

11. The right of the government to place reasonable restrictions on the use of privately held land is known as
    I. a restrictive covenant.
    II. police power.
  A. I only (B.) II only C. Both I and II D. Neither I nor II

12. Which of the following is NOT an example of a government's exercise of its police powers?
  A. Rent controls.   C. Zoning laws.
  B. Building codes.   (D.) Restrictive covenants.

13. A property owner who suffers from a government's exercise of its police powers
  A. may request inverse condemnation of his property.
  (B.) will not be compensated for his loss.
  C. will receive consequential damages from the government.
  D. is entitled to severance damages.

14. A property owner who fails to comply with a government's exercise of its police power may be subject to
    I.   confiscation of his property.
    II. civil penalties.
    III. criminal penalties.
    IV. escheat of his land to the state.
    A. I only   C. II and III only
    B. IV only   D. II, III and IV only

15. Property owned by a person who dies intestate and without heirs will escheat to the
    A. city.   C. state.
    B. county.   D. federal government.

16. A person who is without heirs may avoid having his property pass to the state by
    I.   leaving a valid will containing instructions as to the disposition of his property.
    II. giving it to a charity prior to death.
    A. I only   B. II only   C. Both I and II   D. Neither I nor II

17. Which level of government has the responsibility for protecting the rights of property owners against confiscation by foreign governments?
    A. Federal.   C. County.
    B. State.   D. City.

18. Whereas the United States government is empowered to protect its citizens against forceful takeover by foreign powers, land ownership rights within the U.S. are protected by
    I.   laws.
    II. courts.
    III. contracts.
    A. I and II only   C. I and III only
    B. II and III only   D. I, II and III

19. A property owner who holds fee simple title to land will have all of the following "sticks" in his bundle of rights EXCEPT the right to:
    A. occupy and use it.
    B. restrict the use of the land.
    C. devise it by will.
    D. violate building, health and safety codes.

20. Which of the following rights in land may be held by a private owner?
    A. Refusal to sell to the government.
    B. Rejection of a claim for taxes.
    C. The right to disinherit one's heirs.
    D. Repudiation of zoning laws.

21. The term "estate" refers to
    I.   the quantity of land as shown on a plat of the property.
    II. one's legal rights in the land.
    A. I only   B. II only   C. Both I and II   D. Neither I nor II

22. Charlie and Mabel Brown own their home in fee simple without encumbrances of any kind. Would it be correct to state that they have absolute ownership of the land?
    A. Yes, because there are no limitations as to their use or disposition of the property.
    B. Yes, because a fee simple estate is greater than a life estate.
    C. No, because a life estate is greater than a fee simple estate.
    D. No, because the government retains the rights of eminent domain, taxation, police power and escheat.

23. The holder of a life estate in land derives his rights from
    A. the fee simple title holder.
    B. the laws of inheritance.
    C. a leasehold estate.
    D. governmental rights in the land.

24. The term "title" as used with reference to land refers to
    I. the legal description of the property.
    II. a person's evidence of ownership of the land.
    A. I only   B. II only   C. Both I and II   D. Neither I nor II

25. An impediment to title to real property is called
    A. an encumbrance.   C. an intrusion.
    B. an appurtenance.   D. a domain.

26. All of the following constitute an encumbrance on the fee simple title to real property EXCEPT:
    A. a will conveying the property to the owner's heirs upon death of the owner.
    B. a restrictive covenant in the deed to the property.
    C. a mortgage.
    D. a lease.

27. A right of use and enjoyment held by one person in the lands of another for a special purpose is called
    A. an easement.   C. a license.
    B. an encumbrance.   D. an encroachment.

28. Which of the following easements could be created without a written document?
    I. An easement by necessity.
    II. An easement by prescription.
    A. I only   B. II only   C. Both I and II   D. Neither I nor II

29. An easement is
    I. an appurtenance to the holder of the dominant tenement.
    II. an encumbrance to the holder of the servient tenement.
    A. I only   B. II only   C. Both I and II   D. Neither I nor II

30. An easement acquired by constant use is called an easement by
    A. subscription.   C. condemnation.
    B. necessity.   D. prescription.

31. Morris sold the back half of his lot to Katz, and gave Katz a permanent easement across his land in order for Katz to have access to the road. Which of the following statements is true?
    F I.   The easement is an easement in gross.
    T II. The easement is an easement appurtenant.
    T III. The dominant estate is held by Katz.
    T IV. The servient estate is held by Morris.
    A. I only
    B. II, III and IV only
    C. I, III and IV only
    D. II only

32. Utility easements are
    I.   easements appurtenant.
    II. an encumbrance to the servient estate.
    III. easements in gross.
    IV. an appurtenance to the dominant estate.
    A. I and IV only
    B. II and III only
    C. II, III and IV only
    D. I, II and IV only

33. The right or privilege, by usage or contract, to travel over a designated portion of another person's property is
    A. a party right.
    B. a right-of-way.
    C. a personal easement.
    D. an ease-of-access right.

34. Two adjoining office buildings are separated by a common wall that is located on the property line. All of the following statements would be true EXCEPT:
    T A. The wall is known as a party wall.
    F B. Either owner can demolish his half without liability to the owner of the adjoining property.
    T C. Each owner owns that portion of the wall on his land.
    T D. Each owner has an easement in the other half of the wall for physical support.

35. An easement appurtenant may NOT be terminated
    A. by combination of the dominant and servient tenements.
    B. when the purpose for the easement no longer exists.
    C. by lack of use.
    D. unilaterally by the holder of the servient tenement.

36. Bud is looking for a shorter way to get from the public road to his favorite swimming and fishing spot along the ocean. However, Ray's land stands in the way. Bud could legally cross Ray's land by
    A. obtaining an easement from Ray.
    B. obtaining a license from Ray.
    C. leasing Ray's land.
    D. All of the above.

37. The unauthorized intrusion of a building or other improvement onto another person's land is called
    A. a restrictive covenant.
    B. an appurtenance.
    C. an easement.
    D. an encroachment.

38. Jack planted a tree near the boundary line separating his property from
    that of Dick, his next door neighbor. As the tree grew, its limbs ex-
    tended over the property line into the air space above Dick's land.
    Which of the following statements are correct?
    I.   The intrusion into Dick's air space constituted an encroachment.
    II. Dick could force Jack to remove the tree limbs back to the
         property line.
    III. Failure on Dick's part to force removal for an extended time could
         result in Jack's claiming a legal right to continue the intrusion.
    IV. Since, once it was planted, the tree grew naturally without deli-
         berate assistance from Jack, Dick could not force its removal.
    A. I and IV only   C. I and II only
    B. II and III only   D. I, II and III only

39. Private agreements that govern the use of land are known as
    I.   deed covenants.
    II. deed restrictions.
    A. I only   B. II only   C. Both I and II   D. Neither I nor II

40. Violation of a restrictive covenant in a deed may result in which of the
    following actions against the property owner?
    I.   Criminal action brought by the local government against the
         property owner.
    II. Civil action brought by adjacent property owners.
    III. Civil action brought by the grantor under the deed.
    A. I only   B. II only   C. III only   D. II and III only

41. All of the following may constitute a lien on real property EXCEPT:
    A. a mortgage.   C. a restrictive covenant in a deed.
    B. unpaid real property taxes. D. a judgment against the owner.

42. Which of the following types of liens does NOT arise from operation of
    law?
    A. A mortgage lien.   C. An ad valorem tax lien.
    B. A federal income tax lien. D. A judgment lien.

43. All of the following would be statutory general liens EXCEPT:
    A. federal income tax liens.   C. state income tax liens.
    B. judgment liens.   D. ad valorem tax liens.

44. Which of the following are examples of special liens?
    I.   Mechanic's liens.
    II. Judgment liens.
    III. Ad valorem tax liens.
    IV. Federal income tax liens.
    A. I, II, III and IV   C. II and IV only
    B. I and III only   D. I only

45. Dexter engaged a general contractor to build an addition to his house. The general contractor failed to pay the electrical subcontractor for work which was subcontracted to him. May the subcontractor secure a mechanic's lien on Dexter's house?
    A. Yes, because the work was done on Dexter's property.
    B. Yes, because a mechanic's lien is a general lien which attaches to all real property of the lienee.
    C. No, because Dexter did not directly contract with the subcontractor.
    D. No, because the lien would attach to real property of the general contractor.

46. Once a mechanic's lien is secured, it will attach to
    I. personal property kept within the structure.
    II. the structure and the parcel of land to which it is attached.
    A. I only   B. II only   C. Both I and II   D. Neither I nor II

47. All of the following are true of a mechanic's lien EXCEPT:
    A. it attaches and takes effect when the first item of labor or materials is furnished.
    B. it attaches and takes effect on the date documentation is filed with the county recorder.
    C. to preserve lien rights, a lien statement must be filed with the county recorder.
    D. to preserve lien rights, the lien must be perfected.

48. What forms of liens are superior to all others in terms of lien priority?
    A. Judgment liens.   C. Federal income tax liens.
    B. First mortgage liens.   D. Ad valorem tax liens.

49. In her will, Mrs. Adams left her home to her church, "for so long as it is used for religious purposes." Should religious use of the property ever terminate, the property is to revert to the heirs of Mrs. Adams. The estate created by this will is a
    I. fee simple determinable.
    II. fee simple on condition precedent.
    III. fee simple on condition subsequent.
    IV. qualified fee.
    A. I only   B. II only   C. III only   D. I and IV only

50. Mr. Green donated a parcel of land to the city for use as a public park. The deed was not to become operative until the city had actually established a public park on the land. This established a
    I. qualified fee estate in the land.
    II. determinable fee estate in the land.
    III. fee simple estate subject to condition subsequent.
    IV. fee simple estate subject to condition precedent.
    A. I and II only   C. I and III only
    B. I and IV only   D. IV only

51. Ralph conveyed a house which he owned to his parents for so long as the surviving parent lived. Upon the death of the survivor, title is to be returned to Ralph or his heirs should he predecease his parents. Ralph
      I. has a life estate.
     II. conveyed a life estate to his parents.
    III. conveyed a life estate to his heirs.
     IV. holds a reversion.
    A. I only   C. III and IV only
    B. II and III only   D. II and IV only

52. Earl died and left his real property to his wife for her life, naming Earl, Jr. to receive the fee simple estate upon her death. Which of the following statements are true of the wife's estate in the property?
      I. She has a life estate.
     II. During her life, she is entitled to any income produced by the property.
    III. She cannot sell or dispose of her interest in the property.
     IV. She is responsible for taxes on the property during her lifetime.
    A. I, II, III and IV   C. I, II and III only
    B. II, III and IV only   D. I, II and IV only

53. Mrs. Baker holds a life estate in the home in which she lives. During her lifetime, she
      I. may convey her interest to any other person, as a sale or gift.
     II. must not commit waste on the property.
    III. is obligated to pay the taxes on the property.
     IV. may mortgage the property.
    A. I, II, III and IV   C. II and III only
    B. II, III and IV only   D. III and IV only

54. Which of the following statements is correct?
      I. A husband's rights in his wife's property are called dower rights.
     II. A wife's rights in her husband's property are called curtesy rights.
    A. I only   B. II only   C. Both I and II   D. Neither I nor II

55. An important aspect of dower and curtesy rights is that
    A. the husband has control over marital property.
    B. either spouse can convey marital property.
    C. the wife has control over marital property.
    D. both spouses must sign the deed when marital property is conveyed.

56. According to the laws of various states, homestead protection laws may provide for
      I. exemption from claims of a creditor.
     II. a home for life for a widow or widower.
    III. defeat of a spouse's claims of dower or curtesy.
    A. I only   B. II only   C. I and II only.   D. I, II and III

57. Which of the following is NOT classified as a freehold estate?
    A. An estate created by statute.
    B. A life estate.
    C. A fee simple estate.
    D. A leasehold estate.

58. Which of the following correspond?
     I. Landlord - lessor.
    II. Tenant - lessee.
    A. I only   B. II only   C. Both I and II   D. Neither I nor II

59. The interest that a tenant has in real estate by virtue of a lease is a
     I. leasehold estate.
    II. less-than-freehold estate.
    A. I only   B. II only   C. Both I and II   D. Neither I nor II

60. Real estate held as a leasehold
     I. is used by the owner rather than the tenant.
    II. reverts to the tenant upon termination of the lease.
    A. I only   B. II only   C. Both I and II   D. Neither I nor II

61. An estate for years
     I. is of indefinite duration.
    II. automatically renews itself upon termination.
    A. I only   B. II only   C. Both I and II   D. Neither I nor II

62. A lessee who assigns his rights to another party becomes the
    A. lessor.   C. sublessee.
    B. sublessor.   D. lien holder.

63. A sublessee may be granted
    A. any rights in the property agreed upon between himself and the
       lessee.
    B. those rights in the property which are held by the lessee.
    C. any right held by the fee owner.
    D. all rights held by the fee owner.

64. Unless the landlord or tenant acts to terminate it, an estate from
    period-to-period
     I. automatically renews itself.
    II. continues for an indefinite time.
    A. I only   B. II only   C. Both I and II   D. Neither I nor II

65. An estate which may be terminated by either party at any time is
    A. an estate for years.
    B. an estate from period-to-period.
    C. an estate at will.
    D. a life estate.

66. The lessor holds a reversion in which of the following situations?
      I. Estate for years.
     II. Periodic estate.
    III. Estate at will.
     IV. Tenancy at sufferance.
    A. I only   C. I, II and III only
    B. IV only   D. I, II, III and IV

67. A tenant who retains possession of the premises after the termination of his legal rights is known as a
    I.   tenant at sufferance.
    II. holdover tenant.
    A. I only   B. II only   C. Both I and II   D. Neither I nor II

68. A tenant at sufferance is
    A. a legal tenant.   C. a licensee.
    B. a trespasser.   D. a guest.

69. All of the following are true of a license to use land EXCEPT that it is
    A. revocable by the grantor at any time.
    B. not assignable.
    C. a personal privilege to use another's land.
    D. an encumbrance on the land.

70. Which of the following is an example of a license?
    A. A tenancy at sufferance.   C. A theater ticket.
    B. An encroachment.   D. An easement.

71. A chattel is
    A. an item of personal property.
    B. an item of real property such as a building.
    C. a freehold estate in land.
    D. a term that refers to land used for cattle ranching.

72. Which of the following liens can NOT result in the sale of a debtor's real property in order to gain funds for the satisfaction of a debt?
    A. A chattel mortgage lien.   C. A property tax lien.
    B. A real estate mortgage lien.   D. A mechanic's lien.

73. Common law derives its authority from
    I.   custom and usage over long periods of time.
    II. individual court decisions.
    A. I only   B. II only   C. Both I and II   D. Neither I nor II

74. Statutory law is
    I.   the result of individual court decisions.
    II. created by enactment of legislation.
    A. I only   B. II only   C. Both I and II   D. Neither I nor II

75. Laws requiring the licensing of real estate agents are examples of
    I.   common law.
    II.   statutory law.
    III. case law.
    A. I only   B. II only   C. III only   D. I and III only

Problems

1. A woman bought the lot pictured below for $19,000. A year later the
    state condemned the portion marked off along Main Street. If the land
    is equal in price in all sections, and the state paid her $1.15 per
    square foot for the condemned portion, what is the difference in the
    price of the condemned portion between what she paid and what the state
    paid her for it?

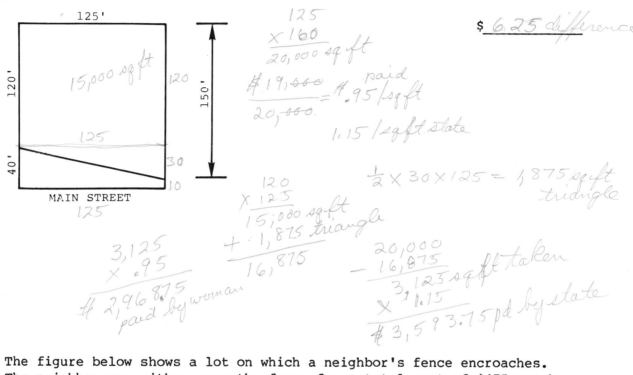

2. The figure below shows a lot on which a neighbor's fence encroaches.
    The neighbor can either move the fence for a total cost of $475, or buy
    the encroached-upon portion at the same price per square foot that the
    owner paid. If the lot cost $30,750, which is the least expensive
    choice? By how much?

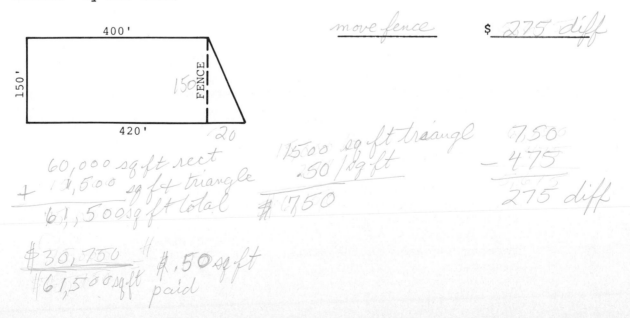

Answers—Chapter 3

Multiple Choice Questions

1.   B   Under the allodial system, individuals may own land. This is not possible under the feudal system.

2.   C   The king, or sovereign, owned the land under the feudal system, and was responsible for providing government services.

3.   A   Property taxes are characteristic of the allodial system.

4.   C   Property taxes may be used to provide revenues for city, county or state governments, but not for the federal government.

5.   D   Governments may acquire ownership of privately held land under eminent domain or escheat, but not through police power or taxation.

6.   A   The power of eminent domain may be used to take private land for public use through the process of condemnation.

7.   C   Severance damages may be paid when a portion of a parcel of land is being taken, or as compensation for damages to the remaining land after a portion was taken through condemnation.

8.   B   A landowner may seek compensation in the form of severance damages, consequential damages, or inverse condemnation.

9.   B   The government's action resulted in consequential damages to the owner's property, and he is entitled to compensation for these damages.

10.   B   Mrs. Murphy might successfully claim consequential damages or be successful in demanding inverse condemnation.

11.   B   Police power is a government's right to make reasonable rules for the use of privately held land.

12.   D   Restrictive covenants are a means of private land-use controls. Rent controls, building codes and zoning laws are examples of a government's exercise of its police powers.

13.   B   Property owners are not compensated for a loss suffered from a government's exercise of its police powers.

14.   C   An owner who fails to comply with the government's exercise of its police powers is subject to civil and/or criminal penalties, but not to confiscation or escheat.

15.   C   Property escheats to the state, not to the city, county or federal government.

16.   C   An owner who is without heirs may avoid having property escheat to the state by leaving a valid will or by giving it away prior to death.

17.   A   The federal government has the responsibility for protecting property owners from acts of foreign governments.

18.   D   Land ownership rights within the U. S. are protected by laws, courts and contracts.

19.   D   The holder of fee simple title to land may not violate building, health and safety codes, but may occupy and use it, restrict its use, and devise it by will.

20.   C   A private owner may disinherit heirs, but may not refuse to sell to the government, reject a claim for taxes or repudiate zoning laws.

21.   B   The term "estate" refers to one's legal rights in the land, not to its quantity in physical terms.

22.   D   The holder of fee simple title is subject to the government's rights of eminent domain, taxation, police power and escheat, so does not enjoy absolute ownership.

23.   A   The holder of a life estate holds whatever rights are conveyed to him by the fee simple title holder.

24.   B   With reference to land, the term "title" refers to evidence of ownership.

25.   A   An encumbrance is anything which impedes or impairs the title to real property.

26.   A   A will is not an encumbrance to the title to real property, but restrictive covenants, mortgages or leases are encumbrances.

27.   A   An easement is a right of use and enjoyment of another's land for a special purpose.

28.   C   An easement by prescription arises from constant use rather than a written document. An easement by necessity can be created in some situations without a written document.

29.   C   An easement benefits the holder of the dominant tenement, but encumbers the property belonging to the holder of the servient tenement.

30.   D   An easement by prescription is acquired by constant use without the existence of a written document.

31.   B   The easement is an easement apppurtenant which runs with the land. The dominant estate is held by the holder of the easement (Katz) and the servient estate is held by the landowner (Morris).

32.   B   A utility easement is an easement in gross, and an encumbrance to the servient estate. There is no dominant estate.

33.   B   A right-of-way is the right to travel over another's land. It may be acquired by usage or by contract.

34.   B   A party wall is jointly owned and neither owner may damage or destroy it without the other's consent.

35.   D   An easement appurtenant may be terminated by combination of the dominant and servient tenements, by abandonment or when its purpose no longer exists. It cannot be terminated unilaterally by the holder of the servient tenement.

36.   D   All of these are possible; however obtaining a license to cross would be the easiest.

37.   D   An encroachment is the unauthorized intrusion of a building or improvement on another's land.

38.   D   The tree's intrusion into the neighbor's air space constituted an encroachment; and its owner could be forced to cut the limbs back to the property line. Failure to do so for an extended time could result in the neighbor's claiming the legal right to continue its use.

39.   C   Deed covenants, also known as deed restrictions, are private agreements that govern the use of land.

40.   D   Failure to abide by a restrictive covenant may result in civil action by the grantor or by adjacent property owners. It will not result in criminal action by the government.

41.   C   A restrictive covenant in a deed is not a lien. Mortgages, unpaid taxes and judgments are liens.

42.   A   A mortgage lien is a voluntary lien which arises from actions of the parties. Tax and judgment liens are statutory liens which arise from operation of law.

43.   D   Ad valorem tax liens are special liens which attach only to the property on which the taxes are delinquent. Income tax and judgment liens attach to all property of the lienee.

44.   B   Mechanic's liens and ad valorem tax liens are special liens. Judgment liens and income tax liens are general liens.

45.   A   The mechanic's lien attaches to the property on which the work was performed or for which materials were supplied.

46.   B   A mechanic's lien attaches to the land and buildings named in the lien, but not to personal property within the structure.

47.   B   A mechanic's lien attaches and takes effect when the first item of labor or material is furnished. However, the lien must be later perfected by recordation to be enforceable.

48.   D   Ad valorem tax liens are superior to all other liens in priority.

49.   D   The estate is a fee simple determinable and a qualified fee.

50.   B   The estate is a qualified fee estate and a fee simple estate subject to condition precedent, i.e., a certain condition must precede title passage.

51.   D   The estate is a life estate held by the parents and Ralph holds a reversion.

52.   D   The estate is a life estate and as the life tenant she is entitled to any income produced during her tenancy. She is responsible for property taxes during her life tenancy and she may sell or convey her life interest.

53.   A   A life tenant may sell or convey his/her interest, must not commit waste on the property, must pay taxes on the property during the life tenancy and may mortgage the property.

54.   D   A husband's rights in the wife's property are called curtesy and a wife's rights in the husband's property are called dower.

55.   D   Both spouses must sign a deed when marital property is conveyed.

56.   C   Homestead laws may provide for exemption from a creditor's claims or provide a home for life for a widow or widower, according to state law.

57.   D   A leasehold estate is an estate less-than-freehold.

58.   C   Both word pairs correspond.

59.   C   An interest acquired by virtue of a lease is a leasehold and an estate less-than-freehold.

60.   D   Real property held as a leasehold is used by the tenant and reverts to the owner upon termination of the lease.

61.   D   An estate for years is of definite duration and does not automatically renew itself upon termination.

62.   B   A lessee who assigns his rights to another party becomes the sub-lessor.

63.   B   A sublessee may be granted only those rights in the property which are held by the lessee.

64.   C   Unless landlord or tenant acts to terminate it, an estate from period-to-period automatically renews itself and continues indefinitely.

65. C An estate at will is terminable by either party at any time.

66. D The lessor holds a reversion in any and all leasehold estates.

67. C A tenant who retains possession of the premises after the termination of his legal rights is known as a tenant at sufferance and a holdover tenant.

68. B A tenant at sufferance is a trespasser.

69. D A license to use land is not an encumbrance on the land. It is a personal privilege, revocable, and not assignable.

70. C A theater ticket is an example of a license. It is a personal privilege and can be cancelled.

71. A Chattels are personal property.

72. A A chattel mortgage lien attaches only to the personal property named in the lien and cannot result in the sale of the lienee's real property.

73. C Common law derives its authority from custom and usage and from individual court decisions.

74. B Statutory law is created by enactment of legislation.

75. B Laws governing the licensing of real estate agents are examples of statutory law, enacted by state legislatures.

Problems

1. 125' x 160' = 20,000 sqft area of lot.
    $19,000 ÷ 20,000 sqft = $.95 per sqft of lot.
    $1.15 - $.95 = $.20 gain per sqft.
    (40' + 10') ÷ 2 x 125' x $.20 = $625 answer.

2. (400' + 420') ÷ 2 x 150' = 61,500 sqft area of lot.
    $30,750 ÷ 61,500 sqft = $.50 per sqft, cost of lot.
    (20' x 150') ÷ 2 x $.50 = $750 to buy encroached portion.
    $750 - $475 = $275 cheaper to move fence.

A note on what to do first: The rule is to perform all calculations inside all parentheses first. Then do the multiplication and division. Then do the addition and subtraction. Thus, in line 1 of number 2 above, the first step is to add 400' and 420'. The sum is then divided by 2 and multiplied by 150'.

Forms of Ownership

Chapter 4

1. Ownership in severalty occurs when
   A. two or more persons have identical interests in the same property concurrently.
   B. husband and wife share ownership of the same property.
   C. property is owned by one person.
   D. two or more persons own the same property in any form of title.

2. A married person can hold as separate property
   I. property bought by that person before marriage.
   II. property inherited by that person after marriage.
   A. I only   B. II only   C. Both I and II   D. Neither I nor II

3. Among the advantages of ownership of real property in severalty is
   I. freedom of choice as to the use or disposition of the property.
   II. the ability to defeat a spouse's claim of dower or curtesy rights.
   A. I only   B. II only   C. Both I and II   D. Neither I nor II

4. All of the following are true of a tenancy in common EXCEPT:
   A. all tenants hold an undivided interest in the entire property.
   B. each tenant must have a separate deed to his/her share.
   C. the tenants may dispose of all or part of their shares without the agreement of the other tenants.
   D. there is no right of survivorship among the tenants.

Note: If you are reading <u>Real Estate: An Introduction to the Profession,</u>
       you may omit the following questions: 32 through 55.

5. Susan and Nancy wish to purchase a condominium unit as co-owners. Susan
    will hold a 60 per cent interest and Nancy a 40 per cent interest. Both
    are single and each wants the other to inherit her share automatically
    upon death. Can title be conveyed to them in this manner?
    A. Yes, by taking title as tenants in common with the right of
        survivorship.
    B. Yes, by taking title as joint tenants with the right of survivorship.
    C. No, because only as tenants in common can two co-owners have unequal
        interests, and there cannot be survivorship among tenants in common.
    D. No, because survivorship can only exist between husband and wife.

6. A tenant in common may NOT
    A. claim a portion of the property for his own use.
    B. convey his interest by will.
    C. use his share of the property as collateral for a mortgage loan.
    D. sell his share without the agreement of the other tenants.

7. Able, Baker and Charles own an investment property as tenants in common.
    Able owns a 20 per cent interest, Baker a 30 per cent interest and
    Charles a 50 per cent interest. Charles needs to raise cash, and offers
    to sell David a 25 per cent interest, or half of his 50 per cent inter-
    est. Able and Baker are opposed to the sale. Can they prevent Charles
    from selling to David?
    A. Yes, because tenants in common may not dispose of their interest
        without agreement of all the other tenants in common.
    B. Yes, because a tenant in common may dispose of all his interest, but
        not of a part of it.
    C. Yes, because a tenant in common may sever his interest only by means
        of a suit for partition.
    D. No, because a tenant in common may dispose of all or part of his
        interest without permission of the other tenants.

8. Chauncey and Cheney, who own 160 acres of land as tenants in common, want
    to terminate this relationship. They may partition their interests by
      I. physical subdivision of the property.
     II. sale of the property and division of the proceeds.
    A. I only   B. II only   C. Both I and II   D. Neither I nor II

9. The difficulty in disposing of undivided interests and joint liability
    for debts against the property are regarded as hazards of
      I. joint tenancy.
     II. tenancy in common.
    A. I only   B. II only   C. Both I and II   D. Neither I nor II

10. Able, Baker, and Charles are going to purchase an investment property as
    co-owners, and will take title as joint tenants. Which of the following
    statements are correct?
      I. All will acquire their interest at the same moment in time.
     II. Each will receive a separate deed for his share.
    III. All will have equal interests in the property.
     IV. All will enjoy equal rights of posession.
    A. I, II, III and IV   C. I, II and III only
    B. I, III and IV only   D. II, III and IV only

11. The surviving co-owner may automatically inherit the deceased co-owner's share when property is held as a
    I.   tenancy in common.
    II. joint tenancy.
    III. tenancy by the entireties.
    A. I only   B. II only   C. II and III only   D. I, II and III

12. All of the following are true of joint tenancy EXCEPT:
    A. Unities of time, title, interest, and possession must be present.
    B. New joint tenants may be added without forming a new joint tenancy.
    C. Survivorship exists among joint tenants.
    D. A husband and wife may hold title as joint tenants.

13. Madora wants to leave her real estate to her nephew Carlos, but wants the flexibility to change her mind in the future. She can accomplish this goal with a
    I.   will naming her nephew as recipient of her real estate.
    II. joint tenancy with her newphew.
    A. I only   B. II only   C. Both I and II   D. Neither I nor II

14. The ABC Corporation and the XYZ Corporation want to purchase a property as co-owners. Each will hold equal shares of ownership, which will be acquired from the same source, at the same time, and by means of a single deed. May they hold title as joint tenants?
    A. Yes, because the four unities of joint tenancy will be present.
    B. Yes, because they hold equal shares in the property.
    C. No, because corporations may not hold title as joint tenants.
    D. No, because the unity of interest will not be present.

15. Joint tenants must acquire their interests in jointly held property
    I.   at the same time.
    II. from the same source.
    III. in the same instrument.
    A. I, II and III   C. I and III only
    B. I and II only   D. II and III only

16. Joint tenants have equal
    I.   rights of possession.
    II. interests in the property.
    A. I only   B. II only   C. Both I and II   D. Neither I nor II

17. If any unity of joint tenancy is broken, the law will regard the estate as
    A. a tenancy by the entireties.
    B. community property.
    C. a tenancy in common.
    D. an estate in severalty.

18. Able, Baker and Charles own a property as joint tenants. Able wants to sell his interest to David. In the absence of documents creating a new joint tenancy,
    I. David will become a tenant in common with Baker and Charles.
    II. Baker and Charles remain joint tenants between themselves.
    III. David will own an individual one-third interest in common with Baker and Charles.
    IV. Baker and Charles will own an individual two-thirds interest as joint tenants.
    A. I, II, III and IV   C. II, III and IV only
    B. I, II and IV only   D. I and IV only

19. Tenancy by the entireties is based upon
    I. English law.
    II. the premise that husband and wife are one legal unit.
    A. I only   B. II only   C. Both I and II   D. Neither I nor II

20. Bob and Ruth own their home as tenants by the entirety with the right of survivorship. Which of the following statements would NOT be true regarding their ownership?
    A. Upon death of one spouse, the survivor automatically becomes the owner in severalty.
    B. Neither spouse has a disposable interest in the property during the lifetime of the other.
    C. Should they be divorced, they would become joint tenants in the ownership of the property.
    D. In most states, the property cannot be attached by a creditor unless the creditor is the creditor of both spouses.

21. Carlos and Demas want to purchase an investment property as co-owners. If they hold title as joint tenants, will either's spouse inherit his share upon his death?
    A. Yes, because of the right of survivorship which exists among joint tenants.
    B. Yes, because a joint tenant's share passes to his heirs upon death.
    C. No, because the spouses were not named as joint tenants on the deed.
    D. No, because a joint tenancy with another party defeats a spouse's dower rights.

22. If tenants by the entireties divorce, barring any other agreement
    A. they become tenants in common with each other.
    B. divorce does not affect the status of the title to the property.
    C. the ex-wife takes title in severalty.
    D. the ex-husband takes title in severalty.

23. Community property laws are derived from legal concepts which have their origin in
    A. Spanish and French law.   C. American statutory law.
    B. English common law.   D. English parliamentary law.

24. The basic concept of community property law is that
    A. husband and wife are merged into one by marriage.
    B. husband and wife are equal partners.
    C. husband and wife are separate owners in severalty.
    D. the husband owns everything in the entirety.

25. Mr. and Mrs. Marvin live in a community property state. Which of the following would most likely be considered their community property?
    A. Property which is inherited by either spouse.
    B. Property conveyed as a gift to either spouse.
    C. Property purchased after they were married.
    D. Property owned by either spouse prior to their marriage.

26. After his marriage to Leslie, Randy took title to real property in severalty, using marital funds to make the purchase. The property is located in a community property state. In order for Randy to sell this property, Leslie must
    A. be given her share as separate property.
    B. surrender her dower rights in the property.
    C. sign the deed as grantor.
    D. receive her share of the property by partition.

27. In states having community property laws, which of the following types of property, purchased with marital funds, is/are classified as community property?
    I. Real property.
    II. Personal property.
    A. I only   B. II only   C. Both I and II   D. Neither I nor II

28. In community property states, which of the following exists?
    I. Dower.
    II. Curtesy.
    A. I only   B. II only   C. Both I and II   D. Neither I nor II

29. Under community property law, a wife is considered to be a co-owner in any property purchased from the husband's earnings
    I. even though her name does not appear on the deed.
    II. if the property was acquired after the marriage took place.
    A. I only   B. II only   C. Both I and II   D. Neither I nor II

30. Adam and Alice own their home as tenants in common in a community property state. Upon Adam's death, which of the following statements will be true?
    A. Alice will inherit his share through her right of survivorship.
    B. By will, Adam may devise his share to anyone.
    C. Alice's dower rights will be vested immediately.
    D. The property will belong to Alice in severalty.

31. In community property states, property not held as community property is designated as
    A. private property.   C. separate property.
    B. personal property.   D. sole property.

32. Smith, Duncan and Robbins formed a partnership to purchase real estate, naming Smith as the general partner. What type of ownership did they create?
   A. A syndicate.
   B. General partnership.
   C. Joint venture.
   D. Limited partnership.

33. Peach and Pear formed a general partnership and took title to real estate in the partnership name. Under this form of ownership, all of the following statements would be correct EXCEPT:
   A. Each has equal rights of possession of the property for partnership purposes.
   B. Upon the death of Peach, his rights in the property are vested in Pear.
   C. The partner's rights in partnership property are subject to claims of dower or curtesy.
   D. The partnership property cannot be attached by creditors of the individual partners.

34. In order to hold property in the name of the partnership, a list of the partners must be published in each county and state
   I. where the partnership does business.
   II. where the partnership owns property.
   A. I only   B. II only   C. Both I and II   D. Neither I nor II

35. In a general partnership,
   I. each partner has unlimited financial liability.
   II. each partner pays individual taxes on his/her share of the partnership's earnings.
   A. I only   B. II only   C. Both I and II   D. Neither I nor II

36. Which of the following would sometimes prove to be a negative factor in the corporate form of ownership?
   A. Limited personal liability.
   B. Liquidity of investment.
   C. The ability to acquire an ownership interest with small capital investment.
   D. Tax considerations.

37. An advantage of the partnership form of ownership is
   I. the aggregation of capital and individual expertise.
   II. individual taxation of profits and/or losses.
   A. I only   B. II only   C. Both I and II   D. Neither I nor II

38. An individual investor who is seeking the partnership advantages of capital aggregation and pass-through of profits, but who wishes to avoid unlimited financial liability, would join a
   I. joint venture.
   II. limited partnership.
   A. I only   B. II only   C. Both I and II   D. Neither I nor II

39. Management of a limited partnership is performed by the
   I. limited partners.
   II. general partners.
   A. I only   B. II only   C. Both I and II   D. Neither I nor II

40. The limited partnership has become popular as a means of owning real estate because of
    A. limited liability.
    B. minimum management responsibility.
    C. direct pass-through of profits.
    D. All of the above.

41. Before investing in a limited partnership, one should
    I. determine if the partnership is suitable for his personal objectives.
    II. investigate the past performance of the general partners.
    A. I only   B. II only   C. Both I and II   D. Neither I nor II

42. A joint venture differs from a partnership in that
    I. a joint venture is formed to carry out a single project.
    II. a joint venturer cannot bind the other joint venturers to a contract.
    A. I only   B. II only   C. Both I and II   D. Neither I nor II

43. Which of the following usually offers the most liquid form of property ownership?
    A. Limited partnership.   C. Sole ownership.
    B. Joint tenancy.   D. General partnership.

44. The homeowners along Birdsnest Lane want to form a nonprofit organization to beautify their street. What would they most likely organize as?
    A. A land trust.   C. A partnership.
    B. A syndication.   D. An association.

45. A business entity owned by stockholders who possess shares of stock as evidence of their ownership is
    I. a general partnership.
    II. an S corporation.
    III. a C corporation.
    A. I only   B. II only   C. II and III only   D. I, II and III

46. The possibility of double taxation on income is a negative factor in
    I. the corporate form of ownership.
    II. the limited partnership form of ownership.
    A. I only   B. II only   C. Both I and II   D. Neither I nor II

47. Protection from personal liability is an advantage of
    I. corporate ownership.
    II. general partnership ownership.
    A. I only   B. II only   C. Both I and II   D. Neither I nor II

48. The day-to-day management of a corporation is the responsibility of its
    I. stockholders.
    II. board of directors.
    A. I only   B. II only   C. Both I and II   D. Neither I nor II

49. Mr. Rose wants to set up a trust to provide income for his minor children, to take effect after his death. What form of trust would this be?
     I. Inter vivos trust.
    II. Testamentary trust.
    A. I only   B. II only   C. Both I and II   D. Neither I nor II

50. Which of the following statements is NOT true with regard to a real estate investment trust?
    A. Investors are known as beneficiaries.
    B. Ownership shares are known as beneficial interests.
    C. Income is taxed at the level of the trust, rather than as income to the beneficiaries.
    D. Ownership shares are freely transferable.

Ownership Situations

1. Charlie and Mabel Brown, husband and wife, owned their home as tenants by the entireties. What course of events would take place in each of the following situations?

    A. In order to raise cash for his business, Charlie sold the home, acting alone. Mabel later refused to sign the deed. What is the status of this sale? *Void*

    B. The deed to this property reads "Charles Brown and Mabel Brown, husband and wife, as tenants by the entireties." If it were located in a state in which survivorship is automatic, what action would be necessary for Mabel to receive the fee in severalty upon Charlie's death? *Nothing*

    C. If Charlie and Mabel were to be divorced, what type of tenancy would be established, assuming no property settlement which awarded the property to one spouse in severalty?

        Tenancy in common

D. If title were granted as in C above, and one person did not wish to continue co-ownership, what possibilities are available to him/her?

Sell, give away, court partition of property

E. If the property was not capable of physical subdivision, how else could the interests of the parties be separated?

By selling, then dividing sale price

F. Suppose Charlie incurred a debt in the form of a bank loan, but without Mabel's signature on the note. If Charlie were to default on the loan, could the property be attached for the satisfaction of the debt?

Not if they are tenants by entirety
Yes if tenants in common

2. Suppose that Charlie and Mabel lived in a community property state. After marriage, they purchased their home. Mabel was not employed and had no funds of her own. The home was purchased entirely from funds produced by Charlie at his employment. Would this be separate or community property?

Community property

A. Upon her parents' death, Mabel inherited real property which was situated in the same state. Would this be community property or would this be Mabel's separate property?

Mabel's separate property

B. Suppose that Charlie died prior to Mabel. When his will was read, it was found that he had left his interest in the family home to his sister. Would this be a legal provision of the will? Would Mabel have any dower rights in this property?

No dower rights in a community property state

C. Upon the death of his parents, Charlie inherited some cash, with which he purchased investment property. If he took title in his name alone, would it be community property or separate property? Would Mabel have any dower rights?

Separate
No dower rights in community property state

3. Ace and Deuce, each of whom were married, purchased a parcel of investment property as joint tenants in a state in which survivorship was presumed among joint tenants. Title was taken in this manner. This was not a community property state.

A. Upon the death of either tenant, who would acquire the interest of the deceased tenant? Could this be defeated by will?

Surviving partner
Cannot be defeated by a will

B. What rights would the widow of the deceased tenant have in the property? Why?

None
Joint tenancy has survivorship rights

4. Brown, Jones and Smith, each of whom were married, purchased a parcel of investment property for a price of $50,000. Brown paid $10,000, Jones paid $15,000, and Smith $25,000 of the purchase price and they took title in those proportions on the deed.

    A. What type of tenancy would be established and why?

        In common
        Unequal interests

    B. What proportionate shares of the property would each tenant hold?

        Brown 20%
        Jones 30%
        Smith 50%

    C. If this were a rental property containing five units, how would ownership of the individual units be divided? Why?

        Wouldn't be divided
        Ten. in common has undivided interest

    D. Should Smith desire to sell a portion of his share to Green, could he do so without the agreement of Jones and Brown? If so, what would be the relationship of Green to the other tenants?

        Yes
        Tenant in common

    E. If one of the owners should die, what disposition would be made of his share, in the absence of a will?

        To his heirs

    F. Suppose the property were in a community property state, and Brown had purchased his share with funds earned from his employment. Would this be community property or separate property? If he should die intestate, to whom would his share be given?

        Separate property
        Partners

G.   How would the earnings of the property be divided for tax purposes?

20%
30%
50%

5.   Suppose that Brown, Smith and Jones had decided to take title in partner-
     ship and the shares of the individual owners were the same as described
     in number 4 above.

B - 10,000
J - 15,000
S - 25,000

A.   Suppose that Brown were to die of a sudden heart attack. What effect
     would this have on the partnership?

*Brown's wife would inherit & become
tenant in common with Jones & Smith*

B.   What liability would each partner have as an individual for the debt
     of the partnership?

Severally and jointly liable

C.   If one partner were to desire to sell his share of the partnership,
     what difficulties might be encountered?

*Other partners might not be able to buy him out
new partner may be incompatible
May need to partition property or sell property
and divide sale price*

D.   If the partners wanted to limit their individual liability to the
     amount invested, what type of partnership could be created to accom-
     plish this?

Limited partnership

E.   Suppose the partnership was founded for the purpose of a specific
     project, and was to be dissolved upon its completion. What type of
     partnership would be created?

Joint venture

Note: If you are reading <u>Real Estate: An Introduction to the Profession</u>
       you may omit questions 5 and 6 above.

6. Suppose that the partners had elected to adopt the corporate form of ownership of this property.

    A. How would the individual partners receive their share of ownership?

    in stocks

    B. How is it possible that the earnings of the property could be subject to double taxation? Explain.

    The corp. is taxed
    Stockholders are taxed on profits

    C. Why is it usually easier for a partner to dispose of his interest in a corporate form of ownership than with other forms of co-ownership?

    Its easier to sell stock rather than property

7. Give a brief explanation of the manner in which a real estate investment trust is operated.

    A. What term is used to describe investors in a REIT?

    B. How are the earnings of a REIT taxed?

    C. Failure of a REIT to follow the rules for its operation may have what effect on the tax situation of its investors?

Note: If you are reading <u>Real Estate: An Introduction to the Profession</u> you may omit question 7 above.

Answers—Chapter 4

Multiple Choice Questions

1. C   Ownership in severalty is ownership by one person. This may be an individual person or a partnership, corporation or other legal entity buying in its name solely.

2. C   Property acquired before marriage and property acquired after marriage through inheritance are usually considered to be separate property.

3. A   An owner of property in severalty has freedom of choice as to use or disposition of the property, but does not necessarily have the ability to defeat a spouse's claim of dower or curtesy.

4. B   Tenants in common do not need separate deeds to their respective shares of ownership in the property. One deed with all their names is sufficient and customary.

5. C   Whenever the co-owners have unequal shares of ownership, they are tenants in common, and there cannot be survivorship among tenants in common.

6. A   Tenants in common hold undivided interests in the entire property and one tenant cannot claim a portion for his own use.

7. D   A tenant in common may dispose of all or part of his interest independently of the other tenants and without their permission.

8. C   Partition of a tenancy in common may be accomplished by physical subdivision of the property or by sale of the property and division of the proceeds.

9. C   Difficulty of disposing of undivided interests and joint liability for debts against the property are hazards of both tenancy in common and joint tenancy.

10. B   They do not receive separate deeds for their shares.

11. C   The right of survivorship exists among joint tenants or tenants by the entireties, but not among tenants in common.

12. B   New joint tenants may not be added to an existing joint tenancy without forming a new joint tenancy.

13. A   Only by using a will can Madora retain the flexibility to change her mind later.

14. C   Corporations may hold title as tenants in common or in severalty, but not as joint tenants.

15.   A   Joint tenants must acquire their interest in jointly held property at the same time, from the same source and in the same instrument.

16.   C   The unities of joint tenancy require that all joint tenants have equal rights of possession and equal interests in the property.

17.   C   Should any unity of joint tenancy be broken, the estate becomes a tenancy in common.

18.   A   The new co-owner (David) will be a tenant in common with the remaining joint tenants, who remain joint tenants among themselves. David will own a one-third undivided interest and Baker and Charles will continue holding a two-thirds undivided interest.

19.   C   The concept of tenancy by the entireties is based upon English law, which treats a husband and wife as one legal unit.

20.   C   Should a tenancy by the entireties be terminated by divorce, the parting spouses become tenants in common with one another.

21.   D   A spouse's right of curtesy or dower is defeated by holding title to property as a joint tenant with another person.

22.   A   In the absence of any other agreement, tenants by the entireties who are divorced become tenants in common with one another.

23.   A   The legal concepts of community property laws are derived from Spanish and French law.

24.   B   The premise that husband and wife are equal partners is fundamental to the concept of community property law.

25.   C   Any property purchased after marriage is treated as community property in states which have community property laws.

— 26.   C   This property will be treated as community property since it was purchased with marital funds, and both spouses' signatures will be required on the deed if it is sold.

27.   C   Both real and personal property purchased with marital funds are treated as community property in states having community property laws.

28.   D   Neither dower nor curtesy exist in community property states.

29.   C   Following marriage, a person's earnings are considered to be marital funds, and any property purchased from these earnings will be treated as community property. The wife's name need not appear on the deed.

— 30.   B   Under community property law, a spouse may devise his or her share to anyone, provided the surviving spouse does not have survivorship rights such as with joint tenancy ownership.

31. C   In community property states, property not held as community property is designated as separate property.

32. D   A limited partnership has a general partner or partners, and all other partners are limited partners.

33. C   Property held in the name of a partnership is not subject to claims of dower or curtesy from the spouse of either partner.

34. B   The list of partners must be published in the county and state where the partnership owns property.

35. C   In a general partnership, each partner has unlimited financial liability, and pays individual taxes on earnings from the partnership.

36. D   Corporate income is taxed to the corporation, and may be taxed as individual income upon disbursement to stockholders.

37. C   The aggregation of capital and individual expertise and individual taxation of profits and/or losses is sometimes an advantage of the partnership form of ownership.

38. B   Limited partnerships permit the pass-through of profits while limiting the financial liability of limited partners to the amount of their investment.

39. B   Limited partnerships are managed by a general partner or partners. Limited partners have little or no voice in management decisions.

40. D   Limited liability, minimum management responsibilities, and direct pass-through of profits have all contributed to the popularity of the limited partnership form of ownership.

41. C   Before investing in a limited partnership one should determine whether it is suitable for one's personal objectives and investigate the past performance of the general partners.

42. C   A joint venture is formed to carry out a single project, and a joint venturer cannot bind the other joint venturers in a contract.

43. C   Sole ownership is usually the most liquid form of ownership because no other person has a voice in disposing of the property.

44. D   An association would provide limitations on individual liability and could be organized so as to be nontaxable.

45. C   Only in a corporation do the owners possess shares of stock as evidence of their ownership.

46. A   The possibility of double taxation on income exists in the corporate form of ownership.

47. A   Protection from personal liability exists within the corporate form of ownership, but not in a general partnership.

48. D   The management policies of a corporation are determined by its board of directors and implemented by its officers. Stockholders have no management functions, but do elect the board of directors.

49. B   A testamentary trust takes effect after the death of its creator.

50. C   If a REIT follows the rules regarding distribution of its earnings, those earnings are taxed only once, at the beneficiaries level.

Ownership Situations

1A. A cloud on the title exists due to rights held by Mabel.

B. None, except that it is customary to file a death certificate and a description of the property in the public records to make the matter clear to anyone searching the title.

C. Tenants in common.

D. Sell the unwanted interest, or buy the other's interest, or petition for partition.

E. The property would be sold and the proceeds divided.

F. The property can be attached and sold only if Mabel dies first. (This is why lenders require both to sign.)

2. Community property.

A. Mabel can keep this as separate property.

B. This is legal. No dower rights exist under community property.

C. Separate property. No dower rights.

3A. The surviving joint tenant would acquire full ownership. This cannot be defeated by will.

B. The widow would have no rights; the surviving joint tenant would.

4A. Tenancy in common due to unequal interests.

B. Brown 20%; Jones 30%; Smith 50%.

C. Ownership would not be split among the apartment units, as each owner holds an undivided interest in the whole property.

D. Smith can sell to Green without the agreement of Jones or Brown. All would be tenants in common.

E. The rules of intestate succession wuld apply.

F. This would be community property. His spouse or his descendents, depending on state law, would acquire his interest if he dies intestate.

G. Earnings would be apportioned among the owners according to their respective interests.

5A. The deceased's partner's rights vest in the remaining partners, but his estate must be reimbursed for the value of those rights.

B. Each partner is fully liable for all the debts of the partnership.

C. Illiquidity is a problem; so is finding a compatible partner.

D. Limited partnership. However, one person must remain as a general partner.

E. Joint venture.

6A. Shares of stock would be held.

B. Earnings could be taxed to the corporation and again to the shareholder when paid as dividends.

C. As a rule, shares of stock are easier to sell and transfer.

7. A REIT is composed of trustees and beneficiaries, the latter providing capital through the purchase of beneficial interests. The trustees invest this capital and the results are allocated and paid to the beneficiaries.

A. The investors are called beneficiaries.

B. REIT earnings are taxed only once at the beneficiary level provided certain rules are met.

C. Double taxation, once to the REIT and once to the beneficiary, results if the rules are not met.

Transferring Title

Chapter 5

1. A written legal document by which ownership of real property is transferred from one party to another is
   A. a bill of sale.
   B. a lease.
   C. a contract of sale.
   D. a deed.

2. The law which requires that transfers of real property ownership be in writing is known as the
   A. Law of Evidence.
   B. Statute of Liberties.
   C. Statute of Frauds.
   D. Statute of Limitations.

3. Oral transfers of land, as practiced in the early centuries of English history, were abolished because
   I. of the increasing numbers of transfers by sale.
   II. as people became more mobile, witnesses were more difficult to locate.
   III. of the susceptibility of fraud through bribed witnesses.
   A. I and II only
   B. I and III only
   C. II and III only
   D. I, II and III

4. The actual act of transferring ownership of land is known as
   A. a grant.
   B. a devise.
   C. a demise.
   D. a curtesy.

5. Which of the following is essential to the validity of a deed?
   I. The grantor must be of legal age.
   II. The grantor must be of sound mind.
   A. I only   B. II only   C. Both I and II   D. Neither I nor II

Note: There are no deleted questions in this chapter for readers of
        Real Estate: An Introduction to the Profession.

6. All of the following are true of the consideration stated in a deed EXCEPT:
   A. The deed may be based on a valuable consideration.
   B. The consideration may be stated as a good consideration.
   C. A deed may be based on a consideration that is both good and valuable.
   D. The actual amount of a valuable consideration must be stated in the deed.

7. One day after the birth of his first son, Reilly signed a deed conveying real estate which he owned to the son. The consideration recited in the deed was stated as the love that Reilly felt for his son. Was this a valid form of consideration?
   A. Yes, because the statement of love constituted a valuable consideration.
   B. Yes, because the deed recited a good consideration.
   C. No, because a deed may not convey title to real estate to an infant.
   D. No, because the son was unable to sign the deed.

8. With the words of conveyance in a deed, the grantor
   I. states that he is making a grant of the property to the grantee.
   II. warrants that he has the right to convey title to the property.
   A. I only   B. II only   C. Both I and II   D. Neither I nor II

9. Which of the following may be conveyed by deed?
   I. Fee simple estate.   III. Easements.
   II. Life estate.   IV. Leasehold estate.
   A. I and II only   C. I, II and III only
   B. I, II and IV only   D. I, II, III and IV

10. Carter conveyed property to Blaine by means of a deed which identified the property as "the property located at 123 W. Maple Street, Anytown, Your State." Is this an acceptable description of the property?
    A. Yes, because the property can be located from this description.
    B. Yes, because Blaine knew the location of the property.
    C. No, because it does not identify the boundaries, and street numbers can be changed.
    D. No, because all land descriptions in a deed must be based on a recorded survey.

11. If only air or mineral rights are being conveyed by deed,
    I. the legal description of the land will be omitted.
    II. words of conveyance will be omitted.
    A. I only   B. II only   C. Both I and II   D. Neither I nor II

12. In order to convey title to real property, a deed must be signed by the
    I. grantee.
    II. grantor.
    A. I only   B. II only   C. Both I and II   D. Neither I nor II

13. A deed must be made under seal if the grantor is
    A. a natural person.   C. illiterate.
    B. a corporation.   D. an infant.

14. In order to convey title, a deed must be
    I. delivered by the grantor to the grantee.
    II. accepted by the grantee.
    A. I only   B. II only   C. Both I and II   D. Neither I nor II

15. A grantee can indicate acceptance of a deed by
    I. retaining the deed.
    II. recording the deed.
    III. encumbering the title.
    IV. taking occupancy of the property.
    A. II only   C. II and IV only
    B. I and II only   D. I, II, III and IV

16. A grantee is assured that he will not be disturbed by someone else
    claiming an interest in the property by the covenant of
    A. seizin.   C. further assurance.
    B. quiet enjoyment.   D. warranty forever.

17. The grantee is assured that the title to property is not encumbered by
    unpaid taxes, judgments, etc. by the covenant of
    I. warranty forever.
    II. further assurance.
    A. I only   B. II only   C. Both I and II   D. Neither I nor II

18. Should additional documents be necessary to perfect the grantee's title,
    this would be required by the
    A. covenant of seizin.
    B. convenant of further assurance.
    C. covenant against encumbrances.
    D. covenant of warranty forever.

19. The covenant which is the absolute guarantee that the title and rights to
    possession of the property are as stated in the deed is the
    A. covenant of seizin.
    B. covenant of quiet possession.
    C. covenant against encumbrances.
    D. covenant of warranty forever.

20. Rex conveyed real estate to Edgar by means of a deed which he prepared
    himself without the assistance of an attorney. For this to be a valid
    deed, which of the following elements must be present?
    I. Consideration, either good or valuable.
    II. Operative words of conveyance.
    III. A legally acceptable description of the property.
    IV. A testimony clause.
    A. I and II only   C. I, II and III only
    B. II, III, and IV only   D. I, II, III and IV

21. Deeds are usually acknowledged to
    A. make them valid.
    B. provide constructive notice.
    C. make them enforceable.
    D. make them admissible to the public records.

22. In addition to the minimum requirements of a deed, all five covenants and warranties are found in all the following deeds EXCEPT a:
    A. special warranty deed.   C. warranty deed.
    B. general warranty deed.   D. full covenant and warranty deed.

23. The deed considered to be the best deed a grantee can receive is a
    A. general warranty deed.   C. bargain and sale deed.
    B. special warranty deed.   D. quitclaim deed.

24. As used in a deed, the word "appurtenances" means
    A. rights that pass with the conveyance.
    B. a deed wherein a full set of covenants and warranties is lacking.
    C. the place where the deed is signed and notarized.
    D. a combination granting clause and habendum.

25. In order to be valid, a deed must show
    I. where it was made.
    II. the date on which it was signed.
    A. I only   B. II only   C. Both I and II   D. Neither I nor II

26. Which of the following are the same?
    I. Grantor--Party conveying title.
    II. Grantee--Party acquiring title.
    A. I only   B. II only   C. Both I and II   D. Neither I nor II

27. The words of conveyance in a deed
    I. state the intent to pass ownership to the grantee.
    II. describe the extent of the estate being granted.
    III. include the habendum clause.
    A. I only   B. II only   C. I and II only   D. I, II and III

28. The phrase "the grantee's heirs and assigns forever" indicates the conveyance of a
    I. fee simple estate.   III. leasehold estate.
    II. life estate.   IV. less than freehold estate.
    A. I only   C. II and III only
    B. I and II only   D. III and IV only

29. The word "assigns" in a deed refers to
    A. anyone to whom the grantee may later deed the property.
    B. creditors of the grantee.
    C. the grantor.
    D. the grantor's heirs.

30. The description of the land in a deed may be by
    A. metes and bounds.   C. recorded plat.
    B. government survey.   D. Any of the above.

31. A grantor who does not wish to convey certain rights of ownership
    A. must note the exceptions in a separate instrument.
    B. may not do so, as a deed conveys the entire premises.
    C. may note the exceptions in the deed.
    D. must convey the entire premises and have the grantee reconvey the right to be retained by the grantor.

32. The description of the land in a deed
    A. automatically includes all buildings on the land.
    B. conveys buildings only if described in the deed.
    C. conveys only the land.
    D. does not convey subsurface rights unless so stated in the deed.

33. The clause which identifies the estate being granted by the deed is
    I. the habendum clause.
    II. sometimes called the "to have and to hold" clause.
    III. a part of the words of conveyance.
    A. I only   C. II and III only
    B. I and II only   D. I, II and III

34. The testimony clause in a deed
    I. states that the grantor caused the deed to be prepared and that
       he signed it on the date noted.
    II. may be omitted as long as the grantor signs the deed.
    A. I only   B. II only   C. Both I and II   D. Neither I nor II

35. The seal may be affixed to a deed by means of
    I. a glued paper seal.   III. the word "seal."
    II. a hot wax seal.   IV. the letters "L. S."
    A. I, II, III and IV   C. III and IV only
    B. I and II only   D. II and IV only

36. The exact form and wording of a deed are
    A. critical to its validity.
    B. set by federal statutes.
    C. determined by state law.
    D. flexible as long as all essentials are present and in conformity
       with state law.

37. In a grant deed, the grantor covenants and warrants all of the following
    EXCEPT:
    A. that he has not previously conveyed the estate being granted to
       another party.
    B. that he has not encumbered the property except as noted in the deed.
    C. that he will convey to the grantee any title to the property that
       he may later acquire.
    D. that he will be responsible for prior encumbrances as well as his
       own.

38. In a grant deed, the grantor is responsible for encumbrances
    I. of future owners as well as his own.
    II. during the period of time he possessed the property.
    A. I only   B. II only   C. Both I and II   D. Neither I nor II

39. A deed wherein the grantor covenants and warrants the property's title
    against defects occurring during the grantor's ownership and not against
    defects existing before that time is a
    A. bargain and sale deed.   C. special warranty deed.
    B. grant deed.   D. quitclaim deed.

40. Which of the following deeds contain only the covenant that the grantor has not encumbered the property?
    I. Guardian's deed.   III. Referee's deed in foreclosure.
    II. Sheriff's deed.   IV. Cession deed.
    A. I and II only   C. I, II and III only
    B. II and III only   D. I, II, III and IV

41. A quitclaim conveys
    I. the grantor's interest in the property at the time of conveyance.
    II. any rights that the grantor may acquire in the future.
    A. I only   B. II only   C. Both I and II   D. Neither I nor II

42. Quitclaim deeds are often used
    I. to remove a cloud from the title.
    II. to convey the grantor's interest without imposing any future obligations to defend the title upon the grantor.
    A. I only   B. II only   C. Both I and II   D. Neither I nor II

43. Gift deeds usually take the form of
    A. sheriff's deeds.   C. warranty deeds.
    B. bargain and sale deeds.   D. grant deeds.

44. In what type of deed must the grantor state the legal authority that permits the grantor to convey the property of a minor?
    A. Gift deed.   C. Sheriff's deed.
    B. Life estate deed.   D. Guardian's deed.

45. You would expect to find the words "remise" and "release" in a
    A. warranty deed.   C. grant deed.
    B. special warranty deed.   D. quitclaim deed.

46. Which of the following could be used to convey title as the result of mortgage foreclosure?
    I. A sheriff's deed.
    II. A referee's deed in foreclosure.
    A. I only   B. II only   C. Both I and II   D. Neither I nor II

47. A deed used to correct an error in a previously executed and delivered deed may be called a
    I. correction deed.
    II. deed of confirmation.
    A. I only   B. II only   C. Both I and II   D. Neither I nor II

48. A court of law with the power to admit and certify wills is called a
    I. probate court.
    II. surrogate court.
    A. I only   B. II only   C. Both I and II   D. Neither I nor II

49. Title acquired as the result of inheritance from a person who dies intes-
     tate is known as
       I.   title by descent.
      II.   a devise.
     III.   title by intestate succession.
     A. I, II and III   C. II only
     B. I and III only   D. III only

50. Under the laws of intestate succession, which of the following would have
     the superior right of inheritance?
     A. The deceased's children.   C. The deceased's brothers and sisters.
     B. The deceased's parents.   D. The deceased's aunts and uncles.

51. The term "escheat" refers to
       I.   the passing of title to real property to the state when no will
            or heirs can be found for a decedent's estate.
      II.   title acquired through undue influence or duress.
     A. I only   B. II only   C. Both I and II   D. Neither I nor II

52. A gift of real property by will is indicated by the term
     A. devise.   C. demise.
     B. bequest.   D. legacy.

53. An executor's deed may be used to
       I.   transfer property to a devisee named in the will.
      II.   sell real property to persons unrelated to the will.
     A. I only   B. II only   C. Both I and II   D. Neither I nor II

54. A handwritten will signed by the testator but not witnessed is known as a
       I.   noncupative will.
      II.   holographic will.
     A. I only   B. II only   C. Both I and II   D. Neither I nor II

55. A person named in a will to carry out its terms may be known by all the
     following terms EXCEPT:
     A. an executor.   C. a surrogate.
     B. an executrix.   D. a personal representative.

56. Title acquired by occupation of another's land is known as title by
     A. dereliction.   C. adverse possession.
     B. accretion.   D. squatter's rights.

57. In order to successfully claim title by adverse possession, the claimant
     must meet all the following requirements EXCEPT:
     A. actual possession of the land.
     B. open and hostile possession.
     C. continuous possession for the statutory period.
     D. occupancy of the land with the permission of the owner of record.

58. Joe has been farming his deceased father's land and paying property taxes on it for so long that everyone in town has come to assume that Joe owns it. A document in the public records seems to indicate that Joe is the owner, but there is no deed or other conveyance from his father. Which of the following is/are true?
    I.   Joe has color of title to the farm.
    II. Joe is an adverse claimant against anyone else claiming ownership of the farm.
    III. Anyone buying the farm from Joe can tack on Joe's claims and rights to his own.
    IV. Joe's occupation of the land will result in it being dedicated to him.
    A. I only   C. I, II and III only
    B. I and II only   D. I, II, III and IV

59. When a person assumes, through adverse possession or assignment, the rights of a previous adverse possessor, it is known as
    A. tacking-on.   C. adversity.
    B. prescription.   D. probate.

60. An easement acquired by prolonged adverse use is acquired by
    A. implied grant.   C. prescription.
    B. necessity.   D. condemnation.

61. An owner can break a claim of adverse possession by
    I.   ejecting the trespasser.
    II. giving the trespasser permission to trespass.
    A. I only   B. II only   C. Both I and II   D. Neither I nor II

62. The process of increasing land due to the gradual deposition of water-borne soil is known as
    A. reliction.   C. accretion.
    B. avulsion.   D. alluvion.

63. When a waterline permanently recedes, exposing dry land, it is known as
    I.   avulsion.
    II. dereliction.
    A. I only   B. II only   C. Both I and II   D. Neither I nor II

64. Land acquired through accretion or dereliction is known as ownership by
    A. accession.   C. assemblage.
    B. appurtenance.   D. alluvion.

65. A conveyance of land by a government to a private citizen is known as a
    A. dedication.   C. public grant.
    B. prescription.   D. private grant.

66. Land may be transferred from the public domain to private ownership by
    I.   dedication.
    II. a land patent.
    A. I only   B. II only   C. Both I and II   D. Neither I nor II

67. A voluntary gift of private land to the public is known as
    A. alienation.   C. dereliction.
    B. dedication.   D. annexation.

68. When a landowner, by act or word, shows that he intends that land be de-
    dicated, even though no written dedication has been made, it is known as
    A. a public devise.   C. statutory dedication.
    B. a public bequest.   D. common law dedication.

69. Forfeiture can result when a grantee
    I. fails to meet a condition or limitation imposed by the grantor.
    II. fails to make mortgage payments.
    A. I only   B. II only   C. Both I and II   D. Neither I nor II

70. The term "alienation" can be used to describe transfers of land by
    I. foreclosure, execution sale, quiet title action or escheat.
    II. eminent domain, partition, forfeiture or marriage.
    A. I only   B. II only   C. Both I and II   D. Neither I nor II

Deed Situations

Each situation described below would be resolved by a certain type of deed.
Examine the situation and determine the type of deed best used in each in-
stance. Justify your selection by showing why the features of that deed
apply.

1. Sally Somebody was named in the will of her late brother to settle his
    estate. In order to raise money for taxes, it was necessary to sell a
    parcel of real estate which was owned by him. Title would be conveyed
    by means of a(n) _____ deed.
    Justification:

2. Charlie Nomoney's real property was sold at a court-ordered foreclosure
    sale. The property was located in a state which allowed Charlie one year
    to pay the debt and redeem the property. For a consideration, Charlie
    agreed to give up this right to the purchaser at foreclosure. He would
    do so by means of a(n) _____ deed.
    Justification:

3. Sam Sunburn, of Palm Springs, California, voluntarily sold his home
    through normal marketing procedures. Title would probably be conveyed
    by means of a(n) _____ deed.
    Justification:

4. George Goodfellow wishes to convey property to his daughter as a gift.
    He is willing to warrant that he has not encumbered the property, but
    will not give any further warranties of title. In this situation, title
    would probably be conveyed in a(n) _____ deed.
    Justification:

5. Sam and Suzy Byers purchased a home in your state through normal mar-
    keting procedures. Sam and Suzy are man and wife. What type of deed
    would they ask for in this situation? _____ deed.
    Justification:

6. Discuss and give several pitfalls in the use of preprinted deed forms for the transfer of real estate ownership.

7. Why would a grantee be willing to accept a deed with fewer covenants than those found in a warranty deed?

8. Identify and discuss one of the more important differences in the transfer of real estate ownership by grant and by will.

9. Define and illustrate the term "color of title."

10. Give several examples of the alteration of one's ownership of land by accession.

Answers—Chapter 5

Multiple Choice Questions

1. D   A deed is a written legal document used for transferring ownership of real property.

2. C   The Statute of Frauds requires that transfers of ownership of real property be in writing.

3. D   The increasing numbers of transfers by sale, mobility of people, difficulty of locating witnesses and susceptibility to fraud through bribed witnesses all led to the abolishment of oral transfers of land ownership.

4. A   The actual act of transferring ownership of land is known as a grant.

5. C   For a deed to be valid, the grantor must be of legal age and of sound mind.

6. D   It is not necessary for the actual amount of a valuable consideration to be stated in a deed.

7. B   The statement of love constituted a good consideration, sufficient for the validity of the deed.

8. A   The words of conveyance are the grantor's statement that he is making a grant of the property to the grantee. They do not warrant that the grantor has the right to convey.

9. C   A fee simple estate, life estate or easement, but not a leasehold, may be conveyed by deed.

10. C   The property description in a deed must be sufficient to identify the boundaries. Street numbers are subject to change, so are not acceptable.

11. D   Even though a deed conveys only air or mineral rights, the deed must contain a legal description of the land and words of conveyance.

12. B   For a deed to convey title, it must be signed by the grantor. The grantee's signature is not necessary.

13. B   If the grantor is a corporation, the deed must be made under seal.

14. C   A deed does not convey title until it is delivered and accepted.

15. D   A grantee can indicate acceptance by retaining or recording the deed, encumbering the title, taking occupancy of the property, or the performance of any other act of ownership.

16.   B   The covenant of quiet enjoyment assures that the grantee will not be disturbed by someone else claiming an interest in the property.

17.   D   The covenant against encumbrances, not the covenant of warranty forever or the covenant of further assurance, assures that the title to the property is not encumbered by undisclosed encumbrances.

18.   B   The covenant of further assurance assures that any additional documents necessary for the perfection of the grantee's title will be executed by the grantor.

19.   D   The covenant of warranty forever is the absolute guarantee that the title and rights to possession are as stated in the deed.

20.   C   A consideration, operative words of conveyance, and legally acceptable property description are essential to a deed's validity. A testimony clause is not essential.

21.   D   Deeds are usually acknowledged to make them admissible to record. An acknowledgement is not essential to the deed's validity or enforceability.

22.   A   A special warranty deed warrants only against defects occurring during the grantor's ownership. It does not contain all five covenants and warranties, as do the other deeds named.

23.   A   A general warranty deed provides the grantee with the most assurances of title, and is the best deed the grantee can receive.

24.   A   Rights that pass with the conveyance are identified as appurtenances.

25.   D   Neither the date nor place of execution need be shown on a deed for it to be valid.

26.   C   The party who conveys title is the grantor, and the party who receives title is the grantee.

27.   D   The words of conveyance in a deed state the intent to pass ownership, describe the extent of the estate being granted, and include the habendum clause.

28.   A   The phrase "the grantee's heirs and assigns forever" indicate the conveyance of a fee simple estate.

29.   A   The word "assigns" in a deed refers to anyone to whom the grantee may later deed the property.

30.   D   The description of the land in a deed may be by metes and bounds, government survey or recorded plat.

31.   C   Rights which are not to be conveyed by deed may be excluded in the deed and will not be conveyed.

32. A   The description of the land in a deed automatically conveys any buildings on the land.

33. D   The habendum clause, also called the "to have and to hold clause," is a part of the words of conveyance and identifies the estate being granted by the deed.

34. C   The testimony clause in a deed states that the grantor caused the deed to be prepared and that he signed it on the date noted. It may be omitted as long as the grantor signs the deed.

35. A   The seal may be affixed by means of a glued paper seal, a hot wax seal, the word "seal" or by the letters "L. S."

36. D   The exact form and wording of a deed are flexible as long as all essentials are present and in conformity with state law.

37. D   In a grant deed the grantor does not covenant or warrant that he will be responsible for prior encumbrances.

38. B   The grantor under a grant deed is responsible for encumbrances during the period of time that he possessed the property. The grantor is not responsible for encumbrances of future owners.

39. C   A special warranty deed warrants against defects occurring during the grantor's ownership, but not against defects existing before that time.

40. C   A guardian's deed, sheriff's deed, and a referee's deed in foreclosure all covenant that the grantor has not encumbered the property. A cession deed is a quitclaim deed and contains no covenants of title.

41. A   A quitclaim deed conveys only the grantor's interest at the time of conveyance.

42. C   Quitclaim deeds are often used to remove a cloud from a title or to convey the grantor's interest without imposing upon the grantor any future obligations to defend the title.

43. B   Gift deeds usually take the form of bargain and sale deeds to avoid committing the grantor to any warranties of title.

44. D   The grantor must state his legal authority to convey the property in a guardian's deed.

45. D   The words "remise" and "release" are most likely to be found in a quitclaim deed.

46. C   Either a sheriff's deed or a referee's deed in foreclosure may be used to convey title as the result of mortgage foreclosure.

47. C   A correction deed, also called a deed of confirmation, may be used to correct an error in a previously executed and delivered deed.

48. C Courts which are empowered to admit and certify wills are called either probate courts or surrogate courts.

49. B Title acquired by inheritance from a person who died intestate is known as title by descent or title by intestate succession.

50. A The deceased's children (and surviving spouse, if any) are the dominant recipients of the deceased's assets in the case of an intestate death.

51. A The term "escheat" refers to the passing of title to the state when no will or heirs can be found for the decedent's estate.

52. A A devise is a gift of real property by will.

53. C An executor's deed may be used to transfer property to a devisee named in a will or to sell real property from the estate to persons unrelated to the will.

54. B A handwritten will signed by the testator but not witnessed is known as a holographic will.

55. C A person named in a will to carry out its terms may be referred to as an executor, executrix or personal representative, but not as a surrogate.

56. C Title acquired by occupation of another's land is known as title by adverse possession.

57. D To successfully claim title by adverse possession, a claimant must have been in actual possession of the land in an open and notorious manner continuously for the statutory period in the jurisdiction. If the claimant had the owner's permission to occupy the land, there would not be any adverse possession.

58. C Joe has color of title, is an adverse claimant to others, and can allow his claims and rights to be tacked-on to those of a future purchaser.

59. A Assumption of the rights of a previous adverse possessor, either through adverse possession or assignment, is known as "tacking on."

60. C An easement by prescription is acquired by prolonged adverse use.

61. C A claim of adverse possession can be forestalled by ejecting the trespasser or by giving the trespasser the right to trespass.

62. C Accretion is the process of increasing the size of a parcel of land by the gradual deposition of water-borne soil.

63. B Dereliction results from the recession of the water line, exposing dry land.

64.   A   Land acquired through accretion or dereliction is known as ownership by accession.

65.   C   A conveyance of land by a government to a private citizen is known as a public grant.

66.   B   Land may be transferred from the public domain to private ownership by means of a land patent.

67.   B.   A dedication is a voluntary gift of privately held land to the public domain.

68.   D   Common law dedication arises when a landowner, by act or word, shows that he intends land to be dedicated, even though no written dedication has been made.

69.   A   Forfeiture can result from a grantee's failure to meet a condition or limitation imposed by a grantor.

70.   C   A change in ownership of any kind is known as alienation.

Short Answer Questions

1.   Executor's deed. This is a legal requirement when probating a will.

2.   Quitclaim deed. Charlie is conveying whatever rights he might still have to the purchaser.

3.   Grant deed. This is the standard deed in California for fee simple land title transfers.

4.   Gift deed. This is a special warranty deed with the wording "for natural love and affection" as consideration. With only one covenant he limits his liability exposure.

5.   The buyer would ask for a warranty deed or grant deed depending upon the state. These would provide the most protection available from a deed.

6.   Preprinted forms may not be correct for the user's state, they may not fit the user's needs, and they may be filled in improperly.

7.   Title insurance may be available. The grantee's purpose may require less than a warranty deed.

8.   A will can be changed until the death of the testator. A grant cannot be changed once it is made.

9.   Color of title is some plausible suggestion of an ownership interest, for example, a relative claiming an interest in a deceased's estate, or a trespasser of longstanding.

10. Examples of accession include receding waterline, buildup of earth, and man-made additions such as the conversion of personalty to realty.

Recordation, Abstracts
and Title Insurance

Chapter 6

1. The Statute of Frauds was enacted in England in the year
   A. 1066   C. 1677
   B. 1492   D. 1776

2. The statute of frauds established the requirement that
   A. written deeds be used to show transfers of ownership.
   B. all deeds be recorded in the public records.
   C. a system of public records be established.
   D. anyone claiming ownership of land visibly occupy the land.

3. Notice provided by recording an instrument in the public records is
   I. legal notice.   III. constructive notice.
   II. actual notice.   IV. inquiry notice.
   A. I only   C. II and IV only
   B. II only   D. I and III only

4. Constructive notice requires that
   I. a landowner give public notice of his/her claim of ownership.
   II. anyone interested in the property inspect the property and the
       public records.
   A. I only   B. II only   C. Both I and II   D. Neither I nor II

5. An investor is considering the purchase of a 100-unit apartment building
   that is fully occupied. Which of the following would be true?
   I. The investor should search the public records for copies of the
      tenant's rental agreements.
   II. By their presence, the tenants are giving constructive notice of
       their rights to be there.
   III. The investor is charged with inquiring as to the rights of each
        tenant.
   A. I and II only   C. II and III only
   B. I and III only   D. I, II and III

Note: If you are reading <u>Real Estate: An Introduction to the Profession</u>,
      you may omit the following questions: 20, 21, 27, 28, 29, 49, 56
      and 57.

6. Once a person is aware of another's rights or interest in property, that person is said to have
   A. constructive notice.   C. inquiry notice.
   B. legal notice.   D. actual notice.

7. The public recorder's office
     I. serves as a central information station for documents pertaining to interests in land.
    II. is an agency of the federal government.
   A. I only   B. II only   C. Both I and II   D. Neither I nor II

8. Farmer Sorensen leases 320 acres adjacent to his ranch. Sorensen can give notice to the world at large by
     I. plowing the land.
    II. storing his equipment on it.
   III. putting a fence around it.
   A. I only   B. II only   C. III only   D. I, II and III

9. Instruments affecting land transfers are recorded in the jurisdiction in which the
     I. parties to the instrument maintain legal residence.
    II. land is situated.
   III. instrument is created.
   A. I only   B. II only   C. III only   D. I, II and III

10. Documents are recorded by
    A. placing the original document on file in the recorder's office.
    B. submitting the original document which is photocopied and placed on file.
    C. posting a photocopy of the original document on the property.
    D. posting the name and mailing address of the owner on the property.

11. An unrecorded deed to land is binding upon
    A. the parties to the deed.   C. the public generally.
    B. subsequent purchasers.   D. subsequent lenders.

12. Adams conveyed property to Bowen, by a deed dated June 1. Bowen did not record the deed or take possession of the property. On June 10 of the same year, Adams conveyed the same property to Cummings, who has properly searched the records and visited the property. Cummings promptly recorded his deed and took possession of the property. Bowen claimed ownership based on his earlier deed. Would his claim be recognized?
    A. No, because Bowen did not provide legally required notice of his his ownership.
    B. No, because priority is given to the deed with the later date.
    C. Yes, because of the earlier date on his deed.
    D. Yes, because Adam's conveyance to Bowen constituted fraud.

13. Priority of a recorded instrument is determined by the date of
    A. acknowledgement.   C. the instrument.
    B. delivery to the grantee.   D. recordation.

14. Which of the following would NOT usually be placed on record?
    A. A mortgage on the property.
    B. A month-to-month rental agreement.
    C. The deed to the property.
    D. An option to purchase the property.

15. Records in the public recorder's office may be inspected by
    I. prospective buyers.   III. prospective lenders.
    II. the general public.   IV. title insurance company employees.
    A. I, III and IV only   C. I, II and IV only
    B. III and IV only   D. I, II, III and IV

16. A prospective purchaser of real estate is presumed by law to have in-
    spected the
    I. land itself.
    II. public records pertaining to the land.
    A. I only   B. II only   C. Both I and II   D. Neither I nor II

17. Deeds and other instruments which affect land titles should be recorded
    I. immediately after delivery or execution.
    II. in order to provide constructive notice.
    A. I only   B. II only   C. Both I and II   D. Neither I nor II

18. The purpose of having a person's signature acknowledged is to
    I. make certain the person signing the document is the same person
       named in the document, and that the signing was voluntary.
    II. make the document admissible to the public records.
    A. I only   B. II only   C. Both I and II   D. Neither I nor II

19. Which of the following statements is NOT true?
    A. Some states require that a document be acknowledged in order to be
       admissible to record.
    B. Some states will admit documents to record if they are witnessed but
       not acknowledged.
    C. Some states require both witnesses and acknowledgement on all
       recorded instruments.
    D. An acknowledgement can only be taken by a notary public.

20. In a jurisdiction which indexes recorded instruments by grantee and
    grantor, if one knew the name of the current owner of a property, and
    wished to search the records to verify that ownership, one would look
    in the
    I. grantee index.
    II. grantor index.
    A. I only   B. II only   C. Both I and II   D. Neither I nor II

21. In completing a title search, in what order would an abstracter normally proceed with the following steps?
    I. Check the grantor index to ascertain that the present owner had not previously conveyed to someone else.
    II. Check the grantee index to verify the present owner's claim of title.
    III. Check other public records such as court records, lien indexes, judgment rolls, and lis pendens index.
    IV. Trace the chain of title back to the original sale or grant of the land.
    A. I, II, IV, III   C. I, II, III, IV
    B. II, I, III, IV   D. II, I, IV, III

22. Modern-day methods of recording documents include
    I. photocopying.
    II. microfilming.
    A. I only   B. II only   C. Both I and II   D. Neither I nor II

23. Instruments are recorded in the public records in what order?
    A. Alphabetical order, based on the grantee's last name.
    B. Chronological order, as received for recordation.
    C. According to the date of the instrument.
    D. Alphabetical order, based on the grantor's last name.

24. When one has traced the ownership of a parcel of land to the beginning of its recorded history, without reference to any encumbrances or other documents affecting the title, the result is
    A. an abstract of title.   C. a chain of title.
    B. a history of title.   D. a record of title.

25. When tracing a chain of title, it may be necessary to look beyond the grantor-grantee index or tract index because of
    I. a break in the chain of title.
    II. delinquent property tax.
    A. I only   B. II only   C. Both I and II   D. Neither I nor II

26. Among the sources which might have to be checked to establish an unbroken chain of title would be
    I. civil court records.   III. mortgage records.
    II. probate court records.   IV. judgment rolls.
    A. I and II only   C. I, II and IV only
    B. I, II and III only   D. I, II, III and IV

27. Depending upon the system used in that state, mortgages on a property may be indexed in the
    I. mortgage index.   III. grantee index.
    II. grantor index.   IV. tract index.
    A. I, II, III and IV   C. II and III only
    B. I only   D. IV only

28. The name of the borrower would be filed alphabetically in the
    I. mortgagee index.
    II. mortgagor index.
    A. I only   B. II only   C. Both I and II   D. Neither I nor II

29. The location of a mortgage and its subsequent release can be found by checking the
    I. mortgagor index.
    II. mortgagee index.
    A. I only   B. II only   C. Both I and II   D. Neither I nor II

30. Which of the following would not ordinarily be checked in searching a title to a parcel of land?
    A. Judgment records.   C. Chattel mortgage records.
    B. Lien records.   D. Lis pendens index.

31. A lis pendens index is
    A. an index of existing leases on property.
    B. an index of pending lawsuits.
    C. a tract index.
    D. a chain of title.

32. It is conceivable that in some circumstances a title searcher may find it necessary to check
    I. birth, death, and marriage records.
    II. divorce, adoption, military, and tax records.
    A. I only   B. II only   C. Both I and II   D. Neither I nor II

33. A person who is engaged in searching land titles as an occupation may be known as a(n)
    I. abstracter.
    II. title searcher.
    A. I only   B. II only   C. Both I and II   D. Neither I nor II

34. A summary of all recorded documents affecting title to a given parcel of land is called
    I. a chain of title.
    II. an abstract of title.
    III. a title report.
    A. I only   B. II only   C. III only   D. I, II and III

35. In the normal course of events, when an abstract of title is sent to an attorney for examination, the attorney will render
    I. an opinion of title based on the facts contained in the abstract.
    II. a certificate of title which guarantees the title to be as reported in the abstract.
    A. I only   B. II only   C. Both I and II   D. Neither I nor II

36. Sherwood, an abstracter, prepared the abstract on property being conveyed to Betts. Should Betts' title later prove to be defective, Sherwood could be held liable if the title defect was based on
    I. a forged deed in the chain of title.
    II. a spouse's unextinguished dower rights.
    III. an unrecorded deed to the property.
    IV. a mistake due to negligence in searching the title.
    A. I, II, III and IV   C. IV only
    B. II and IV only   D. I, III and IV only

37. Protection against incomplete or defective records of the title to land can best be obtained by securing
    A. an abstract of title.   C. an attorney's opinion.
    B. title insurance.   D. a title searcher's opinion.

38. Protection against a loss occasioned by which of the following would not be covered by title insurance?
    A. Forged deeds, or deeds by incompetents.
    B. Unextinguished dower or curtesy rights.
    C. Claims by undisclosed or missing heirs.
    D. Destruction of improvements by a tornado.

39. Title insurance companies were originally organized to provide protection for
    A. the buyer of real property.
    B. the seller of real property.
    C. the real estate agent.
    D. attorneys and abstracters.

40. Before a title insurance company will issue a title insurance policy on a property,
     I. the property must be physically inspected by a representative of the title insurance company.
    II. a title report must be prepared showing the apparent condition of the title.
    A. I only   B. II only   C. Both I and II   D. Neither I nor II

41. Which of the following would commit a title insurance company to issue a title policy?
     I. Preliminary title report.
    II. Binder.
    A. I only   B. II only   C. Both I and II   D. Neither I nor II

42. DiVita purchased a title insurance policy on land which he had purchased. The insurance company's title report included all of the following EXCEPT:
    A. a list of outstanding mortgage loans against the property.
    B. a report of an existing tax lien against the property.
    C. a record of all previous owners of the property.
    D. a list of easements held by utility companies.

43. Which of the following are among the provisions of a typical owner's title insurance policy?
    A. The insurer is responsible for having searched the records pertaining to the property and insures its findings.
    B. The insurer is not responsible for pertinent information that is not found in the public records.
    C. The insurer has not made a visual inspection of the land for signs of notice.
    D. All of the above.

44. Benson purchased real estate from Hedges without making a visual inspection of the land for signs of notice. The American Title Insurance Co. insured the title. Benson later discovered that Hedges had previously conveyed the land to Salem who was in possession at the time of Benson's purchase, but had not recorded his deed. Is Benson's potential loss covered by the title insurance policy?
    A. Yes, because the title insurance protects against any defect in the title.
    B. Yes, because the title insurance company should have made a visual inspection of the land for signs of actual notice.
    C. No, because title insurance never protects against unrecorded deeds.
    D. No, because the title insurance policy would not protect against claims which could have been disclosed by a visual inspection or inquiry of persons in possession.

45. You are standing in the backyard of a house that is offered for sale. You want to buy the house, but the fence surrounding the backyard appears to encroach onto the land of adjacent neighbors. Which of the following would normally disclose such an encroachment?
    A. An abstract of title.
    B. A standard title insurance policy.
    C. An attorney's opinion of title.
    D. A current survey.

46. Depending upon local custom, the premium for title search and insurance may be paid by the
    I.   purchaser.
    II. seller.
    III. purchaser and seller.
    A. I only   B. II only   C. III only   D. I, II and III

47. The premium for a title insurance policy is
    A. paid annually.   C. a single premium, paid upon issuance.
    B. paid semiannually.   D. included in the mortgage payment.

48. Which of the following are true of a lender's policy of title insurance?
    I.   The face amount of the policy is always equal to the acquisition cost of the property.
    II. The coverage declines as the loan is amortized.
    III. It does not make exceptions for claims that could have been anticipated by a physical inspection of the property.
    IV. It is assignable to subsequent holders of the mortgage loan.
    A. II, III and IV only   C. II and IV only
    B. I, II and IV only   D. I, III and IV only

49. When comparing title insurance to casualty insurance, which of the following statements is/are true?
    I.   Title insurance protects against something that has already happened, but has not yet been discovered.
    II. Casualty insurance policies are issued for specified times, but title insurance policies continue indefinitely.
    A. I only   B. II only   C. Both I and II   D. Neither I nor II

50. A title insurance policy issued for the protection of a lender who has taken real estate as collateral for a loan is called
    I.   a lender's policy.
    II. mortgage insurance.
    A. I only   B. II only   C. Both I and II   D. Neither I nor II

51. When both an owner's and a lender's policy of title insurance are purchased simultaneously,
    A. the cost will be the total of normal premiums for both policies.
    B. the combined cost is slightly more than for an owner's policy alone.
    C. there is no extra charge for the lender's policy.
    D. the cost of the lender's policy is deducted from the owner's policy.

52. When a claim is filed against a title insurance policy, the company may elect to
    I.   pay the claim.
    II. fight the claim in court.
    A. I only   B. II only   C. Both I and II   D. Neither I nor II

53. Should a title insurance company elect to fight a claim in court, the legal expenses incurred will be
    A. deducted from the coverage under the policy.
    B. assumed by the title insurance company without affecting the policy coverage.
    C. shared by the insured and the insurance company.
    D. paid by the insured.

54. Brown had a title insurance policy in the amount of $30,000 on his home. A claim was filed against the property, and the title insurance company paid out $10,000 to settle the claim. The coverage under the policy would continue at
    A. $10,000.   C. $30,000.
    B. $20,000.   D. $40,000.

55. Marketable title to real estate is title which is
    A. absolutely free of any possible defect.
    B. free of reasonable doubt as to ownership.
    C. issued by a court after completion of a quiet title action.
    D. insured by a title insurance company.

56. Title insurance protects against
    I.   the seller being unable to make good on his warranty.
    II. the dispossession of the grantee before a claim could be filed against the grantor.
    A. I only   B. II only   C. Both I and II   D. Neither I nor II

57. The use of mortgagee's title insurance has had which of the following effects?
    I.   Makes loans more attractive by removing the risk of losses due to defective titles.
    II. Makes it possible for lenders to charge lower interest because of the elimination of losses due to defective titles.
    A. I only   B. II only   C. Both I and II   D. Neither I nor II

58. The purchase of title insurance eliminates the need for
      I. casualty insurance.
     II. a survey of the property.
    III. constructive notice.
    A. I only   B. II only   C. III only   D. Neither I nor II nor III

59. Which of the following would usually provide the greatest assurance to
    an owner that the title to his property was marketable?
    A. An attorney's certificate of title.
    B. An owner's policy of title insurance.
    C. A preliminary title report.
    D. A mortgagee's policy of title insurance.

60. An outstanding claim or encumbrance which, if valid, would affect or
    impair an owner's title to the real estate is a
      I. title defect.
     II. cloud on the title.
    III. title cloud.
    A. I and II only   C. Both II and III
    B. I and III only   D. I, II and III

61. All of the following are true of a quiet title suit EXCEPT that it
    A. is a judicial proceeding.
    B. removes all claims to title other than the owner's.
    C. quiets those without a genuine interest in the property.
    D. can be used to clear up a disputed title.

62. Because of controversy over how a will was probated, several parties are
    claiming small interests and one person a major interest in a single
    parcel of land. The major owner wants to sell but the title companies
    have refused to insure the title. The major owner's alternatives are to
      I. negotiate and obtain quitclaim deeds from the minor owners.
     II. file a quiet title suit.
    A. I only   B. II only   C. Both I and II   D. Neither I nor II

63. A Torrens certificate of title does which of the following?
      I. Recognizes legitimate claims against the title at the time the
          certificate is issued.
     II. Eliminates the need to search back further in time than the
          quiet title suit.
    A. I only   B. II only   C. Both I and II   D. Neither I nor II

64. A Torrens certificate of title is more meaningful than an attorney's
    certificate of title because
      I. the Torrens certificate is founded on judicial decision.
     II. the attorney's certificate is founded on an opinion of the
          condition of the title.
    A. I only   B. II only   C. Both I and II   D. Neither I nor II

65. A quiet title suit is necessary for a
      I. Torrens certificate.
     II. marketable title act.
    A. I only   B. II only   C. Both I and II   D. Neither I nor II

66. Marketable title acts
     I.   are a system of title registration.
     II. make abstracts easier to prepare.
     III. cut off inactive claims.
     A. I and II   B. I and III   C. II and III   D. I, II and III

67. A certain state has a marketable title act with a statutory period of
     40 years. Which of the following will be true?
     I.   A person with an unbroken chain of title and no defects for 40
          years has marketable title.
     II. Title searches will be concentrated on the first 40 years.
     III. When no document has been recorded for 40 years, the property
          escheats to the state.
     A. I and II only   C. II and III only
     B. I and III only   D. I, II and III

68. States that have passed marketable title acts no longer
     I.   require constructive notice.
     II. allow adverse possession.
     A. I only   B. II only   C. Both I and II   D. Neither I nor II

Short-Answer Questions

1. How does a landowner give notice to the world of his claim of ownership?

2. In most states, what must be accomplished to make an instrument admissible to recordation? Name three officials who are authorized to perform this act.

3. Name five sources (kinds) of records other than indexes of recorded deeds that may have to be checked in completing a title search on a parcel of land.

4. Explain the basic differences in coverage afforded by an owner's title insurance policy versus a mortgagee's policy.

5. How does a casualty insurance policy differ from a title insurance policy?

6. Name and explain briefly three reasons for the popularity of title insurance.

7. Explain what is meant by "marketable title." Name two ways by which an owner who holds less than marketable title can overcome doubts regarding its marketability and make a sale of the property possible.

Note: If you are reading Real Estate: An Introduction to the Profession, you may omit questions 5 and 6 above.

Answers—Chapter 6

Multiple Choice Questions

1. C   The English Statute of Frauds was enacted in 1677.

2. A   The Statute of Frauds established that written deeds be used to show ownership.

3. D   Recording an instrument in the public records provides both legal notice and constructive notice.

4. C   Constructive notice requires that public notice of a claim of owner-ship be given, and that anyone interested in the property inspect the property and the public records.

5. C   The tenants give constructive notice by their occupancy and the investor should make inquiry as to the rights of each tenant. Apart-ment rental agreements are rarely recorded.

6. D   Actual notice is that which is gained by what one has seen, heard, read or observed.

7. A   The public recorder's office serves as a central information station for documents pertaining to interests in land. It is maintained by the local, not the federal, government.

8. D   By plowing the land, storing equipment on it and fencing it, Sorensen gives notice to the world. Persons visiting the property would have actual notice by what they saw.

9. B   Instruments which affect land transfers are recorded in the juris-diction in which the land is situated.

10. B   Documents are recorded by submitting the original document which is photocopied and placed on file.

11. A   An unrecorded deed is binding upon the parties to the deed, but not upon subsequent purchasers, subsequent lenders, or the public generally.

12. A   The first grantee (Bowen) did not provide legally required notice by recordation or by taking possession of the property. Cummings does give notice and becomes the publicly-recognized owner of the property.

13. D   Priority of recorded instruments is established by the date of recordation.

14. B   A month-to-month lease would not usually be recorded. Deeds, mort-gages and options are usually recorded.

15. D   Records in the public recorder's office are public records and available for inspection by anyone.

16. C   A prospective purchaser of real estate is presumed to have inspected both the land itself and the public records pertaining to the land.

17. C   Instruments should be recorded immediately after delivery to provide constructive notice and to establish priority of claim.

18. C   Documents are acknowledged to make certain that the person signing the document is the same person as the one named in the document, that the signing was voluntary, and to make the document admissible for recordation.

19. D   An acknowledgement can be taken by any duly authorized official, including notaries public, officers of a court and commissioned military officers.

20. C   Both the grantee index and the grantor index would be checked; the first to see if title was acquired, the latter to see if it has been subsequently given up.

21. D   An abstracter will usually begin a title search by checking the grantee index, then the grantor index, then tracing the title back to its origin and finally checking other public records as appropriate.

22. C   Both photocopying and microfilming are used as current methods of recording documents.

23. B   Instruments are recorded in chronological order, as received for recordation.

24. C   A chain of title is an historical record of ownership without reference to encumbrances or other documents affecting the title.

25. A   It is necessary to check other sources when a break in the chain of title occurs. Delinquent property tax by itself is not a break.

26. D   Records of the civil courts, probate courts, mortgage records and judgment rolls all might have to be checked to establish an unbroken chain of title.

27. A   Mortgages are sometimes identified in a separate mortgage index, but, depending on the system used in that state, may also be identified in the grantee index, grantor index or tract index.

28. B   The name of the borrower would be filed alphabetically in the mortgagor index.

29. C   The location of a mortgage and its subsequent release can be found by checking either the mortgagee index or the mortgagor index.

30. C   Chattel mortgage records are records of mortgages on personal property and would not normally be checked in searching land titles.

31.   B   Pending lawsuits are indexed in the lis pendens index.

32.   C   In some circumstances an abstracter may find it necessary to check birth, death, marriage, divorce, adoption, military or tax records in order to identify all the parties with an interest in a property.

33.   C   One who is engaged in searching land titles as an occupation may be referred to as an abstracter or as a title searcher.

34.   B   A summary of all documents affecting title to a given parcel of land is known as an abstract of title.

35.   A   An attorney's report as to who holds the fee title to a property and any rights or interest held by others is known as an opinion of title.

36.   C   An abstracter is responsible for mistakes due to negligence, but is not held responsible for forged deeds, unextinguished dower rights or unrecorded deeds.

37.   B   Title insurance provides the best protection against incomplete or defective records of the title to land.

38.   D   Title insurance is not casualty insurance and does not insure against a loss arising from any form of casualty such as a tornado, fire, etc.

39.   D   The original purpose of title insurance was to provide protection for attorneys and abstracters.

40.   B   Title insurance companies require a title report showing the apparent condition of the title before issuing a title insurance policy. No physical inspection of the property is required.

41.   B   A binder is a commitment to insure the title to the property. A preliminary title report is not an insurance policy and does not commit the title insurance company to insure the title.

42.   C   The insurance company's title report does not identify previous owners of the property, but does list all encumbrances and liens now against the property.

43.   D   The title insurer is responsible for searching the records and insuring its findings. The insurer is not responsible for information not in the records. The insurer does not make a visual inspection of the land for a typical owner's policy.

44.   D   Title insurance does not insure against claims which could have been disclosed by a visual inspection or inquiry of persons in possession of the property.

45.   D   A current survey would disclose any encroachments on the property. Encroachments would not be disclosed by an abstract of title, title insurance or an attorney's opinion of title.

46. D   The premium for title insurance may be paid by the purchaser, the seller or shared by both purchaser and seller. Local custom, more than any other factor, determines who pays the premium.

47. C   The premium for a title insurance policy is a single premium, paid only upon issuance.

48. A   A lender's policy of title insurance is issued in an amount equal to the original amount of the mortgage loan, not the acquisition cost. The coverage declines as the loan is amortized; the policy does not make exceptions for claims that could have been anticipated by a physical inspection of the property; and the policy is assignable to subsequent holders of the mortgage loan.

49. C   Title insurance protects against losses arising from past events. While casualty insurance policies insure for a specified time, title insurance policies continue indefinitely.

50. A   A title insurance policy issued for lender's protection is called a lender's policy.

51. B   The combined cost for both an owner's and a lender's title insurance policy is slightly more than the cost of an owner's policy alone.

52. C   At its option, the title insurance company may elect to pay a claim or fight the claim in court.

53. B   Legal expenses incurred in fighting a claim in court are assumed by the title insurance company and are not deducted from any later settlement with the insured.

54. B   The $10,000 paid out to settle the claim would be deducted from the coverage, leaving $20,000 coverage remaining.

55. B   Marketable title is title which is free of reasonable doubt as to ownership of the property.

56. C   Title insurance provides the grantee with protection against the seller being unable to make good on the warranties given in a deed, and also protects the grantee from being dispossessed before he could file a claim against the grantor.

57. C   By protecting the lender against a loss from a defective title to mortgaged property, title insurance makes possible lower interest rates, and encourages the lender to make the loan on more attractive terms.

58. D   Since title insurance insures only the title to the property, the need for casualty insurance, constructive notice and a survey of the property are not eliminated.

59. B   An owner's policy of title insurance provides greater assurance of marketable title than an attorney's certificate of title, a preliminary title report or a mortgagee's policy of title insurance.

60. D   The terms "title defect," "cloud on the title" and "title cloud" are all used to describe a claim or encumbrance which, if valid, would affect or impair an owner's title.

61. B   A quiet title suit does not remove legitimate claims to title such as outstanding mortgages. It is a judicial proceeding which quiets the claims of those without a genuine interest in the property. As such it is used to clear up a disputed title.

62. C   The major owner could file a quiet title suit or negotiate and obtain quitclaim deeds from the minor owners.

63. C   By recognizing legitimate claims against the title at the time the certificate was issued, a Torrens certificate of title eliminates the need to search back further in time than the quiet title suit.

64. C   A Torrens certificate of title is founded on a judicial decision; an attorney's certificate of title is founded on an opinion of the condition of the title.

65. A   A quiet title suit is necessary for a Torrens certificate. Marketable title acts do not require a suit.

66. C   By cutting off inactive claims, marketable title acts make abstracts easier to prepare. The acts are not a system of title registration.

67. A   An unbroken chain of title with no defects for 40 years would establish marketable title; title searches will be concentrated on the first 40 years. A property does not escheat to the state if no document is recorded for 40 years.

68. D   The enactment of a marketable title act does not eliminate the need for constructive notice, nor does it disallow a claim of title by adverse possession.

Short Answer Questions

1. Notice is given by physical occupation of one's land and by recording in the public records.

2. Most states require an acknowledgement by the person executing a document before it can be recorded. Persons authorized to take acknowledgements include notaries public, recording office clerks, commissioners of deeds, judges and consular agents.

3. A title search will include a check of mortgage liens; tax (federal, state and local) liens; mechanics' liens; pending litigation; judgment rolls; birth, marriage and death records; probate records; etc.

4. The owner's policy is good for the face amount of the policy indefinitely while the mortgagee's declines in coverage as the loan is repaid. The mortgagee's policy does not make exceptions for property inspection, while the owner's policy does.

5. A casualty policy protects against losses occurring from an event that has not yet happened. A title policy protects against past events that have not been discovered.

6. Title insurance is popular because (a) the grantor can purchase insurance on the covenants he makes, (b) the grantor feels better protected, and (c) mortgage lending is more attractive.

7. Marketable title is title that is free from reasonable doubt as to who the owner is. Cures for less than marketable title include quiet title suit, title insurance, and quitclaim deeds from those claiming an interest in the property.

Contract Law

Chapter 7

1. Which of the following would be defined as a party to a contract?
   I. Buyer.   III. Landlord.
   II. Seller.   IV. Tenant.
   A. I and II only   C. III and IV only
   B. II and III only   D. I, II, III and IV

2. Which of the following statements regarding contracts are true?
   I. A contract may be an agreement to do a certain thing.
   II. Contracts may be based on an agreement NOT to do a certain thing.
   III. In order to be enforceable, a contract must always be in writing.
   A. I and II only   C. II and III only
   B. I and III only   D. I, II and III

3. Contracts may arise from
   I. the stated intent of the parties.
   II. the actions of the parties.
   A. I only   B. II only   C. Both I and II   D. Neither I nor II

4. Bill agreed orally to purchase a used car from Bob, provided Bill could get a bank loan for a part of the purchase price. Bill gave Bob money as an earnest money deposit. Was this agreement an expressed contract?
   A. Yes, because it resulted from the stated intent of the parties.
   B. Yes, because Bob accepted the earnest money deposit.
   C. No, because the agreement was not in writing.
   D. No, because it was based upon a contingency.

5. An implied contract may arise from
   I. an oral agreement.
   II. a written agreement.
   III. the actions of the parties.
   A. I only   B. II only   C. I and II only   D. III only

Note: There are no deleted questions in this chapter for readers of
Real Estate: An Introduction to the Profession.

6. A contract based upon a promise exchanged for a promise is a
    A. semilateral contract.   C. binary contract.
    B. dilateral contract.   D. bilateral contract.

7. Fowler listed his home for sale with broker Hall. Hall agreed to adver-
    tise the property and to hold "open house" weekly until a purchaser was
    found. Fowler agreed to pay a commission of seven per cent if a pur-
    chaser was found. This agreement constituted a
    A. bilateral contract based on a good consideration.
    B. unilateral contract based on a good consideration.
    C. bilateral contract based on a valuable consideration.
    D. unilateral contract based on a valuable consideration.

8. A contract based upon one party's promise in exchange for an act from
    the other party is classified as
    A. a bilateral contract.   C. an executed contract.
    B. an unenforceable contract.   D. a unilateral contract.

9. A unilateral contract is enforceable against
    A. either party.   C. the offeree.
    B. the offeror.   D. neither party.

10. An agreement in a contract in which one or both parties agree not to act
    in a certain manner is known as
    A. forbiddance.   C. foregiveness.
    B. forbearance.   D. forfeiture.

11. Green agreed to sell his grocery store to Blue provided that Blue agreed
    never to sell alcoholic beverages in the store. Blue agreed to this
    condition. This agreement constituted
      I. an expressed contract.
     II. an implied contract.
    III. a contract for forbearance.
    A. I only   B. II only   C. I and III only   D. III only

12. Which of the following statements is NOT true of a valid contract?
    A. It meets all requirements of law.
    B. It is binding upon all parties.
    C. It is enforceable in a court of law.
    D. It must be accompanied by earnest money.

13. A contract which binds one party but not the other is
    A. unenforceable.   C. voidable.
    B. void.   D. illegal.

14. A contract which is legally insufficient is classified as
    A. voidable.   C. incompetent.
    B. void.   D. invalid.

15. A person who has not reached the age of majority is also known as
     I. a minor.
    II. an infant.
    A. I only   B. II only   C. Both I and II   D. Neither I nor II

16. As a rule, a contract between an adult and a minor is NOT
    A. voidable by the minor.
    B. enforceable against the adult.
    C. enforceable against either party.
    D. enforceable against the minor.

17. Demas and Madora are going to Europe for a month and want to give someone
    at home the authority to sign certain real estate settlement papers for
    them while they are gone. They would do this by appointing
      I. an attorney-in-fact.
     II. a power of attorney.
    A. I only   B. II only   C. Both I and II   D. Neither I nor II

18. An attorney-in-fact derives his powers from
    A. the state bar association.   C. judicial appointment.
    B. a power of attorney.   D. popular election.

19. An attorney-in-fact is legally competent to the extent of the powers
    granted him by the principal so long as
      I. the principal remains legally competent.
     II. both of them are alive.
    A. I only   B. II only   C. Both I and II   D. Neither I nor II

20. Charlie, Jr., age 17, lives in a state which sets the legal age at 18
    years. One week before his 18th birthday, Charlie ordered a new motor-
    cycle from a local dealer. He signed a written purchase contract and
    gave the dealer a $100 deposit. The day after his 18th birthday, Charlie
    attempted to cancel the order. Was Charlie acting within his legal
    rights?
    A. No, because he did not cancel before reaching legal age.
    B. No, because written contracts are not voidable.
    C. Yes, because a minor may usually disavow a contract until reaching
       majority and for a reasonable time thereafter.
    D. Yes, because a contract made by a minor can never be enforced.

21. Bean, who is moving to another city, wants to give his agent, broker
    Bagg, the power to sign a sale contract and deed to real estate which he
    wants to sell. Which of the following statements would NOT be correct?
    A. Bean could give Bagg a written power of attorney to act for him in
       this manner.
    B. Bean could appoint Bagg by means of an oral power of attorney.
    C. Bagg would be an attorney-in-fact for Bean.
    D. The power of attorney would have to be written, acknowledged, and
       recorded.

22. A person who executes a contract for a corporation must derive that
    authority from
    A. the corporation's registered agent.
    B. the state corporation commission.
    C. the corporate board of directors.
    D. a court of competent jurisdiction.

23. A partnership may contract in the name of
    I.   its general partners.
    II. the partnership.
    A. I only   B. II only   C. Both I and II   D. Neither I nor II

24. Any of the following may contract in the name of a decedent's estate EXCEPT
    A. an executor.   C. a trustee.
    B. an administrator.   D. a personal representative of the deceased.

25. For mutual agreement to exist between the parties to a contract, all of the following requirements must be met EXCEPT:
    A. there must be an offer and an acceptance.
    B. the contract must be reduced to writing.
    C. there must be no fraud, misrepresentation or mistake.
    D. the assent must be genuine and freely given.

26. Chet installed a built-in microwave oven in his home. When he sold the home to Ray, he did not mention that the oven was not to be included in the sale. Ray expected it to be included. Was the contract of sale a LEGALLY VALID contract?
    I.   Yes, because once installed, the oven became a fixture and therefore a part of the property.
    II. Yes, if Chet wanted to exclude the oven he would either have to remove it before showing the property to Ray or inform Ray of its exclusion before accepting Ray's offer.
    III. No, because Chet's actions constituted fraud.
    IV. No, because a meeting of the minds was absent.
    A. I only   B. I and II only   C. III only   D. III and IV only

27. An offeree may communicate his acceptance of an offeror's offer
    I.   orally.   III. by his actions.
    II. in writing.   IV. through an agent.
    A. I, II, III and IV   C. I, II and III only
    B. II only   D. II and III only

28. Stump listed his home for sale through broker Welby. Purchaser Peck agreed to all the terms of the listing and signed a purchase agreement. This agreement constituted a contract when
    A. Peck signed the purchase agreement.
    B. Welby accepted the signed offer from Peck.
    C. Welby handed the offer to Stump.
    D. Stump signed the purchase agreement.

29. Mutual agreement cannot exist if
    I.   the terms of the offer are vague.
    II. the offer does not clearly state the obligations of the parties.
    A. I only   B. II only   C. Both I and II   D. Neither I nor II

30. When an offeror makes a valid offer and communicates it to the offeree, the offeree may
    A. reject the offer.   C. make a counteroffer.
    B. accept the offer.   D. All of the above.

31. If an offeree makes a change in the terms of an offer,
    I.   the law considers the offer to be rejected.
    II. this constitutes a counteroffer.
    A. I only   B. II only   C. Both I and II   D. Neither I nor II

32. In his will, Charles, Sr. left his farm to Charles, Jr. The farm had
    never been surveyed, but Charles, Jr. had always understood that it
    contained 110 acres. Charles sold the land to Baker, representing it to
    contain 110 acres. Baker had it surveyed and found that it contained
    only 100 acres. Which of the following statements would be true?
    I.   Charles' statements to Baker constituted fraud.
    II. Charles' statements to Baker constituted innocent misrepresen-
         tation.
    III. At his option, Baker could declare the contract void.
    IV. Either Baker or Charles could declare the contract void.
    A. I, III and IV only   C. II, III and IV only
    B. II and IV only   D. II and III only

33. An offer may be terminated by
    I.   withdrawal of the offer.
    II. refusal from the offeree.
    III. the lapse of time.
    A. I and II only   C. II and III only
    B. I and III only   D. I, II and III

34. Mutual agreement is missing when a contract is made under
    I.   menace.
    II. undue influence.
    III. duress.
    A. I only   B. II only   C. III only   D. I, II and III

35. If a contract is signed under duress,
    I.   the aggrieved party may subsequently declare the contract void.
    II. either party may declare the contract revoked.
    A. I only   B. II only   C. Both I and II   D. Neither I nor II

36. A real estate agent who takes advantage of an elderly property owner's
    ignorance of the value of his property in order to induce him to sell
    below market value would have committed
    I.   undue influence.
    II. duress.
    A. I only   B. II only   C. Both I and II   D. Neither I nor II

37. An act intended to deceive the other party in a contract is
    A. duress.   C. mistake.
    B. menace.   D. fraud.

38. Fraud may consist of
    I.   knowingly telling a lie.
    II. making a promise without any intent of keeping it.
    A. I only   B. II only   C. Both I and II   D. Neither I nor II

39. Which of the following constitute fraud on the part of a real estate agent in dealing with a prospective purchaser?
    I. Failing to disclose pertinent information known to the agent.
    II. Deliberate deceit in statements relative to the property.
    III. Misrepresentation of pertinent information based on incorrect data furnished to the agent by the property owner.
    IV. Making a promise which the agent did not intend to keep.
    A. I, II and III only
    B. I, II, III and IV
    C. I, II and IV only
    D. II and III only

40. A contract based on fraud is
    A. void.
    B. voidable by the injured party.
    C. voidable by either party.
    D. unenforceable.

41. A real estate licensee who committed a fraudulent act in order to make a sale
    A. may be subject to criminal penalties.
    B. may be subject to suit for civil damages.
    C. may have his/her license revoked.
    D. All of the above.

42. Broker Netherby listed a home for sale wherein the seller stated that the existing loan was assumable by the buyer. Netherby told this to prospective buyers, and in time a sales contract was executed. However, the lender refused to allow the assumption to take place. As a result of this,
    A. the seller can rescind the sales contract.
    B. the buyer can rescind the sales contract.
    C. the broker will lose his license.
    D. the broker can be sued for fraud.

43. A contract made as a joke or in jest is precluded from becoming a valid contract because it lacks
    I. contractual intent.
    II. mutual agreement.
    A. I only   B. II only   C. Both I and II   D. Neither I nor II

44. A contract based upon an unlawful objective would be
    A. binding.
    B. enforceable.
    C. void.
    D. voidable.

45. Little borrowed money from Moore at a rate of interest which exceeded the usury ceiling in their state. After making two payments on the loan, Little stopped making payments on the loan. Could Moore bring legal action to collect the loan balance?
    A. Yes, because Little completed partial performance by making two payments.
    B. No, because a contract which requires the breaking of a law cannot be enforced.
    C. Yes, because the principal balance on the loan is an honest debt.
    D. No, because the charging of usurious interest rates constitutes fraud.

46. Lee agreed to purchase real estate from Grant, and gave him an earnest money deposit at the time the agreement was made. Which of the following constituted the consideration in this contract?
    I. The earnest money deposit.
    II. The purchase price of the property.
    A. I only   B. II only   C. Both I and II   D. Neither I nor II

47. Which of the following may constitute the consideration in a contract?
    I. Money paid for property.
    II. A promise given in exchange for a promise.
    III. A promise given in exchange for an act.
    IV. Goods exchanged for services.
    A. I, II and IV only   C. I and IV only
    B. I, III and IV only   D. I, II, III and IV

48. Which of the following would NOT be an example of a valuable consideration?
    A. Barter of goods for services.
    B. A gift of property to a friend.
    C. An even trade of one property for another.
    D. The sale of property for less than market value.

49. In contract law, a "mistake" refers to
    I. ignorance of the law.
    II. innocent misrepresentation.
    III. poor judgment.
    A. I only   C. I and III only
    B. II only   D. Neither I, II nor III

50. A contract which is in the process of being carried out is
    A. executed.   C. executory.
    B. executing.   D. executrix.

51. To execute a contract means to
    I. sign it.
    II. carry out its terms.
    A. I only   B. II only   C. Both I and II   D. Neither I nor II

52. Sales of personal property in excess of $500 must, in many states, be in writing because of the requirements of the
    A. Uniform Commercial Code.   C. statute of frauds.
    B. parol evidence rule.   D. Uniform Vendor and Purchaser Risk Act.

53. Which of the following would NOT have to be in writing in order to be enforceable?
    A. A contract to purchase real estate.
    B. A mortgage.
    C. A month-to-month rental agreement.
    D. A lease for 13 months.

54. When both a written and an oral contract for the same purpose are in existence between the same parties,
    A. both contracts are void.
    B. the written contract will prevail.
    C. the oral contract takes precedence.
    D. neither contract is enforceable.

55. The rule that permits oral evidence to complete an otherwise incomplete written contract is the
    A. Uniform Commercial Code.
    B. rule of specific performance.
    C. parol evidence rule.
    D. statute of frauds.

56. An assignment
    I.   does not release the parties to the original contract from further liability to that contract.
    II. is a special form of power of attorney.
    III. can be used to transfer a right or interest.
    IV. is a form of contract.
    A. I, II, III and IV   C. I and III only
    B. II and III only   D. I, III and IV only

57. When a lessee in a rented property assigns his lease to another party, he assumes the role of
    I. assignor.   III. sublessor.
    II. assignee.   IV. sublessee.
    A. I only   B. I and III only   C. II only   D. I and IV only

58. With regard to the assignment of a contract, which of the following statements is NOT true?
    A. The assignee is bound by the terms of the contract.
    B. Unless prohibited by the terms of the contract, any unfulfilled contract can be assigned.
    C. The assignor is relieved of responsibility under the contract upon its assignment.
    D. The assignment must meet all essential contract requirements in order to be enforceable.

59. Substitution of a new contract and a new party for a previous one is known as
    A. innovation.   C. subrogation.
    B. assignment.   D. novation.

60. Mr. Rhett has been leasing warehouse space for 2 years under a 5 year lease. Business has been good and Mr. Rhett wants to build his own warehouse. He also wants to be fully relieved from liability under the present lease agreement. This can be accomplished by
    I. assignment.   III. novation.
    II. unilateral recission. IV. mutual recission.
    A. I only   B. I and II only   C. III only   D. III and IV only

61. When a contract is only partially performed, which of the following alternatives is open?
   I. Partial performance may be accepted as satisfactory discharge of the contract.
   II. Partial performance plus mutual rescission of the balance of the contract obligations.
   A. I only   B. II only   C. Both I and II   D. Neither I nor II

62. If the objective of a contract becomes legally impossible to accomplish,
   A. the law will consider the contract discharged.
   B. a lawsuit for specific performance is appropriate.
   C. a lawsuit for money damages is appropriate.
   D. liquidated damages would be appropriate.

63. Contracts may be discharged in some situations
   I. by death of one of the parties.
   II. if the property is damaged before title passes.
   A. I only   B. II only   C. Both I and II   D. Neither I nor II

64. In a state which had enacted the Uniform Vendor and Purchaser Risk Act, Green sold his home to Blue, who took possession prior to settlement. After moving in but before settlement took place, the house was destroyed by a tornado. Which of the following statements is true?
   A. The loss will be borne by Green.
   B. The loss will be borne by Blue.
   C. Blue is entitled to a refund of money already paid.
   D. Blue is relieved of his duty to pay the purchase price.

65. The failure of one party to a contract to perform as agreed without a valid excuse constitutes
   I. a form of consideration.
   II. a breach of contract.
   A. I only   B. II only   C. Both I and II   D. Neither I nor II

66. Legal action to force the breaching party to carry out the remainder of a contract is called a suit for
   A. liquidated damages.   C. partial performance.
   B. specific performance.   D. breach of contract.

67. When a contract is breached, the injured party may
   I. rescind the contract unilaterally.
   II. sue for specific performance.
   III. sue for monetary damages.
   IV. accept liquidated damages.
   A. I and II only   C. I and III only
   B. II only   D. I, II, III and IV

68. The law which limits the time in which a wronged party may file legal action for obtaining justice is the statute of
   A. frauds.   C. novation.
   B. limitations.   D. performance.

69. Real estate agents are responsible for
     A. obeying the law.   C. being knowledgeable.
     B. being competent.   D. All of the above.

70. In view of current trends toward consumer protection, the watchwords for
     real estate salespersons and brokers might well be
      I. caveat emptor.
     II. caveat agent.
     A. I only   B. II only   C. Both I and II   D. Neither I nor II

Contract Situations

1. Name three examples of implied contracts, not necessarily associated with real estate, which may be encountered in daily situations. Explain why each constitutes an implied contract.

   1.

   2.

   3.

2. Which of the following constitutes a unilateral contract? Explain your answer.

   A. Marriage.

   B. A reward poster.

3. Each of the following situations comprises a contract which may be either valid, void, voidable, or unenforceable. Identify each situation and explain your answer.

   A. Sally Brown, age 17, purchased a stereo set on the installment plan. After three months, Sally decided to return it to the dealer, who advised Sally that she would be held responsible for the remaining payments under the installment contract. What defense, if any, would Sally have in this situation?

B. In selling a parcel of real estate to a prospect, Joe Salesman iden-
    tified the property as Lot 1, Block 2, Section 3, Spring Valley Sub-
    division. The proper description of the property was Lot 3, Block 1,
    Section 2, Spring Valley Subdivision. What is the status of this
    contract?

C. Harry Homeowner agreed to sell his home to Bob Byer by means of a
    written contract of sale, drawn on a standard form. When Mr. Byer
    had the title examined, an incurable defect was found which made
    transfer by Mr. Homeowner impossible. What is the status of this
    contract?

D. Peter and Penny Purchaser, husband and wife, made an offer to pur-
    chase property from Vera Vendor, a single woman. All parties were
    adults. The purchasers made an earnest money deposit of $2,000 and
    agreed to a down payment of $20,000 on the purchase price of $80,000,
    subject to their ability to secure a first mortgage loan of $60,000
    on acceptable terms. A local savings and loan association agreed to
    make the loan on favorable terms. Miss Vendor signed the agreement,
    but subsequently changed her mind and decided not to sell. What is
    the status of this contract?

4. In the old movie "The Perils of Pauline," the villain tied Pauline to the railroad track in order to force her to sign the deed to the family home. Suppose that Pauline had signed the deed instead of awaiting rescue by Handsome Harry. Could she have later disavowed the contract? If so, on what grounds could she have done so?

5. A grandparent conveys real estate by deed to a grandchild. What would be the consideration if the conveyance was a gift? What type consideration would this be?

6. Brown, the owner of real estate, and Smith, a would-be purchaser, enter into an oral agreement under which Smith agrees to meet Brown at his office next Tuesday morning at 10 A.M., at which time Smith will pay Brown $10,000 in cash and Brown will deliver to Smith a deed to the property.
    A. Smith and Brown meet as agreed and each fulfills his part of the agreement. Is this a valid deed? Justify your answer.

    B. The day after entering into their oral agreement, Brown receives another offer of $11,000 for the property. Can Smith hold him to their agreement? If not, why not? If so, on what grounds?

    C. The law which covers this situation is known as the

Answers—Chapter 7

Multiple Choice Questions

1. D   Buyer and seller are parties to a contract of sale. Landlord and tenant are parties to a lease, which is a contract.

2. A   A contract may be an agreement to do or not to do a certain thing. Certain contracts do not need to be in writing.

3. C   An expressed contract arises from the stated intent of the parties; an implied contract arises from the actions of the parties.

4. A   The agreement to buy and sell the car resulted from the stated intent of the parties. It was not necessary for the contract to be in writing, nor was an earnest money deposit required. The inclusion of a contingency did not affect its status as an expressed contract.

5. D   An implied contract arises from the actions of the parties, and not their stated intent, as would occur with either a written or oral agreement.

6. D   A bilateral contract is based upon an exchange of promises.

7. C   The contract was based upon a valuable consideration in the form of the exchange of promises.

8. D   A unilateral contract is based upon a promise from one party in exchange for an act from the other party.

9. B   A unilateral contract is enforceable against the offeror, but not against the offeree.

10. B   A contract for forbearance is an agreement not to do a certain thing.

11. C   Blue's agreement not to sell alcoholic beverages constituted an agreement not to do a certain thing, thus a contract for forbearance.

12. D   There is no legal requirement that earnest money accompany a contract to make it valid.

13. C   When one party to a contract is not bound by the contract, the contract is voidable by the party who is not bound by it.

14. B   Any contract which does not meet the requirements of law would be classified as void.

15. C   The terms "minor" and "infant" both refer to a person who has not reached the age of majority.

16. D   Generally, a contract between an adult and a minor is enforceable against the adult, but voidable by the minor.

17. A   A power of attorney is a legal instrument which appoints a person as the attorney-in-fact of another person.

18. B   The powers of an attorney-in-fact are derived from a power of attorney.

19. C   The powers of an attorney-in-fact extend for so long as the principal remains legally competent and both are alive.

20. C   A minor may usually disavow a contract until reaching majority and for a reasonable time thereafter. If not, the contract becomes valid.

21. B   A power of attorney may not be granted orally. All other responses are correct.

22. C   The authority to execute a contract in the name of a corporation must be granted by the corporation's board of directors.

23. C   A partnership may contract in the name of the partnership or its general partners.

24. C   The person appointed to settle a decedent's estate may be designated as the executor, administrator, or personal representative of the decedent, but not as a trustee.

25. B   That a contract be in writing is not a requirement of mutual agreement. But there must be an offer and an acceptance, and the assent must be genuine and freely given. Also, there must be no evidence of fraud, misrepresentation, or mistake.

26. B   Built-in appliances become fixtures and a part of the realty unless excluded from the sale or removed prior to the offer to sell.

27. A   An acceptance of an offer may be communicated orally, in writing, by the offeree's actions, or through an agent.

28. D   A contract existed when the seller, Stump, signed the purchase agreement. The purchaser, Peck, had previously signed the agreement but no contract existed until it was signed by the seller.

29. C   Mutual agreement cannot exist until all parties to a contract fully understand their rights, duties, and obligations under the contract, and this agreement is clearly stated in the contract.

30. D   The offeree may accept or reject the offer or make a counteroffer.

31. C   A counteroffer constitutes a rejection of an offerer's offer and the substitution of another offer by the original offeree.

32. D   The statements of the seller, Charles Jr., constituted innocent misrepresentation and made the contract voidable by the buyer, Baker. Charles Jr. did not commit fraud, and the contract could not be voided by him.

33. D   An offer may be terminated by withdrawal, refusal, or the lapse of time.

34. D   There cannot be mutual agreement when a contract is made under menace, undue influence, or duress.

35. A   A contract signed under duress may be disavowed by the injured party only.

36. A   Undue influence is the taking of an unfair advantage. Duress is the use or threat of force to compel the signing of a contract against one's will.

37. D   Fraud occurs when one party deliberately deceives the other party to a contract.

38. C   Fraud is created by deceit, such as telling a lie or making a promise without the intent of keeping it.

39. C   Failure to disclose pertinent information, deliberate deceit, and making false promises constitute fraud. Innocent misrepresentation (response III) is not fraud.

40. B   Only the injured party may disavow a contract based on fraud.

41. D   A licensee who commits fraud may be subject to criminal prosecution, civil action for damages, and license revocation.

42. B   The broker's statement to the purchaser constituted innocent misrepresentation and the contract would be voidable by the purchaser only. Fraud was not present, and the broker would not be subject to license revocation.

43. C   A contract made in jest is not based on mutual agreement and does not reflect contractual intent.

44. C   Contracts with an unlawful objective are treated as void.

45. B   A contract which requires a violation of the law is not enforceable, even though partial performance has taken place.

46. B   The total amount to be paid for the property is the consideration. Earnest money is evidence of good faith.

47. D   The consideration in a contract may be based upon money, other valuables, a promise, an act, or services.

48. B   A gift of property to a friend would be based on a good consideration. Barter, trade, or sale constitute a valuable consideration.

49. D   A mistake in a contract results from ambiguity in negotiations. It is not the result of ignorance, innocent misrepresentation, or poor judgment.

50. C   An executory contract is one in which something remains to be done. An executed contract is one which has been fulfilled.

51. C   As used in this context, the word "execute" has a double meaning. It refers to both the signing of a contract and the carrying out of its terms.

52. A   In many states, the Uniform Commercial Code requires that sales of personal property in excess of $500 be in writing to be enforceable.

53. C   The statute of frauds requires that all contracts for the sale or mortgage of real estate be in writing. This requirement does not apply to month-to-month rentals or leases for one year or less.

54. B   Written contracts will prevail over oral contracts for the same purpose between the same parties.

55. C   The parol evidence rule permits oral evidence to complete an otherwise incomplete contract.

56. D   An assignment is a contract that transfers a right or interest. It does not release the parties from further liability under that contract. It is not a special form of power of attorney.

57. B   A lessee who assigns his lease becomes both the assignor and the sublessor.

58. C   The assignor is not relieved of contract responsibility by the assignment, but remains liable. The assignee is also bound by the contract terms. Any executory contract may be assigned unless the contract terms prohibit an assignment. The assignment must meet all essential contract requirements in order to be enforceable.

59. D   Novation is the substitution of a new contract for an earlier contract, or the substitution of new parties to an old contract.

60. D   Mr. Rhett's objectives could be met by novation or by mutual rescission, but not by assignment or unilateral rescission.

61. C   Partial performance alone, or partial performance plus mutual rescission of the balance of the contractual obligations may be acceptable to the parties involved.

62. A   Should a contractual objective become legally impossible to accomplish, the law will consider the contract to be discharged. Lawsuits for specific performance, monetary damages, and liquidated damages would be inappropriate because a court would not enforce them.

63. C   Contracts may be discharged in some situations by the death of one of the parties or by damage to the property before title passes.

64.   B   Under the Uniform Vendor and Purchaser Risk Act, the risk of loss to the property from casualty remains with the seller until title passes to the purchaser or possession is given to the purchaser, whichever occurs first.

65.   B   Failure to live up to one's contractual obligations constitutes a breach of contract.

66.   B   Legal action to compel a breaching party to carry out the remainder of a contract is known as an action for specific performance.

67.   D   When a contract is breached, the injured party may rescind unilaterally, sue for specific performance or monetary damages, or accept liquidated damages.

68.   B   The statute of limitations limits the time in which a wronged party may bring legal action for obtaining justice.

69.   D   Real estate agents are responsible for obeying the law, being competent and being knowledgeable. This is what persons dealing with them expect, and courts uphold this.

70.   B   Real estate agents should exercise particular caution in their dealings, in view of the current trends toward consumer protection.

Contract Situations

1. Taxicab ride, restaurant meal, barber shop. In each case, the proprietor makes an offer by way of his actions and facilities. When a customer accepts these services, he implies that he will pay, even though no verbal or written contract exists.

2. A marriage is a bilateral contract wherein both parties make promises to each other. A reward poster constitutes a unilateral contract for it is a promise by the offeror, but the offeree does not have to act. If he does, however, the offeror is committed to carry out his promises.

3A. Sally's defense would be that she was a minor and that contracts with minors for nonessential items are voidable by the minor.

3B. The contract is void since there was no mutual agreement as to the parcel of land involved.

3C. The contract is voidable by Mr. Byer and unenforceable by Mr. Homeowner due to the fact that Mr. Homeowner cannot deliver title as specified in the contract.

3D. The contract is still valid and the purchasers can sue the seller for specific performance.

4. Pauline could disavow the contract on the grounds of duress and menace.

5. The consideration would be stated as "love and affection" and be classified as good consideration.

6A. The deed is valid if it meets the requirements of a deed.

6B. A verbal agreement to sell real estate is not enforceable at law. Therefore, Smith cannot hold Brown to the price of $10,000 if Brown changes his mind before delivering the deed.

6C. Statute of frauds.

Real Estate Sales Contracts

Chapter 8

1. A real estate sales contract is entered into between a buyer and seller
    in order to give the buyer time to do all the following EXCEPT:
    A. ascertain that the seller holds marketable title to the property.
    B. arrange for financing.
    C. reach a firm decision to buy the property.
    D. have the title examined.

2. A properly prepared sales contract
    I.   commits each party to its terms.
    II. is enforceable in a court of law.
    A. I only   B. II only   C. Both I and II   D. Neither I nor II

3. A formal real estate sales contract, prepared at the outset by an agent
    using prepared forms, may be identified as any of the following EXCEPT:
    A. a purchase contract.   C. an offer and acceptance.
    B. an option contract.   D. a purchase offer.

4. Normally found provisions of a real estate sales contract include
    I.   a buyer's offer to purchase and provision for earnest money
         deposit.
    II. a seller's acceptance and provision for brokerage commission.
    A. I only   B. II only   C. Both I and II   D. Neither I nor II

5. Martin purchased real estate from Stevens under an agreement which called
    for him to pay for the property in installments, and to receive a deed
    upon payment of the entire purchase price. This agreement could properly
    be identified as a
    I.   land contract.   III. conditional sales contract.
    II. contract for deed.   IV. installment contract.
    A. II, III and IV only   C. I, II, III and IV
    B. III and IV only   D. IV only

Note: If you are reading <u>Real Estate: An Introduction to the Profession,</u>
       you may omit the following questions: 55-60.

6. In normal real estate brokerage practice, the amount of earnest money deposit paid by the purchaser is
   I.   determined by negotiation.
   II. set by state law.
   III. equal to the agent's commission.
   IV. the minimum required to make the contract valid.
   A. I and II only   C. IV only
   B. III and IV only   D. I only

7. Once the buyer and seller have executed a sales contract, paperwork and details of the title transfer may be handled by:
   I.   an escrow agent.   III. an attorney.
   II. the real estate broker.   IV. the lender.
   A. I, II, III and IV   C. II only
   B. I only   D. IV only

8. Property taxes, insurance, loan interest, etc. may be divided between the buyer and seller by the process of
   A. allocation.   C. proration.
   B. appropriation.   D. proportioning.

9. Scott owns a house that he has been renting to a tenant on a month-to-month lease. Scott offers to sell the house to Dale. As part of his offer to purchase, Dale can ask Scott to
   I.   terminate the tenant's lease.
   II. let the tenant continue to lease.
   A. I only   B. II only   C. Both I and II   D. Neither I nor II

10. The inclusion of a termite and dry rot clause in a contract for the sale of real estate is
    A. optional and negotiable.
    B. often required by state law.
    C. essential to an enforceable contract.
    D. required by all mortgage lenders.

11. Typically, physical possession of the property is given to the buyer
    A. upon signing of the sale contract.
    B. before close of escrow (settlement).
    C. the day of close of escrow (settlement).
    D. 30 days following close of escrow (settlement).

12. Kitt sold his home to Park with broker Lee acting as agent for the sale. The contract of sale called for the expenses of settlement to be paid entirely by Park. Was this an enforceable provision of the contract?
    A. Yes, because the seller is required to pay all expenses of settlement.
    B. Yes, because the allocation of expenses is negotiable.
    C. No, because these expenses should be paid by the purchaser.
    D. No, because these expenses should be prorated between buyer and seller.

13. Case sold his home to Fox. They agreed that Case's power lawn mower be included in the sale. Should this agreement be included in the purchase contract?
    A. Yes, because the lawn mower is real property.
    B. Yes, to avoid misunderstandings.
    C. No, because it must be conveyed by a separate bill of sale.
    D. No, because lawn mowers are personal property.

14. Bravos signed a contract to purchase real property from Alcala, subject to his ability to secure a loan for a part of the purchase price within thirty days. After diligent effort, Bravos was unable to secure the loan within the specified time. At the end of thirty days, this contract was
    A. void on its face.   C. voidable by Alcala.
    B. voidable by Bravos.   D. unenforceable.

15. If a seller fails to carry out his obligation under a typical residential contract of sale, the buyer may take any of the following actions EXCEPT:
    A. sue for specific performance.
    B. rescind the contract.
    C. sue for monetary damages.
    D. demand liquidated damages.

16. Green made an offer to purchase property from Blue. The offer was contingent on Blue's acceptance within seven days. Prior to Blue's acceptance, Green found another property which he liked better, and decided to withdraw his offer.
    A. He could not withdraw his offer until Blue had decided to accept or reject the offer.
    B. He could not withdraw his offer until the expiration of the seven days mentioned in his offer.
    C. He could withdraw at any time prior to acceptance of the offer by Blue.
    D. He could withdraw at any time within seven days.

17. The phrase "time is of the essence" in a sales contract means that
    I.   the time limits set by the contract must be faithfully observed or the contract is voidable.
    II. the parties are prohibited from giving each other an extension.
    A. I only   B. II only   C. Both I and II   D. Neither I nor II

18. When a buyer makes an offer to purchase through an agent, such as a real estate broker,
    A. there is never any need to consult an attorney for counsel.
    B. an attorney should be consulted if the buyer has any doubts or questions regarding the legal effects of the offer.
    C. the state bar association requires that an attorney be consulted.
    D. state law requires that an attorney be consulted.

19. If a buyer makes an offer to purchase, and the seller accepts part but not all of its conditions,
    A. this constitutes partial acceptance and is binding upon the buyer as if it were fully accepted by the seller.
    B. those conditions accepted by the seller are binding on the buyer.
    C. this does NOT constitute a rejection of the entire offer.
    D. the entire offer is considered rejected.

20. A property owner wishes to reject a written offer from a prospective purchaser and to make a counteroffer to the prospective purchaser. He may do so by
    I. preparing an entirely new purchase contract and signing it.
    II. listing changes required on the back of the original offer and signing it.
    III. making changes on the face of the original offer to be initialed by all parties.
    IV. advising the agent orally of the required changes, to be conveyed to the prospective purchaser by the agent for agreement.
    A. I, II, III and IV   C. III only
    B. I only   D. I, II and III only

21. Martin is going to purchase a newly built home from the builder. He will finance the purchase by means of a VA-guaranteed loan. The builder must include in the purchase contract
    I. an amendatory clause.
    II. insulation disclosures.
    A. I only   B. II only   C. Both I and II   D. Neither I nor II

22. The purchase agreement used for most real estate sales is
    A. prepared in its entirety by the agent.
    B. prepared in advance by the seller and attached to the listing.
    C. prepared by an attorney especially for the transaction.
    D. prepared by the agent by filling in blank spaces on a form which was prepared by an attorney.

23. Mr. and Mrs. Silver entered into a real estate contract with Mr. and Mrs. Gold. If Mr. Gold dies before settlement takes place,
    I. Mr. and Mrs. Silver are obligated to carry out the contract.
    II. Mr. and Mrs. Silver are NOT obligated to carry out the contract.
    III. Mrs. Gold is obligated to carry out the contract.
    IV. Mr. Gold's estate is obligated to carry out the contract.
    A. II only   C. I and IV only
    B. I and III only   D. I, III and IV only

24. A short form contract used by real estate agents in some states to hold a deal together until a more formal contract can be prepared by an attorney is known as a
    I. rider
    II. binder.
    A. I only   B. II only   C. Both I and II   D. Neither I nor II

25. A binder which has been executed by both purchaser and seller
    I.   meets all requirements of a legally binding contract.
    II. can be used to enforce completion of the sale.
    A. I only   B. II only   C. Both I and II   D. Neither I nor II

26. The major weakness of a binder lies in
    A. its unenforceability.
    B. what it does not say.

27. A letter of intent is
    A. an agreement to enter into a contract.
    B. binding on the seller.
    C. binding on the buyer.
    D. binding on both buyer and seller.

28. Who should be represented by an attorney at the meeting for the purpose
    of preparing a formal contract as provided for in a binder?
      I.   The seller.
     II.   The buyer.
    III.   The agent.
    A. I and III only   C. I, II and III
    B. II and III only   D. I and II only

29. In most states, licensed real estate agents
    A. may fill in blank spaces on a pre-printed contract of sale form
        which was prepared by a lawyer.
    B. may prepare a contract of sale in its entirety.
    C. may NOT participate in the preparation of a formal contract
        of sale.
    D. must engage an attorney to prepare the formal agreement of sale.

30. All of the following terms relate to the same type of instrument EXCEPT:
    A. installment contract.   C. land contract.
    B. contract of sale.   D. contract for deed.

31. When property is sold by means of an installment contract, the
      I. seller delivers a deed at closing.
     II. buyer is NOT given the right to occupy the property until the
          contract terms have been fulfilled.
    A. I only   B. II only   C. Both I and II   D. Neither I nor II

32. Installment contracts may be used when
      I. the buyer does not have the full purchase price in cash.
     II. the buyer is unable to borrow part of the purchase price from
          a lender.
    A. I only   B. II only   C. Both I and II   D. Neither I nor II

33. Traditionally, the language of installment contracts used for the pur-
    chase of real estate has favored the
    A. vendor.   C. grantor.
    B. vendee.   D. grantee.

34. Installment contracts may be used in the sale of
    I. vacant land.
    II. improved property.
    A. I only   B. II only   C. Both I and II   D. Neither I nor II

35. The increasing use of installment contracts for the sale of real estate
    has led to laws in some states designed to protect the interests of the
    A. buyer.   C. lender.
    B. seller.   D. agent.

36. The purchaser under an installment contract may protect his interests by
    requiring that the
    I. seller place a deed in escrow at settlement.
    II. contract be recorded in the land records.
    A. I only   B. II only   C. Both I and II   D. Neither I nor II

37. A well-written installment contract will include language which specifies
    I. any restrictions on the use of the property.
    II. who is responsible for maintenance of the property.
    III. how taxes and insurance will be paid.
    IV. who is responsible for casualty losses to the property.
    A. I, II, III and IV   C. II and III only
    B. I, II and III only   D. III and IV only

38. An installment contract can be
    I. the original purchase contract.
    II. a separate agreement which is an adjunct to a purchase contract.
    A. I only   B. II only   C. Both I and II   D. Neither I nor II

39. A purchaser's right to acquire legal title to real property under the
    terms of a valid purchase agreement is known as
    A. naked title.   C. specific performance.
    B. equitable title.   D. contract title.

40. Equitable title can be
    I. transferred by sale.   III. mortgaged.
    II. inherited.   IV. transferred by deed.
    A. I, II and IV only   C. I and II only
    B. IV only   D. I, II, III and IV

41. Purchaser Patricia and seller Susan entered into a purchase contract for
    the sale of Susan's residence. From the moment the contract was signed
    by both parties, the
    I. legal title to the property was vested in purchaser Patricia.
    II. equitable title to the property was held by seller Susan.
    A. I only   B. II only   C. Both I and II   D. Neither I nor II

42. Adam holds the equitable title to real property under an installment
    contract. Baker wants to purchase the property, and Adam is willing to
    sell to Baker. This can be accomplished by
    I. assignment of the contract by Adam to Baker.
    II. novation, provided the vendor agrees.
    A. I only   B. II only   C. Both I and II   D. Neither I nor II

43. Under the terms of a lease with option to buy, the tenant is given the right to purchase the property
    I. at a price to be negotiated at the time of purchase.
    II. at any time during the option period.
    III. after expiration of the lease.
    IV. at a preset price.
    A. I and II only
    B. III and IV only
    C. I and III only
    D. II and IV only

44. The option portion of a lease-option contract can be attached to the lease as
    I. a rider.
    II. an accord.
    A. I only   B. II only   C. Both I and II   D. Neither I nor II

45. On balance, a lease-option tends to favor the
    A. optioner.
    B. optionee.

46. Lease-option contracts tend to increase in popularity during a
    A. seller's market.
    B. buyer's market.

47. The purchase contract which accompanies a lease-option should be prepared
    A. at the same time as the lease.
    B. when the option is exercised.
    C. during the option period.
    D. after the option expires.

48. Evidence that a tenant has an option to buy a property should be recorded so as to establish
    I. the tenant's rights to the property.
    II. that the tenant's rights date back to the date of recordation.
    A. I only   B. II only   C. Both I and II   D. Neither I nor II

49. An option to buy is an example of
    I. an executory contract.   III. an executed contract.
    II. a bilateral contract.   IV. a unilateral contract.
    A. I only
    B. I and IV only
    C. II and III only
    D. III and IV only

50. Landlord Lewis and tenant Ted entered into an agreement in writing which gave Ted the right to match any valid offer which Lewis might receive for the purchase of the property. Did this agreement constitute a lease-option on the property?
    A. Yes, because it gave the tenant the right to purchase the property.
    B. Yes, because the agreement was in writing.
    C. No, because there was no consideration.
    D. No, because the elements of an option to buy were not present.

51. Under the terms of a right of first refusal, the tenant is given the right to
    I. match an offer to purchase the property.
    II. purchase the property at a previously agreed price.
    A. I only   B. II only   C. Both I and II   D. Neither I nor II

52. The party with the least amount of flexibility in a lease-option agreement is the
    A. optionor.
    B. optionee.

53. Stephanie owns a house worth $150,000. Michael would like to lease it for fair market rental value and have an option to buy it within one year. Stephanie would be most successful in obtaining an option fee in addition to the rent if she sets an option price at
    A. $150,000.   C. $200,000.
    B. $175,000.   D. $250,000.

54. When putting together a lease-option agreement, a real estate agent can charge a commission for
    I. leasing the property.
    II. selling the property if the option is exercised.
    A. I only   B. II only   C. Both I and II   D. Neither I nor II

55. Exchanging of real properties has become popular among sophisticated investors because
    I. trades can be accomplished without large amounts of cash.
    II. income taxes may be deferred on profits from the first property in the transaction.
    A. I only   B. II only   C. Both I and II   D. Neither I nor II

56. When an owner-occupied dwelling is sold for a profit, and a new residence of equal or greater value is purchased within 24 months, taxes on the gain are
    A. due upon the sale of the original residence.
    B. deferred until the second home is sold.
    C. due in the year of purchase of the new residence.
    D. waived under the residence replacement rule.

57. Real estate exchanges are possible only when
    I. all properties are of equal value.
    II. no more than two properties are involved.
    A. I only   B. II only   C. Both I and II   D. Neither I nor II

58. A broker who arranges a four-way trade of real properties will normally expect to receive
    A. one commission.
    B. four commissions.
    C. a commission based on the amount of cash involved.
    D. no commission if no cash is involved in the trades.

59. Under the 1984 Tax Reform Act, in order to qualify for a delayed exchange,
    I. the designated property to be exchanged must be identified
        within 30 days of the original closing.
    II. title to the designated property must be acquired within 90
        days of the original closing.
    A. I only   B. II only   C. Both I and II   D. Neither I nor II

60. Warner wants to trade up to a larger property and at the same time defer
    the capital gain in his present property. He wants Smithson's property
    and would like to trade directly with Smithson. However, Smithson wants
    cash, not Warner's property. Jeddah has cash and wants Warner's
    property. Which of the following would accomplish these goals?
    I. Warner trades with Smithson who, in turn, sells to Jeddah.
    II. Jeddah buys Warner's property, and with the money Warner buys
        Smithson's property.
    III. Jeddah buys Smithson's property and trades with Warner.
    A. I only   B. II only   C. I and III only   D. I, II and III

Math Problems

1. Fletcher bought a parcel of unimproved land measuring 200' by 435.6' for
    $96.50 per front foot. After one year he decides to sell the land. He
    has paid property taxes of $1,000 per acre. He desires to make at least
    a 30% profit. What is the approximate minimum sale price for Fletcher to
    achieve his objective?

    $_____

2. The buildings on a 150' by 180' lot cover 25% of the lot. For road-
    widening purposes, the state buys vacant land along the front amounting
    to 15% of the total area of the lot. How many square feet of land not
    covered with buildings is retained by the owner?

    $_____

3. A subdivider is selling eight lots that are 75' by 120'. Which will give
    her the highest selling price?
    A. $1.50 per square foot   C. $185 per front foot
    B. $13,600 per lot   D. $110,000 for the entire parcel

4. A purchaser buys a lot for $11,000 and pays a $3,000 down payment. He
    pays $72.50 per month for ten years and ten months. How much more than
    the original sales price did he pay?

    $_____

5. Azar, the owner of real estate valued at $77,000, allows Balston, the
    owner of a 60 acre farm, $1,500 an acre as a trade property. How much
    cash difference will be paid to whom?

    $_____ to _____

Real Estate Purchase Contract

As a salesman employed by the Happy Valley Realty Company, 123 Oak Avenue, Midvale, Anystate, you negotiate a sale of a single-family home owned by Otis Land and his wife, Lotta Land. The buyer is Mary Vann, an unmarried woman. The date of the offer is July 15 of this year. Property description is Lot 15, Block 3, Section 5 of West Grove Subdivision as recorded in the land records of Sunshine County in Plat Book 1523, Page 128. Street address is 59 Pine Street, Midvale. Buyer makes a deposit of $2,000 with her offer, and agrees to pay an additional deposit of $3,000 upon acceptance. The balance of the purchase price of $99,500 is to be paid as follows: Buyer to make a total down payment of $20,000 and assume an existing first mortgage held by the Comet Mortgage Company in the amount of $52,450 bearing interest at 9.5 percent per annum. Sellers are to accept a second mortgage for the balance of the purchase price, bearing interest at the rate of 11 percent per annum to be amortized by payments of $400 per month applied first to interest, then to principal, the entire balance due and payable at the end of five years. Refrigerator, washer, and dryer now on the premises are to be included in the sale. Your firm's sales commission is to be 6 percent of the sale price.

The sellers are to furnish at their expense a certificate of termite and wood rot inspection from a licensed inspector, and pay for the inspection and any corrective work needed. Sellers are to convey by warranty deed and furnish a standard title insurance policy insured by Valley Title Company. Prorations and possession are as of the close of escrow. Escrow agent to be Sunrise Escrow Company and escrow shall close 45 days from acceptance of this contract. Escrow costs are to be split equally. There are no outstanding bonds or assessments placed against the property. Earnest money is to be placed into escrow. Conveyance is to be subject to existing covenants and easements of record. Buyer gives seller until noon on July 17 of this year to accept this offer. On July 16 the sellers accept, sign the contract and a copy is delivered to the buyer by you. The contract is prepared in the city of Midvale, Anystate. Mary Vann currently lives at 232 Hemlock, Apt. 4, Midvale. The sellers live at 59 Pine Street.

Using the above information, complete the real estate purchase contract which follows.

Real Estate Purchase Contract

①City of_____, State of_____,
②Date_____.

③_____(herein called the Buyer) agrees to
purchase and④_____(herein called the Seller) agrees
to sell the following described real property located in the City of
⑤_____, County of_____,
State of_____, a_____,
Commonly known as_____,
and legally described as_____
_____
_____
_____.

⑥The total purchase price is_____
_____ Dollars ($),
payable as follows:_____
_____
_____
_____
_____
_____
_____
_____
_____.

⑦Seller will deliver to the buyer a _____deed to said
property. Seller will furnish to the buyer at the _____
expense a standard American Land Title Association title insurance policy
issued by _____Company showing title vested in the
Buyer and that the Seller is conveying title free of liens, encumbrances,
easements, rights and conditions except as follows:_____
_____
_____
_____.

⑧The escrow agent shall be_____
and escrow instructions shall be signed by the Buyer and Seller and
delivered to escrow whithin five days upon receipt thereof. The close
of excrow shall be _____ days after the date of mutual agreement to
this contarct.

⑨Property taxes, property insurance, mortgage interest, income, and
expense items shall be prorated as of_____.

⑩Any outstanding bonds or assessments on the property shall be___
_____

⑪Any existing mortgage indebtedness against the property is to be
_____

continued . . .

⑫Seller will provide Buyer with a report from a licensed pest control inspector that the property is free of termites and wood rot. The cost of the report and any corrective work deemed necessary by the report are to be paid for by the _____.

⑬Possession of the property is to be delivered to the Buyer_____

_____.

⑭Escrow expenses shall be_____.

⑮Documentary tax stamps shall be paid for by the Seller.

⑯The earnest money deposit is to be held_____.

⑰All attached floor coverings, attached television antenna, window screens, screen doors, storm windows, storm doors, plumbing and lighting fixtures (except floor, standing, and swag lamps), curtain rods, shades, venetian blinds, bathroom fixtures, trees, plants, shrubbery, water heaters, awnings, built-in heating, ventilating, and cooling systems, built-in stoves and ranges, and fences now on the premises shall be included unless otherwise noted. Any leased fixtures on the premises are not included unless specifically stated.

⑱Other provisions:_____

_____

_____

_____

_____

_____

_____

_____.

⑲ If the improvements on the property are destroyed or materially damaged prior to the close of escrow, or if the Buyer is unable to obtain financing as stated herein, or if the Seller is unable to deliver title as promised, then the Buyer, at his option, may terminate this agreement and the deposit made by him shall be returned to him in full. If the Seller fails to fulfill any of the other agreements made herein, the Buyer may terminate this agreement with full refund of deposit, accept lesser performance, or sue for specific performance.

continued . . .

(20) If the purchase is not completed by reason of the Buyer's default, the Seller is released from his obligation to sell to the Buyer and shall retain the deposit money as his sole right to damages.

(21) Upon the signature of the Buyer, this document becomes an offer to the Seller to purchase the property described herein. The Seller has until_____to indicate acceptance of this offer by signing and delivering it to the Buyer. If acceptance is not received by that time, this offer shall be deemed revoked and the deposit shall be returned in full to the Buyer.

(22) Time is of the essence in this contract.

Real Estate Broker_____
By_____
Address_____.(23)Telephone_____

(24) The undersigned offers and agrees to buy the above described property on the terms and conditions stated herein and acknowledges receipt of a copy hereof.

Buyer_____
Address_____
Telephone_____

Acceptance

(25) The undersigned accepts the foregoing offer and agrees to sell the property described above on the terms and conditions set forth.

(26) The undersigned has employed_____ as Broker and for Broker's services agrees to pay said Broker as commission the sum of _____ dollars ($_____) payable upon recordation of the deed or if completion of this sale is prevented by the Seller. If completion of this contract is prevented by the Buyer, Broker shall share equally in any damages collected by the Seller, not to exceed the above stated commission.

(27) The undersigned acknowledges receipt of a copy hereof.

Seller_____
Seller_____
Address_____
Telephone_____ Date_____

Notification of Acceptance

(28) Receipt of a copy of the foregoing agreement is hereby acknowledged.

Buyer_____ Buyer_____ Date_____

Offer to Purchase Agreement

Complete the Offer to Purchase Agreement, using the form on the opposite page. Data for the problem is furnished below.

1. Date of offer — August 1, 19 (current year)

2. Purchasers — Hap E. Tymes and wife, Joy S. Tymes

3. Sellers — Lucky Sale and wife, Wanda Sale

4. Broker — Serv-U Realty Company, your name as sales agent.

5. Property description — Lot 4, Block B, Section 3, Pinewood Subdivision, Glendale, Jackson County, Anystate

6. Chattel items included — Kitchen range, refrigerator, washer and dryer

7. Street address — 406 West Vance Street, Glendale

8. Purchase price — $225,000

9. Deposit with offer — $10,000 personal check

10. Cash down payment (including deposit) — $25,000

11. First mortgage loan — $180,000 Offer subject to purchasers' ability to secure a first mortgage loan in this amount at interest not to exceed 12 percent per annum and a loan fee of one percent.

12. Second mortgage — $20,000 This is to be a purchase money loan to be secured by 2nd mortgage to seller at 10 percent per annum, monthly payments of $200 and the unpaid balance to be due and payable at the end of 5 years.

13. Settlement to be held at — East-West Title Company, Glendale

14. Date of settlement — September 15, 19 (current year)

15. Sales commission — 6 percent

16. Special conditions — Seller to pay for termite and wood rot inspection and corrective work.

The sellers accepted this offer. Prepare the agreement on the above terms.

OFFER TO PURCHASE AGREEMENT

This AGREEMENT made as of_____, 19_____,

among_____(herein called "Purchaser"),

and_____(herein called "Seller"),

and_____(herein called "Broker"),
provides that Purchaser agrees to buy through Broker as agent for Seller, and Seller agrees to sell the following described real estate, and all improvements
thereon, located in the jurisdiction of_____,

(all herein called "the property"):_____

_____

_____, and more commonly known as_____

_____(street address).

1. The purchase price of the property is_____

Dollars ($_____), and such purchase price shall be paid as follows:

_____

_____

2. Purchaser has made a deposit of_____ Dollars ($_____)
with Broker, receipt of which is hereby acknowledged, and such deposit shall be held by Broker in escrow until the date of settlement and then applied
to the purchase price, or returned to Purchaser if the title to the property is not marketable.

3. Seller agrees to convey the property to Purchaser by Warranty Deed with the usual covenants of title and free and clear from all encumbrances,
tenancies, liens (for taxes or otherwise), except as may be otherwise provided above, but subject to applicable restrictive covenants of record. Seller further
agrees to deliver possession of the property to Purchaser on the date of settlement and to pay the expense of preparing the deed of conveyance.

4. Settlement shall be made at the offices of Broker or at_____on or before
_____, 19____, or as soon thereafter as title can be examined and necessary documents prepared, with allowance of
a reasonable time for Seller to correct any defects reported by the title examiner.

5. All taxes, interest, rent, and F.H.A. or similar escrow deposits, if any, shall be prorated as of the date of settlement.

6. All risk of loss or damage to the property by fire, windstorm, casualty, or other cause is assumed by Seller until the date of settlement.

7. Purchaser and Seller agree that Broker was the sole procuring cause of this Contract of Purchase, and Seller agrees to pay Broker for services
rendered a cash fee of_____per cent of the purchase price. If either Purchaser or Seller defaults under such Contract, such defaulting party shall
be liable for the cash fee of Broker and any expenses incurred by the non-defaulting party in connection with this transaction.

Subject to:_____

_____

_____

8. Purchaser represents that an inspection satisfactory to Purchaser has been made of the property, and Purchaser agrees to accept the property in
its present condition except as may be otherwise provided in the description of the property above.

9. This Contract of Purchase constitutes the entire agreement among the parties and may not be modified or changed except by written instrument
executed by all of the parties, including Broker.

10. This Contract of Purchase shall be construed, interpreted, and applied according to the law of the jurisdiction of_____and shall
be binding upon and shall inure to the benefit of the heirs, personal representatives, successors, and assigns of the parties.

All parties to this agreement acknowledge receipt of a certified copy.

WITNESS the following signatures and seals:

_____(SEAL)   _____(SEAL)
Seller   Purchaser

_____(SEAL)   _____(SEAL)
Seller   Purchaser

_____(SEAL)
Broker

Deposit Rec'd $_____

Personal Check   Cash

Cashier's Check   Company Check

Sales Agent:

Answers—Chapter 8

Multiple Choice Questions

1. C   The buyer should have reached a firm decision to buy the property before signing a contract, but the contract gives him time to arrange financing, have the title examined, and determine the marketability of the title.

2. C   A properly prepared sales contract commits each party to its terms and is enforceable in a court of law.

3. B   A formal real estate sales contract may be identified as a purchase contract, an offer to purchase, or a purchase offer, but not as an option contract.

4. C   Provision for the buyer's offer, an earnest money deposit, the seller's acceptance, and a brokerage commission are typically found in a real estate sales contract.

5. C   This agreement may be referred to as a land contract, contract for deed, conditional sales contract, or an installment contract.

6. D   The amount of earnest money deposit is determined by negotiation.

7. A   An escrow agent, the real estate broker, an attorney, or the lender may handle the paperwork and details of title transfer.

8. C   The process of apportioning taxes, interest, insurance, etc., is known as proration.

9. C   Since the rental is a month-to-month lease, the seller can terminate the lease on one month's notice, or permit the tenant to continue the lease.

10. A   The inclusion of a termite and dry rot clause in a sales contract is optional and negotiable.

11. C   The buyer is typically given physical possession of the property on the day of close of escrow or settlement.

12. B   The allocation of settlement expenses is negotiable between buyer and seller.

13. B   The power lawn mower should be identified and included in the sales contract to avoid misunderstandings.

14. B   The contract was voidable by the purchaser because it was subject to his ability to secure the necessary financing. The seller does not have this option.

15. D   The buyer may sue for specific performance, rescind the contract, or sue for monetary damages, but not demand liquidated damages, unless the contract provides for them (which is rarely the case).

16. C   An offer may be withdrawn at any time before it is accepted.

17. A   If the term "time is of the essence" is included in a contract, the time limits set by the contract must be faithfully observed or the contract is voidable.

18. B   An attorney should be consulted if the buyer has any doubts or questions as to the legal effects of the offer.

19. D   The entire offer is considered to be rejected if the seller accepts part but not all of its conditions.

20. D   Oral instructions to an agent do not constitute a proper counter-offer.

21. C   Both an amendatory clause and insulation disclosures must be included in contracts calling for VA financing of a new home.

22. D   Most real estate sales contracts are prepared by having the agent fill in blank spaces on a form which was prepared by an attorney.

23. D   Should a party to a sales contract die after its execution but before performance is completed, the contract remains binding on the other party and upon the estate of the decedent.

24. B   In some states real estate agents use a binder to hold a deal together until a more formal contract can be prepared by an attorney.

25. C   A binder which has been executed by both purchaser and seller is a legally binding contract and can be used to enforce completion of the sale.

26. B   A binder's major weakness lies in what it does not say, but it is an enforceable contract.

27. A   A letter of intent is an agreement to enter into a contract, but is not binding on either party.

28. D   Both the seller and the buyer should be represented by an attorney, but there is generally no need for the agent to have legal representation.

29. A   The laws of most states permit a licensed real estate agent to fill in blank spaces of a pre-printed contract form which was prepared by a lawyer.

30. B   A contract of sale calls for the purchaser to pay for the property at settlement and to receive a deed at settlement, while an installment contract, land contract or contract for deed call for the purchase price to be paid in installments and a deed to be delivered upon fulfillment of the contract terms.

31. D   An installment calls for a deed to be delivered upon fulfillment of the contract terms, but gives the purchaser the right of occupancy during the contract period.

32. C   Installment contracts may be used when the borrower does not have the full purchase price in cash and is unable to borrow part of the purchase price from a lender.

33. A   Traditionally, the language of installment contracts for the purchase of real estate has tended to favor the vendor, i.e., the seller.

34. C   Installment contracts may be used for the sale of vacant land or improved property.

35. A   The increasing use of installment contracts in real estate sales has led to some state laws designed to protect the buyer's interests.

36. C   The purchaser's interests may be protected by requiring that the seller place a deed in escrow and having the contract recorded in the land records.

37. A   Specifications as to restrictions on the use of the property, responsibility for maintenance, payment of taxes and insurance, and responsibility for casualty loss are all part of a well-written installment contract.

38. C   An installment contract can be the original purchase contract or a separate contract.

39. B   Equitable title is a purchaser's right to acquire legal title to real property under the terms of a valid purchase agreement.

40. D   Equitable title can be transferred by sale, inherited, mortgaged, or transferred by deed.

41. D   Equitable title passes with the signing of the purchase contract. Legal title passes with the delivery of the deed.

42. C   Equitable title can be transferred by an assignment of a purchase contract or by novation with the seller's agreement.

43. D   A lease with option to buy gives the tenant the right to purchase the property at any time during the option period at a preset price.

44. A   The option portion of a lease-option can be attached to the lease as a rider, but not as an accord, which is something altogether different.

45. B   A lease-option tends to favor the optionee because the option may or may not be exercised by the optionee and the optionor has no choice but to accept the optionee's decision.

46. B   A buyer's market will lead to an increase in popularity of lease-options because property is not selling quickly.

47. A   The lease-option and purchase contract should be negotiated at the same time to avoid future disagreements.

48. C   Evidence of the tenant's option to buy should be recorded to establish the tenant's rights and the fact that these rights date back to the date of recordation.

49. B   An option to buy is an executory contract because it is unfulfilled, and a unilateral contract because it is based on a promise in exchange for an act.

50. D   The agreement was not a lease-option because it did not contain the elements of an option to buy.

51. A   A right of first refusal gives the tenant the right to match an offer to purchase the property, but not at a previously agreed price.

52. A   The optionor has the least amount of flexibility in a lease-option because the optionee can choose whether or not to exercise the option and the optionor must abide by the optionee's decision.

53. A   The tenant would be more likely to agree to an option fee if the purchase price under a lease-option were set at or near the current market value of the property.

54. C   A real estate agent can charge a fee for both leasing and selling the property if a lease-option is exercised, provided the owner will agree to these terms.

55. C   Property exchanges are popular among investors because of low cash requirements and possible deferral of income taxes on otherwise taxable gain from the first property.

56. B   Taxes on the gain from the sale of an owner-occupied dwelling are deferred if a new residence of equal or greater value is purchased within 24 months.

57. D   Properties that are being exchanged need not be of equal value, and more than two properties may be exchanged.

58. B   Normally, a broker receives a commission based on the value of each property involved in an exchange.

59. D   The 1984 Tax Reform Act requires that the designated property to be exchanged be identified within 45 days of the original closing, that title be acquired within 180 days of closing, and that the property be received before the designating party's tax return is due.

60.   C   This trade can be successfully approached from either end using either response I or response III. It won't work for Warner if he accepts the money offered by Jeddah in response II.

Math Problems

1.   (200' x $96.50 + 2 x $1,000) x 1.30 = $27,690
Note that 200' x 435.6' = 2 acres.

2.   150' x 180' x .75 = 20,250 sqft, portion without buildings
150' x 180' x .15 = 4,050 sqft, sold to state
20,250 sqft - 4,050 sqft = 16,200 sqft answer

3.   A. = 75' x 120' x $1.50 x 8 lots = $108,000
B. = $13,600 x 8 lots   = $108,800
C. = 75' x $185 x 8 lots   = $111,000 answer
D. =   = $110,000

4. $3,000 + $72.50 x 130 months - $11,000 = $1,425

5.   60 acres x $1,500 - $77,000 = $13,000 paid to Balston

Mortgage and Note

Chapter 9

1. Evidence of the amount and terms of a borrower's debt to a lender is provided by means of a
   I. mortgage.
   II. promissory note.
   A. I only B. II only C. Both I and II D. Neither I nor II

2. To be valid evidence of a borrower's debt, a note must
     I. be in writing, between parties having contractual capacity.
    II. state the borrower's promise to repay a certain sum of money.
   III. show the terms of payment.
    IV. be recorded in the public records.
     V. be delivered and accepted.
   A. I, II, III, IV and V   C. I and II only
   B. I, II and III only   D. I, II, III and V only

3. In order to be enforceable, a promissory note must be signed by the
   I. borrower.
   II. lender.
   A. I only B. II only C. Both I and II D. Neither I nor II

4. A promissory note which fails to state that it is to be secured by a mortgage or deed of trust is
    I. a personal obligation of the borrower.
   II. an unsecured obligation of the borrower.
   A. I only B. II only C. Both I and II D. Neither I nor II

5. The purpose of putting the location of the execution on a promissory note is to
    I. establish applicable state laws.
   II. tell the borrower where to send the payments.
   A. I only B. II only C. Both I and II D. Neither I nor II

Note: There are no deleted questions in this chapter for readers of
      Real Estate: An Introduction to the Profession.

6. The words "or order" in a promissory note make it
    I.   possible for the lender to transfer the right to collect the note
         to another party.
    II. a negotiable instrument.
    A. I only   B. II only   C. Both I and II   D. Neither I nor II

7. Under a note secured by a mortgage, the obligor is the
    A. lender.   C. note holder.
    B. borrower.   D. mortgagee.

8. A promissory note may state that
    I.   the note may not be prepaid.
    II.   there will be a penalty for prepayment.
    III. the note may be prepaid without penalty.
    A. I only   B. II only   C. III only   D. I, II and III

9. Should a borrower fail to make payments when due, the lender may demand
    immediate payment of the entire balance under the terms of the
    A. prepayment clause.   C. acceleration clause.
    B. defeasance clause.   D. hypothecation clause.

10. Customarily, which of the instruments associated with a mortgage loan
    is/are recorded in the public records?
    I.   The promissory note.
    II. The mortgage.
    A. I only   B. II only   C. Both I and II   D. Neither I nor II

11. Which of the following statements is/are correct?
    I.   A promissory note is evidence of a borrower's debt to a lender.
    II. A mortgage hypothecates property as collateral for a loan.
    A. I only   B. II only   C. Both I and II   D. Neither I nor II

12. A borrower's property serves as collateral while the borrower retains the
    rights of possession and use of it by the process of
    A. alienation.   C. amortization.
    B. hypothecation.   D. acceleration.

13. The mortgagee under the terms of a mortgage is the
    I.   obligee under the promissory note.
    II. lender.
    A. I only   B. II only   C. Both I and II   D. Neither I nor II

14. In states which subscribe to the title theory of mortgages
    I.   the mortgage deeds title to the mortgaged property to the lender.
    II. the borrower retains the rights of possession and use of the
         property.
    A. I only   B. II only   C. Both I and II   D. Neither I nor II

15. At the time of origination, a mortgage creates a lien on the mortgaged property in states which subscribe to the
   I. lien theory.
  II. title theory.
 III. intermediate theory.
A. I only
B. III only
C. I, II and III
D. I and III only

16. A mortgage becomes null and void when the note is paid in full under the terms of the
A. defeasance clause.
B. prepayment clause.
C. alienation clause.
D. hypothecation clause.

17. Which of the following covenants will NOT appear in a mortgage?
A. Covenants to pay taxes and insurance.
B. Covenant against removal.
C. Covenant against encumbrances.
D. Covenant of good repair.

18. Norman wishes to purchase Wilma's house for $100,000, giving her a $20,000 cash down payment and a note and mortgage for the remaining $80,000. Norman can expect to hypothecate which of the following with the mortgage?
A. The lot and house.
B. The house, but not the lot.
C. The lot, but not the house.
D. Norman's other real estate holdings.

19. The clause which gives the lender the right to call in the note if the mortgaged property is sold or otherwise conveyed by the borrower is known as the
   I. due-on-sale clause.
  II. alienation clause.
A. I only   B. II only   C. Both I and II   D. Neither I nor II

20. If all or part of a mortgaged property is taken by eminent domain, the condemnation clause requires that
A. any money received be used to reduce the balance owed on the note.
B. the entire loan balance be paid in full.

21. When Jack paid off his mortgage loan in full, the lender gave him a satisfaction of mortgage document. Should this instrument be recorded in the public records?
A. Yes, because recordation is required by state law.
B. Yes, because the records would otherwise indicate that the obligation was still outstanding.
C. No, because the mortgage was terminated by the defeasance clause once the debt was paid.
D. No, because the note was not recorded in the public records.

22. Marginal releases of mortgage satisfaction recordations are made in order to
    I. strike the mortgage from the public records.
   II. assist title searchers in completing abstracts of the title to the mortgaged property.
A. I only.   B. II only.   C. Both I and II.   D. Neither I nor II.

23. Loren hypothecated the title to two equally-valued properties as collateral for a loan of $50,000. When he had repaid $25,000 of the principal amount, one of the properties was removed from the mortgage obligation by means of a
A. mortgage satisfaction.   C. defeasance.
B. partial release.   D. release of mortgage.

24. Elmer sold his home to Baker, subject to an existing mortgage loan. Baker later defaulted on the loan. Which of the following statements is correct?
A. The lender has recourse to the assets of Baker for the balance due.
B. Baker is jointly responsible for the loan balance along with Elmer.
C. The mortgagee can look to Elmer for the loan balance.
D. Elmer was relieved of liability for the loan balance when Baker accepted title subject to the existing loan.

25. Who may be held responsible for mortgage loan repayment when a loan is assumed as part of a real estate sale?
    I. The purchaser.
   II. The seller.
A. I only   B. II only   C. Both I and II   D. Neither I nor II

26. When a loan is assumed, the
    I. seller can be relieved of liability by novation.
   II. the buyer should verify the loan balance with the lender.
A. I only   B. II only   C. Both I and II   D. Neither I nor II

27. When a lender wants to sell a loan to another investor, the borrower may sometimes be asked to verify the loan balance by means of
A. a certificate of novation.   C. a certificate of reduction.
B. an estoppel certificate.   D. a verification of certificate.

28. The lien priority of mortgages is determined by the
A. date of the mortgage instrument.
B. date of the promissory note.
C. language of the mortgage instrument.
D. order of recordation.

29. A mortgage which is lower in lien priority than another mortgage on the same property is known as a
    I. first mortgage.
   II. junior mortgage.
A. I only   B. II only   C. Both I and II   D. Neither I nor II

30. Martin is preparing an offer to buy a lot on which the seller will carry back a mortgage. Martin wants to build a house on the lot and has applied for a construction loan, but the lender will make the loan only if it can be secured by a first mortgage. This can be accomplished by asking the seller to execute
    A. an estoppel certificate.   C. a mortgage reduction certificate.
    B. a release of lien.   D. a subordination agreement.

31. The rights of a creditor who is owed for chattels which have been affixed to real property may be protected by recording a
    I. chattel mortgage.
    II. financing statement.
    A. I only   B. II only   C. Both I and II   D. Neither I nor II

32. Most mortgage foreclosures are the result of the borrower's
    A. violation of mortgage covenants.
    B. failure to make loan payments on time.
    C. noncompliance with the terms of the mortgage agreement.
    D. violation of the alienation clause.

33. A real estate borrower who is behind in his loan payments would first take which of the following steps?
    A. Sell the property before the next loan payment is due.
    B. Wait for the lender to accelerate the loan.
    C. Wait for the statutory redemption period.
    D. Meet with the lender as soon as possible.

34. Given a choice of foreclosure methods, in a simple and straightforward case, a lender will usually prefer which method of loan foreclosure?
    A. Judicial.
    B. Nonjudicial.

35. In a foreclosure action, the lender asks the court for a judgment directing that the
    I.   mortgagor's interests in the property be cut off.
    II. property be sold at public auction.
    III. lender's claim be paid from the sale proceeds.
    A. I and II only   C. II and III only
    B. I and III only   D. I, II and III

36. Harold holds a second mortgage on Baker's property. The first mortgage holder has begun foreclosure action because of Baker's default in mortgage loan payments. In order to protect his interests, Harold may
    I. make the delinquent payments for Baker and add them to Baker's indebtedness to Harold.
    II. file a surplus money action.
    A. I only   B. II only   C. Both I and II   D. Neither I nor II

37. A mortgagee may inform the public of a pending foreclosure action by recording a notice of
    A. acceleration.   C. estoppel.
    B. lis pendens.   D. subordination.

38. The period of equitable redemption given to a borrower
    I.   begins when the loan goes into default.
    II. ends when the property is sold at foreclosure.
    A. I only   B. II only   C. Both I and II   D. Neither I nor II

39. When a real estate mortgage is foreclosed, unpaid real estate tax liens against the property
    A. are cut off.
    B. become a lien on the personal property of the delinquent mortgagor.
    C. remain in force against the property.
    D. are added to the purchase price at the foreclosure sale.

40. When the amount received from a foreclosure sale is insufficient to pay off the mortgage loan and the other expenses of the sale, the lender may sometimes secure
    A. a deficiency judgment.   C. an estoppel lien.
    B. a mechanic's lien.   D. a statutory lien.

41. The deed given to the purchaser at foreclosure by the sheriff or other officer of the court usually takes the form of a
    A. general warranty deed.   C. special warranty deed.
    B. quitclaim deed.   D. bargain and sale deed.

42. The period of time set by state law after a foreclosure sale, during which the mortgagor may redeem the property is known as the period of
    A. equitable redemption.   C. voluntary redemption.
    B. legal redemption.   D. statutory redemption.

43. Bidders tend to offer more at a foreclosure sale if the property is located in a state which
    A. has a short statutory redemption period.
    B. has a lengthy statutory redemption period.
    C. permits the mortgagee to occupy the property during the statutory redemption period.
    D. gives title and possession to the high bidder immediately following the foreclosure auction.

44. When a delinquent loan is foreclosed by strict foreclosure,
    I.   the borrower is given a period of time to exercise the equitable right of redemption.
    II. title is vested in the lender if the borrower does not redeem within the time allowed.
    A. I only   B. II only   C. Both I and II   D. Neither I nor II

45. Strict foreclosure may be advantageous to the borrower if
    I.   the mortgage debt exceeds the value of the property.
    II. deficiency judgments are prohibited.
    A. I only   B. II only   C. Both I and II   D. Neither I nor II

46. Lenders may sometimes avoid judicial foreclosure if the mortgage has a
    I.   power of sale clause.
    II. waiver of deficiency judgment rights.
    A. I only   B. II only   C. Both I and II   D. Neither I nor II

47. A borrower who feels mistreated by a power of sale foreclosure can
    I. obtain a judicial foreclosure.
   II. appeal the issue to the courts.
   A. I only   B. II only   C. Both I and II   D. Neither I nor II

48. Judicial foreclosure may sometimes be avoided by
    I. power of sale.
   II. entry and possession.
   A. I only   B. II only   C. Both I and II   D. Neither I nor II

49. By voluntarily giving the lender a deed in lieu of foreclosure, a delinquent borrower can avoid
    I. foreclosure proceedings.
   II. possible deficiency judgments.
   A. I only   B. II only   C. Both I and II   D. Neither I nor II.

50. Adam gave the first mortgage holder a deed in lieu of foreclosure when he became delinquent in his mortgage loan payments. There is also a second mortgage on the property. Which of the following statements are correct?
    I. The first mortgagee is responsible for the balance due on the second mortgage.
   II. The second mortgagee loses the right to foreclose.
  III. The second mortgage becomes a first mortgage.
   A. I and II only   C. II and III only
   B. I and III only   D. I, II and III

51. Mortgages which are secured by personal property
    I. are known as chattel mortgages.
   II. must be foreclosed by judicial foreclosure.
   A. I only   B. II only   C. Both I and II   D. Neither I nor II

52. Generally, lenders ask borrowers to sign whatever security instrument
    I. is permitted by state law.
   II. permits the smoothest foreclosure proceedings in that state.
   A. I only   B. II only   C. Both I and II   D. Neither I nor II

53. When an installment contract to buy real estate goes into default, the
    I. vendee can rescind the contract.
   II. contract can be judicially foreclosed.
   A. I only   B. II only   C. Both I and II   D. Neither I nor II

54. A document that for all intents and purposes is a mortgage, although not labeled one, would most likely be
   A. an installment contract.   C. an equitable mortgage.
   B. a deed of trust.   D. a deed as security.

55. A three-party financing arrangement wherein title is held by a neutral third party until the debt is paid is
   A. an installment contract.   C. an equitable mortgage.
   B. a deed of trust.   D. a deed as security.

56. The borrower under a deed of trust is the
    A. beneficiary.   C. trustor.
    B. trustee.   D. assignor.

57. The lender under a deed of trust is the
    A. beneficiary.   C. trustor.
    B. trustee.   D. assignee.

58. An investor borrowed $100,000 to be repaid as follows: $10,000 at the end of the 1st, 2nd, 3rd and 4th years, and $60,000 at the end of the 5th year. The interest rate was as follows: 10.5% for the 1st year, 11% for the 2nd year, 11.5% for the 3rd year, 12% for the 4th year, and 12.5% for the 5th year. How much interest did he pay?

$_____.

59. Peggy took out a mortgage loan one year ago in the amount of $120,000. Since then she has made twelve monthly payments of $1,200 each and the interest paid to date on this loan is $12,000. If she asks the lender for a certificate of reduction at this time, how many dollars would it show?

$_____.

60. A property has a first mortgage loan balance of $70,000 against it; a second mortgage loan balance of $40,000 against it; a third mortgage loan balance of $15,000 against it and a fourth mortgage loan balance of $5,000 against it. At foreclosure the property sold for $88,000 and sale expenses and back taxes take $3,000 of that. Who gets what?

First $_____.

Second $_____.

Third $_____.

Fourth $_____.

Answers—Chapter 9

Multiple Choice Questions

1. B   The promissory note is evidence of the borrower's debt to the lender. A mortgage provides collateral for the debt.

2. D   It is not necessary for a note to be recorded in the public records in order to be valid evidence of a borrower's debt.

3. A   Only the borrower need sign a note for it to be enforceable.

4. C   A promissory note which does not state that it is to be secured by a mortgage or deed of trust is both a personal obligation and an unsecured obligation of the borrower.

5. A   The location of the execution of a note is stated on the note in order to establish which state's laws govern the note.

6. C   The words "or order" in a promissory note make it a negotiable instrument, thus giving the lender the right to transfer collection rights to another party.

7. B   The borrower is the obligor under a note secured by a mortgage. The note is the borrower's obligation.

8. D   A promissory note may set a prepayment penalty, waive a prepayment penalty, or prohibit prepayment of the note.

9. C   The acceleration clause in a note permits the lender to demand immediate payment of the entire balance due.

10. B   Customarily, the mortgage is recorded but the promissory note is not.

11. C   A promissory note is evidence of the borrower's debt, and a mortgage hypothecates property as collateral for a loan.

12. B   Hypothecation is the process by which a borrower's property serves as collateral for a debt without the borrower giving up possession of the property.

13. C   The lender is both the mortgagee under the terms of the mortgage and the obligee under the terms of the promissory note.

14. C   Under the title theory of mortgages, the mortgage deeds title to the property to the lender but allows the borrower the use of the property.

15. D   The lien and intermediate mortgage theories hold that the mortgage creates a lien on the mortgaged property at the time of origination.

16.   A   The defeasance clause states that the mortgage becomes null and void when the note is paid in full.

17.   C   The covenant against encumbrances appears in a general warranty deed, and not in a mortgage.

18.   A   The mortgage will hypothecate the house and lot on which it is located, but not any other real estate holdings of the mortgagor.

19.   C   An alienation clause permits the lender to demand immediate repayment of the note if the mortgaged property is sold or otherwise conveyed. It is also known as a due-on-sale clause.

20.   A   The condemnation clause in a mortgage requires that any money received from a sale under eminent domain be used to reduce the balance owed on the note.

21.   B   A satisfaction of mortgage should be recorded in the public records in order to give public notice that the debt has been satisfied.

22.   C   Marginal releases of mortgage satisfaction are made in order to strike the mortgage from the public records and to assist title searchers in completing abstracts of the property title.

23.   B   A partial release is used to release one or more properties from the obligations of a blanket mortgage.

24.   C   A person who takes property "subject to" is not personally liable to the lender or the seller. The seller, however, is still liable to the lender under the original terms of the note and mortgage.

25.   C   The purchaser is responsible to the seller, and the seller to the lender when a loan is assumed.

26.   C   A seller can be relieved of liability for an assumed loan by novation, the substitution of the purchaser for the seller as the mortgagor under the original note and mortgage. The balance on a loan which is being assumed should be verified with the lender.

27.   B   An estoppel certificate is used to secure verification from the borrower of the outstanding balance on a loan when the loan is being sold by the mortgagee or noteholder.

28.   D   Under the so-called "race statutes," the priority of a mortgage lien is determined by the order of recordation.

29.   B   A junior mortgage is any mortgage that is lower in lien priority than the first mortgage on a property.

30.   D   By means of a subordination agreement, the holder of a mortgage agrees to accept a position of lower lien priority than a subsequent mortgage on the same property.

31. C   A creditor may protect his rights in chattels which have been in-
          stalled on mortgaged property by filing either a chattel mortgage
          or a financing statement.

32. B   Most mortgage foreclosures are the result of the borrower's failure
          to make loan payments on time.

33. D   A borrower who is behind in mortgage payments should first meet with
          the lender as soon as possible.

34. B   Nonjudicial foreclosure is usually less expensive and faster than
          judicial foreclosure, so will usually be the lender's preference when
          a choice is permitted.

35. D   The purpose of a foreclosure action is to terminate the mortgagor's
          rights in the mortgaged property, cause the property to be sold at
          public auction, and satisfy the lender's claims from the proceeds of
          the sale.

36. C   The holder of a junior mortgage has the option of making the delin-
          quent payments on any mortgage senior to him and adding the amounts
          paid to the obligations under his mortgage, or filing a surplus
          mortgage action.

37. B   A notice of lis pendens is a public notice of pending legal action,
          filed in the public records of the jurisdiction of the mortgaged
          property.

38. C   The period of equitable redemption begins when the loan is in
          default, and ends when the property is sold at a foreclosure sale.

39. C   Foreclosure of a mortgage does not eliminate real estate tax liens.
          They remain in force against the property.

40. A   Should the amount received from a foreclosure sale be insufficient
          to satisfy the indebtedness, when permitted by law a lender may
          request a deficiency judgment against other property of the mortgagor
          as a means of recovering the amount due on a loan.

41. C   The purchaser at foreclosure will usually receive a special warranty
          deed signed by the officer of the court who handled the foreclosure
          sale.

42. D   The statutory redemption period begins at the time of the foreclosure
          sale, and terminates upon expiration of the statutory period in the
          jurisdiction.

43. D   A successful bidder who receives title and possession immediately
          following the foreclosure sale will tend to be willing to pay more
          for the property than in circumstances where title and possession
          will be delayed because of the mortgagor's statutory redemption
          rights.

44.   C   When a loan is foreclosed by strict foreclosure, the borrower is given a period of time to exercise his equitable redemption rights. Title vests in the lender if redemption does not occur within this time.

45.   C   Strict foreclosure may be advantageous to the borrower if the mortgage debt exceeds the property value and a deficiency judgment can be avoided.

46.   A   Where permitted by law, a power of sale clause in a mortgage permits the lender to conduct the foreclosure and auction and avoid judicial foreclosure.

47.   B   The borrower whose loan has been foreclosed by power of sale has the right to appeal the issue to the courts, but not to obtain a judicial foreclosure.

48.   C   Judicial foreclosure may sometimes be avoided by power of sale or by entry and possession.

49.   C   A voluntary deed in lieu of foreclosure avoids foreclosure proceedings and possible deficiency judgments.

50.   B   A first mortgagee who accepts a deed in lieu of foreclosure becomes liable for any junior mortgages on the property. A previous second mortgage will become a first mortgage. The second mortgagee retains the right to foreclose.

51.   A   A mortgage secured by personal property is a chattel mortgage. Judicial foreclosure is not required.

52.   B   Lenders tend to favor the form of security instrument that permits the smoothest foreclosure proceedings in that state.

53.   B   An installment contract which is in default may be judicially foreclosed. The vendee may not rescind the contract.

54.   C   A document which constitutes a mortgage, although not labeled as such, would most likely be considered to be an equitable mortgage.

55.   B   A deed of trust vests title in a neutral third party, called a trustee, to be held until the debt is paid.

56.   C   In a deed of trust, the borrower is referred to as the trustor.

57.   A   The lender is referred to as the beneficiary in a deed of trust.

58.   1st yr: $100,000 balance x 10.5% = $10,500 interest.
          2nd yr: $ 90,000 balance x 11.0% = $ 9,900 interest.
          3rd yr: $ 80,000 balance x 11.5% = $ 9,200 interest.
          4th yr: $ 70,000 balance x 12.0% = $ 8,400 interest.
          5th yr: $ 60,000 balance x 12.5% = $ 7,500 interest.
                                              $45,500 total interest.

59. $1,200 payment x 12 months = $14,400 total payments.
       $14,400 - $12,000 interest paid = $2,400 principal reduction.
       $120,000 loan - $2,400 = $117,600 loan balance, answer.

60. $88,000 - $3,000 expenses and tax = $85,000 available.
       1st mortgagee gets $70,000
       2nd mortgagee gets $15,000
       3rd mortgagee gets -0-
       4th mortgagee gets -0-

Deed of Trust

Chapter 10

1. Stevens obtained a loan on real estate by means of an instrument which conveyed title to the property to a trustee. This instrument is a
   I. deed of trust.
   II. trust deed.
   III. mortgage.
   A. I and II only
   B. I and III only
   C. II and III only
   D. I, II and III

2. When a debt secured by a deed of trust is paid off, title is reconveyed to the borrower by the
   A. beneficiary.
   B. trustor.
   C. trustee.
   D. lienee.

3. Adam defaulted on the obligations of his note which had been secured to the trustee by a deed of trust. Upon request of the beneficiary, may the property be sold in order to secure funds with which to satisfy the indebtedness?
   A. Yes, because of the provisions of the due-on-sale clause.
   B. Yes, because of the provisions of the power of sale clause.
   C. No, because loans on real property require foreclosure through court action.
   D. No, because of the statutory redemption period granted to delinquent borrowers.

4. The quantity of title conveyed to a trustee by means of a deed of trust is
   I. fee simple absolute.
   II. fee simple conditional.
   III. naked title.
   IV. that which is necessary to protect the note.
   A. I only   B. II only   C. III only   D. III and IV only

Note: There are no deleted questions in this chapter for readers of
Real Estate: An Introduction to the Profession.

5. A difference between a deed of trust and a mortgage is that when the loan is made the borrower
   A. delivers a note but not the mortgage to the lender.
   B. delivers a mortgage but not the note to the lender.
   C. delivers the note and deed of trust to the trustee.
   D. conveys bare title to the trustee.

6. When a deed of trust is recorded, bare title is conveyed by the
   A. lender to the borrower.   C. borrower to the trustee.
   B. borrower to the lender.   D. trustee to the lender.

7. When a deed of trust is foreclosed, title is conveyed by the
   A. borrower to the lender.   C. borrower to the trustee.
   B. trustee to the borrower.   D. trustee to the purchaser at
                                       foreclosure.

8. Which of the following clauses would be found in a deed of trust but not in a mortgage?
   I. A reconveyance clause.
   II. A power of sale clause.
   A. I only   B. II only   C. Both I and II   D. Neither I nor II

9. In order for a deed of trust to be cleared from the public records, which of the following documents are delivered to the trustee?
   I. Request for reconveyance.
   II. Promissory note.
   A. I only   B. II only   C. Both I and II   D. Neither I nor II

10. Which of the following documents would be recorded in the public records in order to clear an existing deed of trust?
    I. The promissory note.
    II. A reconveyance.
    A. I only   B. II only   C. Both I and II   D. Neither I nor II

11. Billings was the successful bidder at the foreclosure sale of a loan on property which had been secured by a deed of trust. He would receive
    I. an absolute fee simple title to the property.
    II. a trustee's deed.
    III. whatever right, title, and interest the borrower had deeded to the trustee.
    IV. a general warranty deed to the property.
    A. I and IV only   C. II and IV only
    B. II and III only   D. I, II, III and IV

12. In what order of priority are the following claims against the proceeds of a deed of trust paid after a trustee's sale under a defaulted deed of trust?
    I. The unpaid loan balance.
    II. The claims of junior lien holders.
    III. The trustor.
    IV. The expenses of the sale.
    A. III, I, II and IV   C. I, IV, III and II
    B. IV, I, II and III   D. I, IV, II and III

13. Which of the following would a lender like to have in a deed of trust or mortgage?
    I. Power of sale.
    II. Assignment of rents.
    A. I only   B. II only   C. Both I and II   D. Neither I nor II

14. Which of the following instruments is the most common form of security for a loan on real estate, on a nationwide basis?
    A. Deed of trust.   C. Security deed.
    B. Mortgage.   D. Trust deed.

15. Where trust deeds are used, their popularity may be attributed to which of the following reasons?
    I.   The time between default and foreclosure is shortened.
    II. There is usually no statutory redemption period.
    III. The provisions of the assignment of rents clause.
    IV. Less expensive foreclosure proceedings.
    V.   Title is already in the name of the trustee.
    A. I, II, III, IV and V   C. I, III, IV and V only
    B. I, II, IV and V only   D. I, II, III and V only

16. Should the trustor die before a deed of trust is paid off,
    A. the debt is automatically forgiven.
    B. the debt would be an obligation of the trustor's estate.
    C. the trustor's estate would be relieved of liability for the debt.
    D. the debt becomes immediately due and payable.

17. If the trustee should die or be dissolved before the debt secured by a deed of trust is paid off, a successor may be named by the
    A. trustor.
    B. beneficiary.

18. Appointment of a trustee for a deed of trust can be by which of the following methods?
    I.   Automatic form where the trustee is notified of the appointment and accepts.
    II. Automatic form where the trustee is NOT personally notified of the appointment.
    III. Accepted form where the trustee is notified of the appointment and accepts.
    IV. Accepted form where the trustee is NOT personally notified of the appointment.
    A. II only   B. III only   C. I and IV only   D. II and III only

19. Comparing a deed of trust to a mortgage, which of the following would be unique to the deed of trust?
    I.   Reconveyance.
    II. Power of sale.
    III. Statutory redemption.
    A. I only   B. II only   C. Both I and II   D. Neither I nor II

20. Real estate can be purchased subject to an existing
    I.   deed of trust.
    II. mortgage.
    A. I only   B. II only   C. Both I and II   D. Neither I nor II

21. A real estate purchaser can agree to assume an existing
    I.   deed of trust.
    II. mortgage.
    A. I only   B. II only   C. Both I and II   D. Neither I nor II

22. A deed of trust that is one step lower in priority than a first deed of
    trust would be called a
    I.   senior deed of trust.
    II.   junior deed of trust.
    III. second deed of trust.
    A. I only   B. II only   C. III only   D. II and III only

23. A deed of trust that has been subordinated cannot hold which of the
    following debt priority positions?
    A. Senior.   C. Second.
    B. Junior.   D. Third.

24. Which of the following real estate methods does NOT require the purchaser
    to give a promissory note to the lender?
    I.   Mortgage.
    II.   Deed of trust.
    III. Land contract.
    A. I only   B. II only   C. III only   D. I and II only

25. Which of the following can be foreclosed by judicial foreclosure?
    I.   Mortgage.
    II.   Deed of trust.
    III. Land contract.
    A. I only   B. II only   C. III only   D. I, II and III

26. When the debt is fully repaid, under which of the following financial
    instruments will the buyer receive a deed from the seller?
    I.   Mortgage.
    II.   Deed of trust.
    III. Land contract.
    A. I only   B. II only   C. III only   D. II and III only

27. The purpose of the assignment of rents clause in a deed of trust is to
    I.   preserve the value of the note's security.
    II. expedite the sale of the property at auction.
    A. I only   B. II only   C. Both I and II   D. Neither I nor II

28. Generally, state laws regarding foreclosure on deeds of trust require
    that
    I.   the lender demonstrate conclusively to the trustee that the loan
         is in default.
    II. the property be sold at public auction.
    A. I only   B. II only   C. Both I and II   D. Neither I nor II

Answers—Chapter 10

Multiple Choice Questions

1. A The terms "deed of trust" and "trust deed" are synonymous, and refer to an instrument which transfers title to a trustee as security for a loan. A mortgage does not transfer title to a third party.

2. C Title held by a trustee is reconveyed to the borrower by the trustee upon request of the beneficiary.

3. B The power of sale clause empowers the trustee to sell the property upon the borrower's default on the terms of the note or deed of trust.

4. D Naked title, that which is necessary to protect the note, is conveyed by a deed of trust.

5. D A deed of trust delivers bare, or naked, title to the trustee.

6. C The borrower conveys bare title to the trustee when a deed of trust is recorded.

7. D Title is conveyed by the trustee to the purchaser at foreclosure when a deed of trust is foreclosed.

8. A A reconveyance clause is found in a deed of trust, but is not contained in a mortgage. A power of sale clause is used in trust deeds and, in some states, in mortgages.

9. C Both the cancelled note and a request for reconveyance must be delivered to the trustee to get a reconveyance, which is then recorded to clear the public records.

10. B A reconveyance must be recorded in the public records in order to clear the deed of trust.

11. B The successful bidder at a deed of trust foreclosure sale will receive a trustee's deed, which coneys whatever right, title, and interest had been deeded to the trustee.

12. B Claims against the proceeds would be paid in the following order:
(1) expenses of the sale, (2) the unpaid loan balance, and (3) claims of junior lien holders. The trustor would receive any surplus money.

13. C A lender would normally like to have both a power of sale clause and an assignment of rents clause because both provide the lender protection in case of default.

14. B   Nationwide, mortgages are more commonly used as security instruments for real estate loans than any other form of instrument. Trust deeds are next most popular.

15. A   The reasons stated in responses I, II, III, IV and V all favor the lender and therefore all contribute to the popularity of trust deeds where state law favors their use.

16. B   A debt secured by a deed of trust becomes an obligation of the trustor's estate if death occurs before it is satisfied.

17. B   The beneficiary is empowered to name a substitute trustee by the language of the deed of trust.

18. D   A trustee can be appointed by automatic form where the trustee is not personally notified of the appointment, or by accepted form where the trustee is notified and accepts the appointment.

19. A   Only the reconveyance clause would be unique to a deed of trust as compared to a mortgage.

20. C   Real estate may be purchased subject to an existing deed of trust or mortgage, provided the lender does not object.

21. C   Both an existing deed of trust or a mortgage can be assumed by a purchaser, provided the lender does not object.

22. D   A deed of trust which is one step lower than a first deed of trust is both a second deed of trust and a junior deed of trust.

23. A   To subordinate is to accept a position of lower lien priority; therefore, a deed of trust which has been subordinated cannot be a senior deed of trust.

24. C   A land contract does not require the purchaser to give a promissory note to the lender. Both a mortgage and a deed of trust require the execution of a promissory note.

25. D   A mortgage, deed of trust, or land contract can be foreclosed by judicial foreclosure, although only mortgages are commonly foreclosed in this manner.

26. C   With a mortgage or deed of trust, the seller delivers a deed immediately. With a land contract, title is delivered when the property has been paid for.

27. A   An assignment of rents clause allows the lender to take possession of the property, manage it, and collect the rents while the trustor is in default and before the foreclosure sale occurs.

28. C   Courts watch carefully when foreclosure is conducted outside the courtroom. Thus, the loan must clearly be in default, all foreclosure rules followed to the letter of the law, and the property sold at public auction.

Lending Practices

Chapter 11

1. A loan wherein the principal is all repaid in one lump sum payment at the end of the loan's life is known as a
   I. straight loan.
   II. term loan.
   A. I only   B. II only   C. Both I and II   D. Neither I nor II

2. The last day of a loan's life is known as the
   I. settlement date.
   II. maturity date.
   A. I only   B. II only   C. Both I and II   D. Neither I nor II

3. A straight or term loan for the purpose of purchasing real estate will usually require the borrower to do all the following EXCEPT:
   A. execute a note or bond, promising to pay interest on the loan at regular intervals.
   B. make periodic payments toward reduction of the principal balance.
   C. repay the loan balance at maturity.
   D. hypothecate the real estate as collateral for the loan.

4. To determine the amount of loan payments by using an amortization table, you must know all the following EXCEPT:
   A. loan-to-value ratio.   C. interest rate.
   B. frequency of payments.   D. amount of loan.

5. When a loan is fully amortized,
   I. each payment is applied first to payment of interest due, then to reduction of the principal balance.
   II. principal payments are scheduled so as to have the entire principal repaid by the loan's maturity date.
   A. I only   B. II only   C. Both I and II   D. Neither I nor II

Note: If you are reading <u>Real Estate: An Introduction to the Profession</u>, you may omit the following questions: 25, 31 and 40.

6. East and West each borrowed $10,000 at an annual interest rate of 10 per cent. Both loans matured in five years. East's loan was a term loan with interest payable annually. West's loan was amortized with monthly payments of $212.50. Which of the following statements is/are true?
    I. East will pay a total of $5,000 in interest.
   II. West will make total payments of $12,930, including principal and interest.
  III. West's total expense will be $2,070 less than East's.
   A. I only
   B. I, II and III
   C. I and II only
   D. II and III only

7. The amount of each periodic payment necessary to amortize a loan in a given time can be determined by consulting
    I. a loan balance table.
   II. an amortization table.
   A. I only   B. II only   C. Both I and II   D. Neither I nor II

8. Amortization tables may be used by real estate agents to determine which of the following?
    I. Frequency of payment.
   II. Interest rate.
  III. Maturity.
   IV. Amount of loan.
    V. Amount of each payment.
   A. I, II, IV and V only
   B. II, IV and V only
   C. II, III and IV only
   D. I, II, III, IV and V

9. Which of the following would result in the least interest expense to the borrower if all loans were made at the same annual percentage rate of interest?
   A. An amortized loan, ten year maturity.
   B. An amortized loan, five year maturity.
   C. A term loan, five year maturity.
   D. A term loan, ten year maturity.

10. Clyde borrowed money to purchase a home under terms which required him to make monthly payments which included loan amortization plus prorated insurance premiums and annual real property tax payments. This loan is referred to as a
    I. budget loan.
   II. package loan.
  III. blanket loan.
   IV. PITI loan.
   A. I, II and IV only
   B. I and IV only
   C. II and IV only
   D. I, II, III and IV

11. A balloon note is characterized by
    I. equal monthly payments of principal and interest.
   II. a final payment larger than preceding payments.
   A. I only   B. II only   C. Both I and II   D. Neither I nor II

12. A major negative of balloon loan financing is that the borrower may have difficulty
    I. meeting the final payment when it becomes due.
   II. refinancing when the final payment comes due.
   A. I only   B. II only   C. Both I and II   D. Neither I nor II

13. A loan calling for a series of amortized payments followed by a payment at maturity that is substantially larger than previous payments would be a
    I. balloon loan.
   II. partially amortized loan.
  A. I only   B. II only   C. Both I and II   D. Neither I nor II

14. Kevin wants to know what portion of a 30-year, fully amortized loan would be paid off by the fourth year of the loan's life. Kevin would consult
    I. an amortization table.
   II. a loan progress chart.
  A. I only   B. II only   C. Both I and II   D. Neither I nor II

15. Mai and Ming want to borrow $100,000 to purchase a house and lenders are offering a 15-year loan at 10 per cent and 30-year loans at 11 per cent. Using Table 11:1 in the text, which of the following statements would be true?
    I. Total payments over the life of the 15-year loan will be $193,500.
   II. Total payments over the life of the 30-year loan will be $343,080.
  III. Interest on the 15-year loan will total $93,500.
   IV. Interest on the 30-year loan will total $243,080.
  A. I only   C. III and IV only
  B. I and II only   D. I, II, III and IV

16. Compared to monthly payments, biweekly payments of one-half of the monthly payment will
    I. reduce the total amount of interest paid over the life of the loan.
   II. shorten the life of the loan.
  III. lengthen the life of the loan.
  A. II only   B. III only   C. I and II only   D. I and III only

17. At which one of the following interest rates would earlier mortgage loan repayment be most effective in reducing the interest paid by the borrower?
  A. 4 per cent.   C. 12 per cent.
  B. 8 per cent.   D. 16 per cent.

18. By the tenth year of an 11 1/2 per cent 30-year amortization period, how much of the principal balance will have been repaid under a monthly amortization of equal installments? Use Table 11:2 in the text.
    I. One-half.
   II. One-third.
  III. Two-thirds.
  A. I only   C. III only
  B. II only   D. Neither I nor II nor III

19. Mrs. North is purchasing a house and a lender will make a loan on it at an 80% loan-to-value ratio. The house is appraised at $98,000, but the actual sale price is $96,000. Which of the following statements will be true?
    I. The cash down payment will be $19,200.
    II. The loan will be in the amount of $78,400.
    III. The cash down payment will be $17,600.
    IV. The loan will be in the amount of $76,800.
    A. II and III only   C. III and IV only
    B. I and IV only   D. I and II only

20. The difference between a property's market value and the debts against it is known as the
    I. loan-to-value ratio.
    II. owner's equity.
    A. I only   B. II only   C. Both I and II   D. Neither I nor II

21. As used in real estate finance, the term "point" means
    A. one per cent of the purchase price.
    B. the down payment expressed as a percentage of price.
    C. one per cent of the loan amount.
    D. the borrower's equity expressed as a percentage of value.

22. The loan origination fee stated to a purchaser for setting up a loan may be charged as
    I. a percentage of the loan.
    II. an itemized billing for expenses incurred by the lender.
    A. I only   B. II only   C. Both I and II   D. Neither I nor II

23. When a lender charges discount points to make a loan,
    A. the yield to the lender will decrease.
    B. the yield to the lender will increase.
    C. the yield to the lender will not change.
    D. the cost of the loan to the borrower decreases.

24. Discount points on mortgage loans will tend to
    I. increase during periods of tight money.
    II. increase during periods of loose money.
    III. decrease during periods of tight money.
    IV. decrease during periods of loose money.
    A. I only   C. II and III only
    B. III only   D. I and IV only

25. In evaluating applications for FHA mortgage insurance, the FHA considers
    I. the borrower's capability of repaying the loan.
    II. the value of the property as collateral for the loan.
    A. I only.   B. II only.   C. Both I and II.   D. Neither I nor II.

26. Which of the following statements regarding the FHA is NOT correct?
    A. The FHA was established in response to the depression of the 1930s.
    B. The FHA offers to insure lenders against losses due to the non-payment of home loans.
    C. The FHA will insure loans on condominiums and cooperatives.
    D. The FHA operates entirely at the taxpayers' expense.

27. The premium for FHA mortgage insurance
     I. is paid by the borrower.
    II. is based on loan amount.
  III. must be paid in cash by the borrower at settlement.
   IV. may be added to the loan amount and paid in monthly installments over the life of the loan.
  A. I, II and III only   C. II and III only
  B. I, II and IV only   D. I and II only

28. Which of the following statements are true?
     I. A nonmilitary borrower desiring an FHA-insured loan must make a down payment.
    II. An FHA-insured borrower can borrow the down payment using a second mortgage against the property.
  A. I only   B. II only   C. Both I and II   D. Neither I nor II

29. Which of the following statements regarding FHA-insured loans are true?
     I. The maximum amount the FHA will insure is changed from time to time.
    II. The maximum amount the FHA will insure varies from city to city.
  A. I only   B. II only   C. Both I and II   D. Neither I nor II

30. Mr. and Mrs. Scott purchased a home for $80,000 with an FHA-insured loan equal to 97 per cent of the first $50,000 of appraised value and 95 per cent of the remaining $30,000. Which of the following statements are NOT true?
  A. The amount of the loan was $77,000.
  B. Up to 50 per cent of the difference between the loan and the purchase price could have been secured by a second mortgage against the home.
  C. The Scotts will pay an insurance premium for the FHA insurance.
  D. The required cash down payment was $3,000.

31. The FHA has been influential in bringing about acceptance of
     I. long-term amortization of loans.
    II. standardized construction techniques.
  A. I only   B. II only   C. Both I and II   D. Neither I nor II

32. FHA mortgage insurance programs are available for
     I. private, single-family residences.
    II. multi-family residential buildings.
  A. I only   B. II only   C. Both I and II   D. Neither I nor II

33. Which of the following loans are fully assumable without increase in the interest rate?
     I. FHA-insured.
    II. VA-guaranteed.
  A. I only   B. II only   C. Both I and II   D. Neither I nor II

34. Which of the following loans can be repaid in full ahead of schedule without penalty?
     I. FHA-insured.
    II. VA-guaranteed.
  A. I only   B. II only   C. Both I and II   D. Neither I nor II

35. Which of the following statements regarding FHA-insured loans is/are true?
    I. Borrowers who have fully repaid their FHA-insured loans may be entitled to a partial refund of their mortgage insurance premiums.
    II. Interest rates on FHA-insured loans are set by the government.
    A. I only   B. II only   C. Both I and II   D. Neither I nor II

36. Which of the following loans are referred to as "conventional loans"?
    I. FHA-insured.
    II. VA-guaranteed.
    A. I only   B. II only   C. Both I and II   D. Neither I nor II

37. FHA rules that took effect in late 1983 allow all of the following EXCEPT:
    A. interest rates to float.
    B. the buyer and seller to negotiate who will pay how many points.
    C. the seller to pay the buyer's mortgage insurance premium.
    D. a junior mortgage on the property at loan origination.

38. Which of the following loan pairs correspond?
    I.   FHA Section 203(b) = Single family homes.
    II. FHA Section 234 = Condominium homes.
    III. FHA Section 213 = Cooperative homes.
    IV. FHA Section 203(k) = Home improvement loans.
    A. I, II and IV only   C. I, III and IV only
    B. I, II and III only   D. I, II, III and IV

39. The FHA will insure graduated payment loans under
    I. Section 235.
    II. Section 245.
    A. I only   B. II only   C. Both I and II   D. Neither I nor II

40. The FHA has played a major role in
    I. formulating loan qualification criteria.
    II. imposing minimum construction standards.
    A. I only   B. II only   C. Both I and II   D. Neither I nor II

41. The Federal Housing Administration
    I. lends money.
    II. insures lenders.
    A. I only   B. II only   C. Both I and II   D. Neither I nor II

42. FHA and VA loans can be obtained from
    I.   savings and loans associations.
    II. banks.
    III. mortgage companies.
    A. I and II only   C. II and III only
    B. I and III only   D. I, II and III

43. Under VA loan guarantee programs
    I. loans are available without down payment for the veteran purchaser.
    II. the VA loan guarantee is a substitute for the protection normally provided a lender by a down payment requirement.
    A. I only   B. II only   C. Both I and II   D. Neither I nor II

44. Which of the following statements are correct regarding VA-guaranteed loans?
    I. An appraisal of the property is required by the VA.
    II. The VA will guarantee fixed-rate loans for as long as 30 years.
    A. I only   B. II only   C. Both I and II   D. Neither I nor II

45. Which of the following is required for a veteran to secure a VA-guaranteed loan?
    I. Certificate of eligibility.
    II. Certificate of reasonable value.
    A. I only   B. II only   C. Both I and II   D. Neither I nor II

46. VA-guaranteed loans are available for
    I. single-family homes.
    II. mobile homes.
    A. I only   B. II only   C. Both I and II   D. Neither I nor II

47. In the event of foreclosure and a loss suffered by the VA or FHA
    I. the VA borrower must reimburse the VA.
    II. the FHA borrower need not reimburse the FHA.
    A. I only   B. II only   C. Both I and II   D. Neither I nor II

48. A home-selling veteran who took out a VA loan can be relieved of liability to the VA by
    I. selling subject to the loan.
    II. requiring the buyer to obtain new financing.
    A. I only   B. II only   C. Both I and II   D. Neither I nor II

49. Because of loan default losses being suffered by the VA, the VA now charges new VA borrowers
    A. an annual funding fee.
    B. a one-time funding fee upon default.
    C. a one-time funding fee when the loan is made.
    D. a mortgage insurance premium like the FHA.

50. Regarding mortgage insurance, which of the following statements are true?
    I. PMI insures only the top 20 or 25 per cent of the loan.
    II. FHA insures the entire loan.
    A. I only   B. II only   C. Both I and II   D. Neither I nor II

51. James purchased a home for $90,000 and secured a 90% L/V loan which was protected by private mortgage insurance, the premium for which was 1/2 of 1% for the first year and 1/4 of 1% annually thereafter. Which of the following statements would be correct?
    I. The first year's premium would be $405.
    II. The premium would be paid by the lender.
    III. At the lender's option, when the loan is partially repaid, the premiums and coverage may be terminated.
    IV. The first year's premium would be $450.
    A. I, II and III only   C. II, III and IV only
    B. I and III only   D. II and IV only

52. Which of the following statements regarding the FmHA are correct?
     I.   FmHA guarantees loans on farms and rural homes.
     II. FmHA makes loans on farms and rural homes.
     A. I only   B. II only   C. Both I and II   D. Neither I nor II

53. The federal Truth in Lending Act requires that, in certain types of loans,
     I.   the borrower be told how much it is costing to borrow the money.
     II. the borrower be given the right to rescind the transaction within
          three days after signing the loan papers.
     A. I only   B. II only   C. Both I and II   D. Neither I nor II

54. All of the following are exempt from the provisions of the federal Truth
     in Lending Act EXCEPT:
     A. commercial loans.
     B. personal property loans in excess of $25,000.
     C. financing extended to corporations.
     D. consumer loans to natural persons.

55. The abbreviation APR stands for
     A. average percentage rate.   C. approximate percentage rate.
     B. allotted percentage rate.   D. annual percentage rate.

56. The purposes of the federal Truth in Lending laws include
     I.   a requirement that creditors disclose the full cost of obtaining
           credit.
     II.   provisions which allow a consumer to rescind credit transactions
           in certain instances.
     III. regulations limiting the cost of credit.
     A. I, II and III   C. II and III only
     B. I only   D. I and II only

57. Regulations governing the administration of the Truth in Lending Simpli-
     fication and Reform Act are
     I.   contained in Revised Regulation Z.
     II. issued by the Federal Reserve Board.
     A. I only   B. II only   C. Both I and II   D. Neither I nor II

58. The annual percentage rate is
     I.   usually lower than the interest rate.
     II. made up of the interest rate combined with the other costs of the
          loan.
     A. I only   B. II only   C. Both I and II   D. Neither I nor II

59. Which of the following loans would be exempt from the disclosure require-
     ments of the truth in lending laws?
     A. An unsecured personal loan of $3,000.
     B. An educational loan from a commercial bank.
     C. A second mortgage loan on a residence.
     D. A $30,000 loan for the purchase of a $40,000 automobile.

60. Which of the following advertisements would be in violation of the federal truth in lending laws?
    A. For sale, $5,000 down, payments of $483.20 per month.
    B. For sale, VA financing available.
    C. For sale, assume large FHA loan.
    D. For sale, seller will carry.

61. The truth in lending laws require that a lender show the borrower all of the following EXCEPT:
    A. the number of payments.
    B. computation of early payment credits.
    C. the amount of any balloon payments.
    D. the lender's net yield from the loan.

62. Penalties for violation of the truth in lending laws include
    I. a fine of up to $5,000 and/or imprisonment for up to one year.
    II. civil penalties up to twice the amount of the finance charge up to a maximum of $1,000.
    III. court costs, attorney fees, and actual damages.
    A. I, II and III   C. I and III only
    B. I and II only   D. II and III only

63. A borrower does not have the right, under the truth in lending laws, to rescind a credit transaction
    I. for a consumer loan on personal property.
    II. for the acquisition of the borrower's principal dwelling.
    A. I only   B. II only   C. Both I and II   D. Neither I nor II

64. When evaluating a loan application, a loan officer will consider the
    I. value of the property being offered as security.
    II. condition of the title to the property.
    III. ability of the borrower to repay the loan.
    IV. applicant's past credit record.
    A. I, III and IV only   C. I, II and IV only
    B. I, II and III only   D. I, II, III and IV

65. Which of the following pairs correspond?
    A. Duplex = two units.   C. Fourplex = four units.
    B. Triplex = three units.   D. All of the above.

66. The practice of some lenders of not making loans on properties in certain neighborhoods is known as
    I. blockbusting.
    II. redlining.
    A. I only   B. II only   C. Both I and II   D. Neither I nor II

67. Which of the following is/are generally true?
    I. As a borrower's equity in his real estate increases, the probability of default on the loan is diminished.
    II. Insured loans are generally made at higher loan-to-value ratios than uninsured loans.
    A. I only   B. II only   C. Both I and II   D. Neither I nor II

68. Generally, before a lender will approve a loan, the borrower must
    I.   have sufficient funds for the down payment.
    II. sign a statement if the borrower intends to occupy the property.
    A. I only   B. II only   C. Both I and II   D. Neither I nor II

69. Assuming no loan insurance guarantee, a lender would most likely give its lowest interest rate on a loan to buy
    A. an owner-occupied house, 80% LV.
    B. a rental house, 80% LV.
    C. an owner-occupied house, 90% LV.
    D. an apartment building, 80% LV.

70. Which of the following is given consideration in evaluation of a loan application?
    A. Race.   C. Sex.
    B. Marital status.   D. Income adequacy.

71. The Federal Equal Credit Opportunity Act prohibits a lender from
    I.   granting a loan to a member of a minority race.
    II. investigating the credit record of a member of a minority race.
    A. I only   B. II only   C. Both I and II   D. Neither I nor II

72. As a general rule of thumb regarding home loans,
    I.   monthly housing expense should not exceed 25% to 30% of gross monthly income.
    II. total fixed monthly expenses should not exceed 33% to 38% of gross monthly income.
    A. I only   B. II only   C. Both I and II   D. Neither I nor II

73. Which of the following would be more favored by a lender in evaluating a loan application?
    A. U.S. Savings Bonds having cash value of $10,000.
    B. Ownership of a recreational lot in another state worth $10,000.

74. A lender can legally discriminate in loan terms based on the applicant's
    A. religion.   C. race or skin color.
    B. marital status.   D. intention to occupy (or not occupy) the mortgaged property.

75. The right of an individual to inspect his or her file at a credit bureau is found in the
    I.   Truth in Lending Act.
    II. Fair Credit Reporting Act.
    A. I only   B. II only   C. Both I and II   D. Neither I nor II

Finance Problems and Situations

1. Calculate the total interest charged for borrowing $5,000 for seven years at 10% interest, on a term loan.

   $_____

   What would be the total amount of principal and interest repaid by the borrower?

   $_____

2. On a term loan of $12,000, what will be the interest payment for 3 years, 10 months and 20 days? The interest rate is 9% per year. Use a 30-day month.

   $_____

3. Which of the following simple interest loans will produce the greatest number of dollars of interest?

   $60,000 at 10% for 2 months = $_____

   $ 5,000 at 10% for 2 years = $_____

   $10,000 at 5% for 2 years = $_____

4. If an interest payment of $115.50 is made every three months on a $4,200 loan, what is the annual rate of interest?

   $_____

5. One month, a principal and interest payment of $900 reduced the principal balance by $80. If the principal balance at the time of payment was $120,000, calculate the annual rate of interest.

$_____

6. What will the interest be on $40,000 borrowed at 8% per annum if the principal is borrowed from November 1 through the following June 15?

$_____

7. Rolls Siroyce purchased a home for $100,000 by making a cash down payment of $20,000 and securing a first mortgage loan for the balance of the purchase price. Rolls agreed to pay 10.5% annual interest on the loan, which was to be amortized over a 30-year period in monthly installments. The taxes on the home are $1,320 per year and the annual homeowner's insurance premium is $240. Use the amortization table in Table 11:1 of the text to determine the principal and interest payment.

$_____

Compute the PITI payment on this loan. $_____

8. Armand Legg borrowed $50,000 at 11.5% annual interest, to be amortized on a 15 year schedule, but with the entire balance due and payable at the end of 10 years. Use the remaining balance table in Table 11:2 of the text to determine the amount due at the end of ten years.

$_____

9. Charlie Vett, who has $27,500 in GI loan benefits available to him, decides to purchase a home using the benefits. He finds a lender who agrees to make a no down payment loan at a 75% loan-to-value ratio, plus the veteran's benefits. Assuming adequate financial ability on Charlie's part, what would be the maximum price he could pay for the home on these terms?

$_____

10. Inna Jam borrowed $10,000 at 12% annual interest, and agreed to make payments of $120 per month on an amortized loan. Of the first month's payment, how much was applied to interest?

$_____

How much went to reduce the principal balance?

$_____

How much of the second month's payment went to interest?

$_____

How much of the second month's payment went to reduce the principal balance?

$_____

At the end of these two monthly payments, what is the principal balance of the loan?

$_____

11. Compute the down payment and maximum insurable loan on the purchase of a $98,000 home, using FHA-insured financing. Use the following information for determining loan amounts.

    First $50,000:   97% of value
    Remainder: 95% of value to a maximum loan of $90,000

Down Payment: $_____   Loan Amount: $_____

12. Rosie Tymes and Hardy Tymes, who have reached retirement age, have decided to sell their home and move to an apartment. They find a buyer who offers to pay them 20% of the agreed purchase price of $78,000 as a down payment and give them a mortgage for the balance, amortized at 9% annual interest for 20 years, in equal monthly installments, including principal and interest. What would be the loan-to-value ratio of this mortgage?

_____%

What would be the amount of the down payment?

$_____

What would be the amount of the mortgage debt?

$_____

Using the amortization table in the text (Table 11:1), what monthly payment is required to fully amortize this loan?

$_____

13. Mr. and Mrs. E. G. Lye have found a home which they would like to purchase at a price of $90,000. Their local savings and loan association agreed to make a loan of 90% of the purchase price or appraisal, whichever is lower. The S&L appraised the home for $86,000. Assuming they decide to purchase the property in spite of the appraisal, what would be their down payment?

$_____

What would be the amount of the mortgage loan?

$_____

14. The Last National Bank lent Rochanna Hardspot $120,000 to purchase a new home. The loan was 75% of the purchase price and the interest rate was 9.6% per year. What was the purchase price of the home?

$_____

What was the down payment?

$_____

If the loan is interest-only the first year, how much interest did she pay the second month?

$_____

15. As a real estate agent you are showing homes to Mr. and Mrs. Hope. Through interview, you determine they can afford a monthly payment up to $500, PITI. They have approximately $8,500 cash available for a down payment plus money for anticipated closing costs. You estimate that in your community the combined expense of taxes and insurance approximates 20% of total monthly PITI payments. Present market conditions in your community indicate an interest rate of 9.0% for 30-year conventional loans. Use the amortization table in Table 11:1 in the text to determine the maximum loan the Hopes can afford and the maximum price they could afford to pay for a home.

Maximum loan: $_____   Maximum Price: $_____

Answers—Chapter 11

Multiple Choice Questions

1. C   The terms "straight loan" and "term loan" are both used in reference to a loan wherein the principal is repaid in a lump sum at the end of the loan term.

2. B   The maturity date is the day on which the final payment on a loan is due; the last day of a loan's scheduled life.

3. B   There is no repayment of principal until the maturity date on a straight or term loan. The borrower signs a note or bond, hypothecates the real property as collateral, and agrees to repay the loan balance at maturity.

4. A   The use of an amortization table does not require knowledge of the loan-to-value ratio, but does require knowledge of the frequency of payments, interest rate and amount of loan.

5. C   To fully amortize a loan, payments are calculated so that the entire principal will be repaid by the maturity date, with each payment applied first to interest due, then to the reduction of the principal balance.

6. B   Response   I. $10,000 loan x 10% interest x 5 years = $5,000 interest
        Response   II. $215.50 payment x 60 months = $12,930 total P & I
        Response   III. $5,000 (East) - $2,930 (West) = $2,070 less expense to West than to East

7. B   An amortization table will show the amount of each periodic payment necessary to amortize a loan in a given time. A loan balance table shows the loan balance after given periods of time.

8. D   Amortization tables may be used to determine frequency of payment, interest rate, maturity amount of loan and amount of each payment.

9. B   An amortized loan with a five-year maturity would require less in interest payments than either of the other examples given. This is because it repays faster.

10. B   A loan that calls for amortization payments of principal and interest plus prorated payments of taxes and insurance is called a budget loan or PITI loan.

11. B   A balloon note is one which calls for a final payment larger than the preceding payments, in order to pay the remaining loan balance. It may or may not call for equal monthly payments of principal and interest.

12. C   The possibility that the borrower may have difficulty meeting the
         final payment when it becomes due, and that the borrower may have
         difficulty refinancing when the final payment becomes due are
         negative aspects of balloon financing.

13. C   A balloon loan calls for a final payment substantially larger than
         previous payments. A partially amortized loan is a balloon loan
         because of its larger final payment.

14. B   A loan balance table will show the balance owed on a loan at
         intervals during the loan's life. This is not shown in an amortiza-
         tion table.

15. D   I.   Payments on 15 year loan = $10.75/$1,000/month
                  $10.75 x 100 = $1,075/month payment
                  $1,075 x 180 months = $193,500 total payments
            II.   Payments on 30 year loan = $9.53/$1,000/month
                  $9.53 x 100 = $953/month payment
                  $953 x 360 months = $343,080 total payments
           III. $193,500 - $100,000 principal = $93,500 interest
            IV. $343,080 - $100,000 principal = $243,080 interest
         All responses are correct.

16. C   Biweekly payments of one-half the monthly payments will substan-
         tially reduce the amount of interest paid over the life of the loan,
         and will shorten the life of the loan.

17. D   The higher the interest rate, the more effective earlier mortgage
         loan repayment would be in reducing interest payments.

18. D   At the end of the tenth year, the balance owing on a 30-year,
         11 1/2 per cent loan will be $929 per $1,000. This is far more than
         any of the answer choices given.

19. D   Lenders calculate their loan-to-value ratio on price or appraised
         value, whichever is lower. The loan will be calculated as follows:
         $96,000 sale price x 80% LVR = $76,800 loan
         $96,000 sale price - $76,800 loan = $19,200 down payment

20. B   Equity is the market value of the property less the debts against it.
         Loan-to-value ratio is the amount a lender will lend on a property
         divided by the appraised value or sale price, whichever is lower.

21. C   As used in real estate, a "point" is one per cent of the loan amount.

22. C   Loan origination fees may be stated as a percentage of the loan or an
         itemized billing for expenses incurred by the lender.

23. B   When a lender charges discount points to make a loan, the yield to
         the lender increases and the cost of the loan to the borrower
         increases.

24. D   Discount points on mortgage loans tend to increase when money is
         tight and decrease when money is loose.

25. C   The FHA considers both the borrower's capability of repaying the loan and the value of the property as collateral for the loan when evaluating an application for mortgage insurance.

26. D   The FHA does not operate at taxpayer expense. It charges borrowers a mortgage insurance premium.

27. B   FHA mortgage insurance premiums are based on the loan amount and paid by the borrower. The premiums may be paid in cash or added to the loan amount, at the borrower's option.

28. A   A nonmilitary borrower desiring an FHA-insured loan must make a down payment. The borrower may not borrow the down payment using a second mortgage against the property.

29. C   Maximum FHA-insured loans change from time to time as average sale prices increase, and vary from city to city depending on average sale prices in the area.

30. B   Response A. $50,000 x 97% = $48,500
                      $30,000 x 95% = $28,500
                      $48,500 + $28,500 = $77,000 loan
            B. There cannot be junior financing at the origination of an FHA-insured loan.
            C. There is a mortgage insurance premium on all FHA-insured loans.
            D. $80,000 price - $77,000 loan = $3,000 down payment.

31. C   Through its insurance programs the FHA has been instrumental in bringing about acceptance of long-term amortized loans. Its minimum construction standards have led to standardized construction techniques.

32. C   FHA mortgage insurance programs are available for single or multi-family residential properties.

33. C   Both FHA-insured and VA-guaranteed loans are fully assumable without increase in the interest rate.

34. C   Both FHA-insured and VA-guaranteed loans can be repaid in full ahead of schedule without penalty.

35. A   Borrowers who have fully repaid their loans ahead of schedule may be entitled to a partial refund of their mortgage insurance premiums. Interest rates on FHA-insured loans are not set by the government.

36. D   A conventional loan is one which is not insured or guaranteed by a government agency.

37. D   FHA rules do not allow a junior mortgage at the origination of an FHA-insured loan. Since late 1983, interest rates are allowed to float with the market, points are negotiable between buyer and seller, and the seller may pay the borrower's MIP.

38.   D   All loan pairs correspond as indicated.

39.   B   The FHA insures graduated payment loans under Section 245 of its Title II loan programs.

40.   C   The FHA has played an important role in the formulation of loan qualification criteria and the imposition of minimum construction standards.

41.   B   The FHA does NOT lend money. It insures lenders against a loss brought about by the borrower's default on an FHA-insured loan.

42.   D   Banks, savings and loan associations, and mortgage companies all make FHA-insured loans.

43.   C   VA-guaranteed loans are available without down payment, and the VA loan guarantee substitutes for the protection normally provided to a lender by a down payment.

44.   C   The VA requires that an appraisal be made, and the VA will guarantee fixed-rate loans for as long as 30 years.

45.   C   Both a certificate of eligibility and a certificate of reasonable value are required for a veteran to secure a VA-guaranteed loan.

46.   C   VA-guaranteed loans are available for houses and mobile homes.

47.   C   VA borrowers are required to reimburse the VA for a loss suffered because of foreclosure, but FHA borrowers pay for and are protected by FHA mortgage insurance and are therefore not required to reimburse the FHA for any such losses.

48.   B   New financing, which would pay off the existing VA loan, would relieve the selling veteran of financial responsibility to the VA. Selling "subject to" would not.

49.   C   Veteran borrowers must pay a one-time funding fee to the VA at the time of origination of a VA-guaranteed loan.

50.   C   Private mortgage insurance insures only the top 20 or 25 per cent of the loan, whereas the FHA insures the entire loan amount.

51.   B   I. $90,000 price x 90% = $81,000 loan
                   $81,000 loan x .005 = $405 MIP for 1st year
             II.   Mortgage insurance premiums are paid by the borrower, not the lender
            III.   Mortgage insurance may be terminated at the lender's option, usually when the LVR is 80% or less.
             IV.   The first year's premium would be $405, not $450.
            Responses I and III are correct; responses II and IV are incorrect.

52.   C   FmHA guarantees loans on farms and rural homes, and also makes loans on farms and rural homes.

53. C   The Truth in Lending Act requires that, in loans covered by the act, the borrower be advised of the cost of borrowing, and that the borrower be given the right of rescission within three days after signing loan papers.

54. D   Consumer loans to natural persons are covered by the TIL Act, but commercial loans, personal property loans in excess of $25,000 and business loans are exempt.

55. D   APR represents "annual percentage rate."

56. D   The TIL laws require a creditor to disclose the full cost of obtaining credit, and allow credit transactions to be rescinded in certain instances. TIL does not regulate the cost of credit.

57. C   Regulations governing the Truth in Lending Simplification Act are issued by the Federal Reserve Board and are contained in Revised Regulation Z.

58. B   The annual percentage rate is made up of the interest rate combined with the other costs of the loan. It is usually higher than the interest rate alone.

59. D   The loan on the automobile is a personal property loan in excess of $25,000 and therefore is exempt from the requirements of the TIL act.

60. A   Advertisements offering real estate for sale may state the price and interest rate, but if any "trigger terms" such as down payment or monthly payment are stated, the ad must include other specific disclosures. Advertising may also be in general terms, such as those given in responses B, C and D.

61. D   The lender's net yield from the loan need not be shown, but the number of payments, computation of early payment credits, and the amount of any balloon payments must be stated.

62. A   The penalties defined in responses I, II and III may all be imposed for a violation of the TIL laws.

63. B   The right to rescind applies to consumer loans but not to a loan for the acquisition of the borrower's principal dwelling.

64. D   The value of the property, condition of the title, ability to repay the loan, and past credit record are all considered in evaluating a loan application.

65. D   All of the pairs correspond.

66. B   Redlining is refusing to make loans in certain neighborhoods.

67. C   As equity increases, the probability of default diminishes. Insured loans are generally made at higher LVRs than uninsured loans.

68.   C   Generally, before loan approval, a borrower must have sufficient funds for the down payment and state if he intends to occupy the property.

69.   A   The lowest interest rate would be given to owner-occupied dwellings. Also, the lower the LVR, the lower the interest rate.

70.   D   Income adequacy is considered in evaluating a loan application. Race, marital status and sex are not considered.

71.   D   Responses I and II are both incorrect. The act prohibits racial discrimination.

72.   C   The criteria stated in responses I and II are generally applied in evaluating a loan application.

73.   A   U. S. Savings Bonds are much more liquid assets than a recreational lot, and would be more favored by a lender in evaluating a loan application.

74.   D   A lender may consider the applicant's intention to occupy the property in evaluating a loan application, but may NOT consider religion, marital status, or race.

75.   B   The Fair Credit Reporting Act gives an individual the right to inspect his or her file at a credit bureau.

Finance Problems and Situations

1. $5,000 x 10% x 7 years = $3,500
     Principal and interest would be $3,500 + $5,000 = $8,500.

2. $12,000 x 9% = $1,080 interest per year.
     $1,080 ÷ 12 = $90 interest per month.
     $90 ÷ 30 = $3 interest per day.
     $1,080 x 3 + 90 x 10 + 3 x 20 = $4,200

3.   All produce the same:
     $60,000 x 10% ÷ 12 x 2 = $1,000
     $ 5,000 x 10% x 2   = $1,000
     $10,000 x 5% x 2   = $1,000

4. $115.50 x 4 ÷ $4,200 = 11%

5.   ($900 - $80) x 12 ÷ $120,000 = 8.2%

6. $40,000 x .08 ÷ 12 x 7.5 months = $2,000

7. $9.15 x 80 = $732 the monthly P + I payment.
     Property taxes are $1,320 ÷ 12 = $110 per month.
     Insurance is $240 ÷ 12 = $20 per month.
     Therefore monthly PITI is $732 + $110 + $20 = $862.

8. A 15-year loan at 11 1/2% interest that is 10 years old has a remaining balance of $531 per thousand. Therefore $531 x 50 = $26,650.

9. $27,500 ÷ 25% = $110,000

10. First month's interest is $10,000 x 12% ÷ 12 months = $100
    First month's principal reduction is $120 - $100 = $20
    Second month's interest is $9,980 x 12% ÷ 12 months = $99.80
    Second month's principal reduction is $120.00 - $99.80 = $20.20
    Principal balance after two payments is $10,000 - $20.00 - $20.20 = $9,959.80

11. 97% x $50,000 + 95% x $48,000 = $94,100
    However, the loan maximum is $90,000. This makes the down payment $8,000 and the loan $90,000.

12. Loan-to-value ratio is 80%.
    Down payment would be 20% x $78,000 = $15,600.
    Mortgage debt would be 80% x $78,000 = $62,400.
    Monthly P + I is $9.00 per thousand: $9.00 x 62.4 = $561.60

13. Down payment is 10% x $86,000 + $4,000 = $12,600.
    Loan will be 90% x $86,000 = $77,400.

14. $120,000 ÷ .75 = $160,000 purchase price.
    $160,000 - $120,000 = $40,000 down payment.
    $120,000 x .096 ÷ 12 months = $960 interest.

15. $500 less 20% for taxes and insurance leaves $400 for principal and interest payments. A 30-year, 9% loan requires monthly payments of $8.05 per thousand. Thus, $400 per month would support a $400 ÷ $8.05 = $49,689 loan. Adding their cash down payment gives a maximum purchase price of $58,189.

Sources and Types of Financing

Chapter 12

1. The place where a real estate borrower makes a loan application, receives
    a loan and makes loan payments describes the
    A. primary mortgage market.   C. first loan market.
    B. secondary mortgage market. D. second loan market.

2. Historically, the foremost single source of funds for residential mort-
    gage loans in this country has been
    A. commercial banks.   C. mortgage companies.
    B. insurance companies.   D. savings and loan associations.

3. Certificates of deposit issued by savings and loan associations carry
    higher rates of interest than passbook accounts in order to
    I. compete with higher yields available from other investments.
    II. prevent disintermediation.
    A. I only   B. II only   C. Both I and II   D. Neither I nor II

4. When savings are removed from thrift institutions in large amounts for
    investment in Treasury securities,
    I. the real estate market enjoys an increase in activity.
    II. disintermediation occurs.
    A. I only   B. II only   C. Both I and II   D. Neither I nor II

5. Savings and loan associations combat the problems of rising interest
    rates by
    I. enforcing due-on-sale clauses in mortgages.
    II. encouraging borrowers to accept adjustable rate loans.
    A. I only   B. II only   C. Both I and II   D. Neither I nor II

Note: If you are reading Real Estate: An Introduction to the Profession,
       you may omit the following questions: 29-32.

6. If the nation's commercial banks are considered as a whole, which of the following statements are correct?
    I.   Total deposits exceed those in the nation's savings and loan associations.
    II. They are less active in long-term real estate loans than the savings and loan associations.
    III. The bulk of their deposits are in demand accounts.
    IV. They are active in construction loans.
    A. I, II, III and IV   C. I and II only
    B. II and IV only   D. I, II and III only

7. Mutual savings banks are
    I.   located primarily in the northeastern United States.
    II. owned by their depositors.
    A. I only   B. II only   C. Both I and II   D. Neither I nor II

8. Life insurance companies are ideally suited to make long-term investments because
    I.   premiums are received in predictable amounts on regular dates.
    II. payoffs can be calculated from actuarial tables.
    A. I only   B. II only   C. Both I and II   D. Neither I nor II

9. Life insurance companies invest premium dollars in all the following types of investments EXCEPT:
    A. corporate bonds.
    B. loans secured by personal property.
    C. real estate loans.
    D. government bonds.

10. Generally, life insurance companies are LEAST LIKELY to be interested in originating which of the following type of real estate loans?
    A. Industrial real estate loans.
    B. Multi-family housing loans.
    C. Commercial real estate loans.
    D. Single-family housing loans.

11. A real estate loan which calls for the lender to receive interest plus a percentage of the rental income from a property is
    I.   designed to protect the lender from inflation.
    II. known as a participation loan.
    A. I only   B. II only   C. Both I and II   D. Neither I nor II

12. Mortgage companies
    I.   originate loans.
    II. service loans which they have sold on the secondary mortgage market.
    A. I only   B. II only   C. Both I and II   D. Neither I nor II

13. Mortgage banking activities are regularly carried on by all of the following EXCEPT:
    A. insurance companies.   C. mutual savings banks.
    B. commercial banks.   D. savings and loan associations.

14. A lender who does not lend money, but brings borrowers and lenders together is known as a
    A. mortgage agent.   C. mortgage banker.
    B. mortgage broker.   D. mortgage dealer.

15. Servicing of loans which they have originated and sold on the secondary mortgage market is regularly carried on by all the following EXCEPT:
    A. commercial banks.
    B. savings and loan associations.
    C. mortgage companies.
    D. mortgage brokers.

16. Municipal bond issues as a source of funds for real estate loans provide
    I. tax free interest for investors.
    II. a source of below-market-rate funds for low- and middle-income families.
    A. I only   B. II only   C. Both I and II   D. Neither I nor II

17. Which of the following is the LEAST LIKELY to originate second mortgage loans on residential real estate?
    A. Finance companies.   C. Credit unions.
    B. Pension funds.   D. Individual investors.

18. The secondary mortgage market provides
    I. a means for investors to acquire real estate loans without origination and servicing facilities.
    II. a way for a lender to sell real estate loans.
    A. I only   B. II only   C. Both I and II   D. Neither I nor II

19. A large measure of the success of the secondary mortgage market is attributable to
    I. standardized loans and loan procedures.
    II. government and private mortgage loan insurance programs.
    A. I only   B. II only   C. Both I and II   D. Neither I nor II

20. All of the following are true of the Federal National Mortgage Association EXCEPT that it is
    A. a privately owned corporation.
    B. managed by the federal government.
    C. active in buying FHA and VA mortgage loans.
    D. known as Fannie Mae.

21. When Fannie Mae issues a commitment to purchase a specified dollar amount of mortgage loans within a fixed period of time,
    I. Fannie Mae must purchase all loans delivered under the terms of the commitment.
    II. participating lenders become obligated to sell their loans to Fannie Mae.
    A. I only   B. II only   C. Both I and II   D. Neither I nor II

22. Which of the following statements is NOT true of Fannie Mae's loan buying policies?
    A. Loans must be made using FNMA-approved forms.
    B. Loans must meet FNMA loan approval criteria.
    C. FNMA sets annual limits on the size of individual loans which it will buy.
    D. FNMA buys second and third mortgages for up to 90% loan-to-value.

23. FNMA will purchase
     I. first mortgage loans.
    II. second mortgage loans.
    III. government-insured or guaranteed loans.
     IV. conventional loans.
    A. I, II, III and IV   C. I and III only
    B. I, III and IV only   D. I, II and III only

24. Charles sold his home to David, and agreed to carry back a fixed-rate mortgage on the property. The note and mortgage were prepared by a Fannie Mae approved lender using FNMA qualification procedures. Could this loan be sold to a lender for later resale to FNMA?
    A. Yes, because it is a fixed-rate mortgage.
    B. Yes, because it meets the criteria for the FNMA Home Seller Program.
    C. No, because it is not an insured loan.
    D. No, because it cannot be packaged with lender-originated loans.

25. Fannie Mae will purchase
     I. adjustable rate mortgages.
    II. fixed rate mortgages.
    III. second mortgages.
     IV. first mortgages.
    A. I and III only   C. I, II and IV only
    B. II and IV only   D. I, II, III and IV

26. All of the following are true of the Government National Mortgage Association EXCEPT that it
    A. is a federal agency.
    B. operates a mortgage-backed securities program.
    C. is owned by stockholders.
    D. deals in FHA, VA and FmHA mortgages.

27. Under Ginnie Mae's mortgage-backed securities program,
     I. principal and interest payments are passed through to investors.
    II. the pool as a whole is guaranteed by Ginnie Mae.
    A. I only   B. II only   C. Both I and II   D. Neither I nor II

28. The Federal Home Loan Mortgage Corporation
     I. deals primarily in conventional mortgages.
    II. was established to serve as a secondary market for members of the Federal Home Loan Bank System.
    III. issues securities against its own mortgage pools.
     IV. is an agency of the federal government.
    A. I, II, III and IV   C. II and IV only
    B. II, III and IV only   D. I, II and III only

29. Participation certificates issued by Freddie Mac can be
    I. sold for cash.
    II. used as collateral for loans.
    A. I only   B. II only   C. Both I and II   D. Neither I nor II

30. The Friendly Federal Savings and Loan Association owns a participation certificate issued by Freddie Mac. Should any of the mortgages in the pool represented by the certificate default, the losses
    I. are passed on to the participants.
    II. will be entirely covered by private mortgage insurance.
    A. I only   B. II only   C. Both I and II   D. Neither I nor II

31. Basic problems experienced by investors in mortgage-backed securities include unpredictable
    I. yields.
    II. maturity.
    A. I only   B. II only   C. Both I and II   D. Neither I nor II

32. Collateralized mortgage obligations issued by the FHLMC provide an investor with investments of
    I. predictable maturity.
    II. guaranteed yields.
    A. I only   B. II only   C. Both I and II   D. Neither I nor II

33. Private financial institutions serving the secondary mortgage market
    I. do NOT compete with Fannie Mae, Ginnie Mae, nor Freddie Mac.
    II. specialize in markets not served by the "big three."
    A. I only   B. II only   C. Both I and II   D. Neither I nor II

34. A large measure of the success of the secondary mortgage market is attributable to the advent of
    I. computers.
    II. electronic data transmission systems.
    A. I only   B. II only   C. Both I and II   D. Neither I nor II

35. Computerized mortgage networks serve as conduits between
    I. lenders and real estate brokerage offices.
    II. investors and the secondary mortgage markets.
    A. I only   B. II only   C. Both I and II   D. Neither I nor II

36. Which of the following forms of money represents unconsumed labor and materials?
    A. Real savings.
    B. Fiat money.

37. In the arena of money and capital, home buyers face strong competition for loan funds from
    I. business borrowers.
    II. consumer credit borrowers.
    III. governmental borrowers.
    A. I, II and III   C. III only
    B. I and II only   D. I and III only

38. Generally, attempts to hold down interest rates on home loans by usury laws have met with
    A. success.
    B. failure.

39. The rate of interest charged to borrowers for home loans is determined LEAST of all by
    A. the cost of money to the lender.
    B. reserves for default and loan servicing costs.
    C. available investment alternatives.
    D. usury laws.

40. Due-on-sale clauses in mortgages may be used by lenders to
      I. refuse loan assumption by uncreditworthy buyers.
     II. increase the rate of interest when the property is sold.
    A. I only   B. II only   C. Both I and II   D. Neither I nor II

41. The provisions of the Garn Act apply to
    A. mortgage loans made after October 15, 1982 by deposit institutions in the United States.
    B. carryback financing by sellers.
    C. mortgage companies.
    D. all mortgage loans made before October 15, 1985.

42. Enforcement of a due-on-sale clause can result from the creation of
      I. an installment sale contract.
     II. a lease-option with option to buy.
    III. a lease of one year's duration.
     IV. foreclosure of a junior lien.
    A. I, II, III and IV   C. I and IV only
    B. I only   D. I, II and IV only

43. Loan contracts sometimes contain a prepayment clause in order to
      I. discourage the borrower from shopping for a new loan at a lower interest rate.
     II. decrease the yield from the loan.
    A. I only   B. II only   C. Both I and II   D. Neither I nor II

44. In order to make adjustable rate mortgage loans more attractive to borrowers, lenders offer
      I. lower initial interest rates.
     II. gifts such as appliances, trips, etc.
    A. I only   B. II only   C. Both I and II   D. Neither I nor II

45. Prior to the introduction of adjustable rate mortgages, the FHLBB approved the use of
      I. variable rate mortgages.
     II. renegotiable rate mortgages.
    A. I only   B. II only   C. Both I and II   D. Neither I nor II

46. The purpose of adjustable rate mortgages is to more closely match what the lender receives in interest to
    I.   the yield available from other types of investments.
    II. what it must pay to attract funds.
    A. I only   B. II only   C. Both I and II   D. Neither I nor II

47. To the borrower, as compared to a fixed-rate loan of the same maturity, an ARM mortgage loan offers a borrower the following advantages EXCEPT:
    A. the ability to qualify for a larger loan.
    B. decreasing monthly payments if market interest rates fall.
    C. lower settlement costs.
    D. assumability and prepayment privileges without penalty.

48. Which of the following indexes are used in connection with ARM loans?
    I.   One-year U. S. Treasury securities.
    II. Cost of funds to thrift institutions.
    III. Six-month Treasury bills.
    A. I and II only   C. II and III only
    B. I and III only   D. I, II and III

49. Adam was offered an ARM loan by lender A at a 2 per cent margin and a comparable loan by lender B at a 3 per cent margin. The loan from lender A would result in
    A. lower loan payments.   C. identical loan payments.
    B. higher loan payments.   D. higher interest rate charges.

50. Under the terms of an ARM loan,
    I.   when market rates are rising, the buyer benefits from longer adjustment periods.
    II. when market rates are falling, the buyer benefits from shorter adjustment periods.
    A. I only   B. II only   C. Both I and II   D. Neither I nor II

51. ARM loans are available that contain provisions for
    I.   an annual cap on interest rate increases.
    II. a lifetime cap on interest rate increases.
    A. I only   B. II only   C. Both I and II   D. Neither I nor II

52. ARM loans which contain a payment cap in order to limit possible increases in the borrower's monthly amortization payments can result in
    I.   negative amortization.
    II. an increase in the balance owed on the loan.
    III. the loan balance exceeding the property value.
    A. I only   C. II and III only
    B. I and II only   D. I, II and III

53. When considering an ARM loan, the lender must explain to the borrower, in writing, the
    I.   worst-case scenario.
    II. best-case scenario.
    A. I only   B. II only   C. Both I and II   D. Neither I nor II

54. ARM loans with teaser rates are avoided by
    I.   mortgage insurers.
    II. secondary market buyers.
    A. I only   B. II only   C. Both I and II   D. Neither I nor II

55. All of the following are true of a graduated payment mortgage EXCEPT:
    A. the maturity date is NOT determined at origination.
    B. the interest rate may be fixed or adjustable.
    C. monthly payments increase as the loan matures.
    D. negative amortization occurs during the early years.

56. Under the terms of a shared appreciation mortgage,
    I.   the loan is made at a below-market interest rate.
    II. the lender receives a portion of the property's appreciation.
    A. I only   B. II only   C. Both I and II   D. Neither I nor II

57. The concept of equity sharing may be applied to
    I.   commercial property transactions.
    II.   multi-family residential property transactions.
    III. single-family residential property transactions.
    A. I, II and III   C. I and II only
    B. I only   D. III only

58. Equity sharing is based on the concept of someone who has assets sharing those assets in exchange for
    I.   a share of the ownership.
    II. tax benefits.
    A. I only   B. II only   C. Both I and II   D. Neither I nor II

59. Baker is purchasing a new condominium unit. His purchase agreement calls for the refrigerator in the unit to be financed along with the purchase of the unit. Which of the following statements is NOT true?
    A. The refrigerator will be itemized and included in the mortgage.
    B. The mortgage will be called a package mortgage.
    C. Baker may not sell the refrigerator without the lender's permission.
    D. The rate of interest on the value of the refrigerator will be higher than that on the real property.

60. Which of the following statements is NOT correct with regard to blanket mortgages?
    A. More than one property serves as security for a single mortgage.
    B. Neither property may be sold until the entire debt is repaid.
    C. The mortgage may contain a partial release clause.
    D. The sale of either property may invoke a due-on-sale clause.

61. Charlie and Mabel, both 65 years old, own their home free and clear. They are retired and need supplementary income for living expenses. They have been offered a reverse mortgage by their local savings and loan association. Which of the following statements is NOT correct?
    A. They will receive monthly checks from the lender.
    B. The loan balance plus interest will be due upon sale of the home.
    C. They must make monthly payments of interest only on the loan.
    D. Upon death of the survivor, the property will be sold through the estate and the loan repaid from the proceeds.

62. Kevin is building a new home and secured a construction loan from his local bank. When the house is finished, he plans to pay it off with a permanent loan from a savings and loan association. Which of the following statements is correct?
    I. Money from the construction loan will be advanced to Kevin as construction takes place on the house.
    II. The permanent loan will be a take-out loan.
    A. I only   B. II only   C. Both I and II   D. Neither I nor II

63. When an existing loan at a low interest rate is refinanced by a new loan at an interest rate between the current market rate and the rate on the old loan, the result is a
    A. combined loan.   C. wraparound loan.
    B. blended loan.   D. merged loan.

64. Which of the following statements is NOT true of buy-downs?
    A. They are most often used in the sale of new homes by builders.
    B. The interest rate on the buyer's loan is lower than market rates.
    C. The "buy-down" is accomplished by having the buyer pay discount points to the lender at origination.
    D. Most builders will offer a lower purchase price on the property if the buyer will forego the buy-down.

65. Tom and Alice own their home which is presently worth approximately $150,000. They have an existing fixed-rate first mortgage of $50,000 on the property. To help pay for their child's college expenses, they have arranged for an equity loan on the home. Which of the following statements would NOT be correct?
    A. Assuming that they can qualify, they can probably secure approval of a loan up to $112,500 based on their equity.
    B. The equity loan will be a second mortgage loan.
    C. They may draw against the approved loan amount as money is needed.
    D. The interest rate will probably be based on the prime rate plus a lender's margin of from 1 to 3 percentage points.

66. All of the following statements are true of carryback financing EXCEPT:
    A. the seller of the property is the mortgagee under the mortgage.
    B. mortgage terms and interest rates are negotiable between the seller and buyer.
    C. if repayment is spread over two or more years, income taxes are calculated on the installment reporting method.
    D. carryback mortgages are usually salable to investors without discount.

67. Which of the following is NOT true of wraparound mortgages?
    A. They are junior mortgages, subordinate to an existing first mortgage.
    B. The interest rate on the buyer's note is usually the same as the market rate.
    C. They are useless when the first mortgage carries a due-on-sale clause.
    D. The yield to the seller (mortgagee) is usually greater than the interest rate specified on the note.

68. When the holder of a mortgage agrees to accept a position of lower lien priority, and to allow another mortgage to advance in priority, the process is known as
    A. subrogation.   C. subordination.
    B. substitution.   D. subterfuge.

69. A sale may be made and financed under a contract for deed
    I. only when the seller owns the property free and clear.
    II. by combining wraparound financing with an existing mortgage loan on the property, provided the existing mortgage does not contain a due-on-sale clause.
    A. I only   B. II only   C. Both I and II   D. Neither I nor II

70. Possession without the need to immediately finance the full purchase price of a property can be achieved by using a
    I. lease with option to buy.
    II. right of first refusal.
    A. I only   B. II only   C. Both I and II   D. Neither I nor II

71. Real estate agents who participate in creative financing arrangements in order to make sales should be careful to avoid participating in deals which could result in
    I. overencumbered properties.
    II. the loss of their license.
    A. I only   B. II only   C. Both I and II   D. Neither I nor II

72. Individuals can invest in real estate mortgages by
    I. investing in mortgage loan pools through certificates guaranteed by Ginnie Mae and Freddie Mac.
    II. buying junior mortgages at a discount.
    A. I only   B. II only   C. Both I and II   D. Neither I nor II

73. An individual who is contemplating the purchase of a mortgage as an investment should have
    I. the property appraised.
    II. a credit check made on the borrower.
    III. the title searched.
    A. I, II and III   C. II only
    B. I and II only   D. II and III only

74. In addition to mortgage financing, real estate can be financed through
    I. rentals.   III. sale-leaseback.
    II. leases.   IV. ground leases.
    A. III and IV only   C. I, II, III and IV
    B. I and II only   D. IV only

75. It is probably true of real estate financing that
    I. it will always change as economic conditions change.
    II. all possible means of financing have been utilized, and nothing new will appear in the future.
    A. I only   B. II only   C. Both I and II   D. Neither I nor II

Answers—Chapter 12

Multiple Choice Questions

1. **A**   Lenders in the primary mortgage market accept loan applications, make loans and administer loans. Secondary market investors purchase existing loans.

2. **D**   Savings and loan associations have historically been the foremost source of funds for residential mortgage loans in this country.

3. **C**   Certificates of deposit carry higher interest rates than passbook accounts in order to compete with higher yields from other investments and thereby prevent disintermediation.

4. **B**   Disintermediation occurs when large amounts of money are removed from thrift institutions for investment in government or corporate securities. This results in a decrease in activity in the real estate market.

5. **C**   S&Ls combat the problems of rising interest rates by enforcing due-on-sale clauses in mortgages and by encouraging borrowers to accept adjustable rate loans.

6. **A**   Deposits in commercial banks exceed those in S&Ls and are largely in demand accounts. Commercial banks tend to be less active in long-term real estate loans, but are often active in construction loans.

7. **C**   Both answers are correct.

8. **C**   Their ability to calculate payoffs from actuarial tables and receipt of premiums in predictable amounts make life insurance companies ideally suited to long-term investments.

9. **B**   Life insurance companies invest premium dollars in corporate bonds, real estate loans and government bonds, but do not invest in personal property loans.

10. **D**   Generally, life insurance companies prefer to originate industrial, multi-family or corporate real estate loans.

11. **C**   Participation loans are those in which the lender receives both interest and a part of the rental income from a property, and are designed as a protection against inflation.

12. **C**   Mortgage companies originate loans and service loans which they have sold on the secondary mortgage market.

13. **A**   Commercial banks, mutual savings banks and S&Ls regularly carry on mortgage banking activities. Insurance companies do not engage in this activity.

14. B   Mortgage brokers do not lend money, but bring borrowers and lenders together.

15. D   Mortgage brokers do not ordinarily service loans. This activity is engaged in by commercial banks, S&Ls and mortgage companies.

16. C   Municipal bonds provide a source of below-market-rate real estate loans by paying tax-free interest income to investors.

17. B   Pension funds do not ordinarily originate second mortgage loans. These loans are more readily available from finance companies, credit unions and individual investors.

18. C   The secondary mortgage market provides a means for lenders to sell real estate loans, and a means for investors to acquire these loans without origination and servicing facilities.

19. C   Standardized loan procedures and government and private mortgage insurance programs have contributed substantially to the success of the secondary mortgage market.

20. B   FNMA (Fannie Mae) is a privately owned corporation which is active in buying FHA and VA mortgage loans. It is not managed by the federal government.

21. A   Once Fannie Mae has issued a commitment to purchase a specified dollar amount of loans within a fixed time, it must purchase all loans delivered under the agreement, but participating lenders are not obligated to sell their loans to Fannie Mae.

22. D   FNMA does not buy third mortgages and does not exceed 70% or 80% loan-to-value on seconds.

23. A   FNMA will purchase first or second mortgage loans, government-insured or guaranteed loans, and conventional loans.

24. B   FNMA will purchase carryback mortgages which meet the criteria for their Home Seller Program. This loan meets these criteria.

25. D   Fannie Mae will purchase first or second mortgages, fixed rate or adjustable rate.

26. C   GNMA is a federal agency, not owned by stockholders. It deals in FHA, VA and FmHA and operates a mortgage-backed securities program.

27. C   Under Ginnie Mae's mortgage-backed securities program, principal and interest are passed through to investors, and the pool as a whole is guaranteed by Ginnie Mae.

28. D   FHLMC deals primarily in conventional mortgages, serves as a secondary market for members of the Federal Home Loan Bank System, and issues securities on its own mortgage pools. It is not an agency of the federal government.

29. C   Participation certificates issued by Freddie Mac can be sold for cash and may be used as collateral for loans.

30. D   Freddie Mac guarantees that interest and principal on participation certificates will be paid in full and on time.

31. B   Mortgage-backed securities are of unpredictable maturity, but yields are predictable.

32. C   Collateralized mortgage obligations issued by FHLMC are of predictable yield and maturity.

33. B   Private financial institutions which serve the secondary mortgage market avoid competing with Fannie Mae, Ginnie Mae and Freddie Mac by specializing in markets not served by these institutions.

34. C   Computers and electronic data transmission systems have contributed substantially to the success of the secondary mortgage markets.

35. A   Computers and mortgage networks serve as conduits between lenders and real estate brokerage offices.

36. A   Real savings represents unconsumed labor and materials. Fiat money is printing-press money.

37. A   Business, government and consumer credit borrowers compete strongly with home buyers for investment capital.

38. B   Usury laws have generally met with failure in attempting to hold down interest rates on home loans.

39. D   The interest rate charged to a home buyer is determined by the cost of money to the lender, reserves for default and loan servicing costs, and available interest alternatives. Usury laws have little impact, if any.

40. C   Due-on-sale clauses in mortgages are used by lenders to refuse loan assumption by uncreditworthy borrowers. They are also used to increase the rate of interest when the property is sold by requiring repayment or renegotiation.

41. A   The provisions of the Garn Act apply to mortgage loans made after October 15, 1982 by any deposit institution.

42. D   Enforcement of a due-on-sale clause can result from an installment sale contract, a lease with option to buy, or foreclosure of a junior lien. It cannot result from a lease of one year's duration.

43. A   Prepayment clauses discourage the borrower from shopping for a new loan at a lower interest rate unless there has been a substantial drop in rates.

44. A   Lenders increase the attractiveness of adjustable rate mortgage loans by offering lower initial interest rates than on fixed-rate loans.

45. C   Both variable rate and renegotiable rate mortgages were approved by the FHLBB prior to the introduction of adjustable rate mortgages.

46. B   The purpose of ARM loans is to more closely match the lender's loan yield to the lender's cost of funds.

47. C   ARM loans do not lower settlement costs, but do increase the borrower's ability to qualify for a larger loan, decrease the monthly payments if market interest rates fall, and allow assumption and prepayment without penalty.

48. D   ARM loans may be indexed to one-year U. S. Treasury securities, six-month Treasury bills, or the cost of funds to thrift institutions.

49. A   A one per cent lower margin would result in lower loan payments because the monthly interest charge would be lower.

50. C   A borrower under an ARM loan would benefit from longer adjustment periods when interest rates are rising and shorter adjustment periods when interest rates are falling.

51. C   ARM loans are available with both an annual and a lifetime cap on interest rate increases.

52. D   A payment cap on monthly mortgage amortization payments can result in negative amortization, an increase in the loan balance, and a loan balance in excess of the property value by continual addition of unpaid interest to the loan balance.

53. A   The lender must explain the worst-case scenario to a buyer who is considering an ARM loan.

54. C   ARM loans with teaser rates are avoided by mortgage lenders and secondary mortgage market buyers because they can lead to early foreclosure when rates are increased.

55. A   The maturity date of graduated payment mortgage loans is set at origination. Interest rates may be fixed or adjustable. Monthly payments increase as the loan matures, and there is negative amortization in the early years.

56. C   Shared appreciation mortgages are made at below-market rates in exchange for the lender's receipt of a portion of the appreciation in the mortgaged property.

57. A   The concept of equity sharing may be applied to commercial, multi-family residential or single-family residential property transactions.

58. C   Under equity sharing, the person with assets receives both a share of ownership and tax benefits.

59. D   The loan will be a package mortgage, with the refrigerator included in the mortgage. The refrigerator may not be sold without the lender's permission, but the interest rate will be the same as that on the real property.

60. B   Blanket mortgages include more than one property as security for a single loan, and the sale of either property could invoke a due-on-sale clause. If the mortgage contained a partial release clause, it would be possible to sell a property before the entire mortgage debt was repaid.

61. C   Under the terms of a reverse mortgage, no payment is made of interest or principal prior to maturity. All other responses are correct.

62. C   Advances on the construction loan are disbursed as construction progresses. A take-out loan is secured from another lender to pay off a construction loan.

63. B   A blended loan incorporates an existing loan at a low interest rate with a new loan at a rate of interest between the old rate and the current market rate.

64. C   Discount points on "buy-downs" are paid by the builder, not by the buyer. All other responses are correct.

65. A   A loan of $112,500 would exceed their equity of $100,000 in the property. All other responses are correct.

66. D   Carryback mortgages, when sold to investors, are usually sold at large discounts. All other responses are correct.

67. B   When wraparound financing is used, the interest rate on the buyer's note is usually at a below-market rate. This is what makes it attractive to the buyer. All other responses are correct.

68. C   Subordination occurs when a mortgage holder agrees to accept a position of lower lien priority, thus allowing another mortgage to advance in priority.

69. B   A sale may be made under a contract for deed by using wraparound financing provided there is no due-on-sale clause in the existing mortgage. It is not necessary for the property to be owned free and clear.

70. A   A lease with option to buy eliminates the need for immediate financing of the full purchase price of the property. A right of first refusal does not accomplish this objective as it lacks possession.

71. C   A real estate agent who participated in creative financing which resulted in an overencumbered property could be penalized by the loss of his/her license.

72. C   Individuals can invest in real estate mortgages by purchasing Ginnie Mae or Freddie Mac participation certificates or by buying junior mortgages at a discount.

73. A   Before purchasing a mortgage as an investment, one should have the property appraised, a credit check made on the borrower, and the title searched.

74. C   Rentals, leases, sale-leaseback and ground leases are all ways to finance real estate other than through mortgages.

75. A   Financing methods have always changed to meet current market conditions, and can be expected to continue to do so.

Taxes and Assessments

Chapter 13

1. Local government programs and services are financed primarily through
    A. property taxes.
    B. federal income taxes.
    C. state income taxes.
    D. state sales taxes.

2. Taxes on real property are levied
    I. on an ad valorem basis.
    II. according to the value of the property.
    A. I only   B. II only   C. Both I and II   D. Neither I nor II

3. All of the following governmental services are paid for by taxes on real property EXCEPT:
    A. fire and police protection.
    B. local parks and recreation.
    C. interstate highways.
    D. public libraries.

4. In determining the amount of taxes to be levied on a parcel of real estate, the necessary steps will be completed by the local government officials in which of the following sequences?
    I. Determine the budget requirements of the community.
    II. Assessment of all the taxable real property in the community.
    III. Determine the revenue to be derived from sources other than real property taxes.
    IV. Set the tax rate on all taxable real property.
    A. I, II, III, IV
    B. I, III, II, IV
    C. II, I, III, IV
    D. IV, I, III, II

5. The dollar amount of taxes to be levied on a property may be increased by which of the following means?
    I. Increasing the tax rate.
    II. Raising the assessment ratio.
    III. Increasing the assessed value of the property.
    A. I, II and III
    B. I only
    C. II only
    D. III only

Note: If you are reading <u>Real Estate: An Introduction to the Profession</u> you may omit the following questions: 22, 26, 27, 28 and 29.

6. The assessment ratio of real property in a community may be
   I. one hundred per cent of its appraised value.
   II. less than its fair market value.
   III. more than its appraised value.
   A. I, II and III   B. I and II only   C. II only   D. III only

7. Which of the following properties has the highest assessed value?
   A. Market value $75,000, assessed at 75% of value.
   B. Market value $50,000, assessed at 100% of value.
   C. Market value $90,000, assessed at 50% of value.
   D. Market value $130,000, assessed at 35% of value.

8. Tax rates may be expressed as
   I. a millage rate.
   II. dollars of tax per hundred dollars of valuation.
   III. dollars of tax per thousand dollars of valuation.
   A. I and II only   C. II and III only
   B. I and III only   D. I, II and III

9. The budget for the city of Westview requires $600,000 from real property
   taxes for the current year. The value of all taxable real property in
   the city is 24 million dollars. Which of the following tax rates would
   NOT produce the necessary revenues?
   A. .025 per $1.00.   C. $25. per $1,000.
   B. $2.50 per $100.   D. 2.5 mills.

10. Which of the following would be the highest tax rate?
    A. 38 mills.   C. $38/$1,000.
    B. $3.80/$100.   D. No difference.

11. If a property owner fails to pay his taxes,
    I. the community may attach other assets such as his bank account.
    II. the property owner will lose the property.
    A. I only   B. II only   C. Both I and II   D. Neither I nor II

12. Property named in a tax certificate following a sale for delinquent taxes
    may be redeemed by
    I. the owner.
    II. a lienholder.
    III. anyone who will pay the taxes and interest.
    A. I only   C. II only
    B. I, II and III   D. I and II only

13. In a state where the redemption period follows the tax sale, a tax deed
    is issued to the successful bidder
    A. at the conclusion of the sale.
    B. upon the expiration of the redemption period.
    C. at the beginning of the tax delinquency.
    D. upon waiver of redemption rights by lienholders.

14. In a state in which the sale of property for delinquent taxes occurs only after the expiration of a redemption period, the purchaser at a tax sale will receive a
    A. tax certificate.   C. tax deed.
    B. tax lien.   D. tax receipt.

15. Jeff plans to bid on real estate being offered at a tax auction. Before bidding on a parcel he would be wise to
    I. conduct a title search.
    II. purchase title insurance.
    A. I only   B. II only   C. Both I and II   D. Neither I nor II

16. George has a deed from local tax authorities granting him all the right, title and interest a delinquent owner had in a particular real property. To enhance the marketability of his title, George could
    I. purchase title insurance.
    II. conduct a quiet title suit.
    A. I only   B. II only   C. Both I and II   D. Neither I nor II

17. Which of the following liens holds the highest degree of lien priority?
    A. Federal income tax liens.   C. Ad valorem tax liens.
    B. Mechanic's liens.   D. First mortgage liens.

18. The assessed value of land and buildings in a community is
    A. a matter of public record.
    B. available only to the owner of the property.
    C. available only to those who have a financial interest in the property.
    D. known only to the officials who need to know this information.

19. Records of the assessed valuations of all properties within a jurisdiction are known as
    A. appraisal rolls.   C. appropriation rolls.
    B. allocation rolls.   D. assessment rolls.

20. Richard feels that the taxes on his real property are too high. Through the appeal process he can demand a review of the
    A. amount of tax on the property.
    B. assessed value of the property.
    C. rate of taxation.
    D. assessment ratio.

21. Among the functions of the Board of Equalization are to
    I. equalize assessments between counties.
    II. equalize assessments between individual property owners.
    A. I only   B. II only   C. Both I and II   D. Neither I nor II

22. Assessment procedures between counties may be equalized by
    I. requiring all counties to use the same appraisal procedure and assessment ratio.
    II. allowing each county to use its own method and applying a correction factor as determined by the Board of Equalization.
    A. I only   B. II only   C. Both I and II   D. Neither I nor II

23. The City of Grandview wants to attract a new manufacturing plant to locate within the city. As an inducement, may the city officials offer an exemption from real property taxes?
    A. Yes, on the basis that the cost to the public is outweighed by the economic benefits.
    B. Yes, because the government's power of eminent domain permits exemptions to private owners.
    C. No, because this would increase the tax burden to other property owners.
    D. No, because only publicly owned land can be exempt from taxation.

24. Land and buildings may be exempted from property taxation
    I. as a means of attracting industry to a community.
    II. if they are used for religious or educational purposes.
    A. I only   B. II only   C. Both I and II   D. Neither I nor II

25. All of the following types of property are usually exempt from taxation EXCEPT:
    A. government-owned utilities.
    B. residences owned by elderly homeowners.
    C. property owned by charitable organizations.
    D. hospitals.

26. Homes of the same value may bear different tax burdens because of
    I. delays in reassessment.
    II. different services being provided by the government in different neighborhoods.
    A. I only   B. II only   C. Both I and II   D. Neither I nor II

27. Taxes on real property of the same value are different in various communities because of
    I. varying sources of revenue from city to city.
    II. varying services provided by different cities.
    A. I only   B. II only   C. Both I and II   D. Neither I nor II

28. The property tax burden of an individual owner is NOT influenced by
    A. the efficiency of the government.
    B. the owner's ability to pay.
    C. local debt service.
    D. services furnished by the government.

29. Real property taxes are sometimes limited by laws which limit
    I. the amount of taxes that can be collected.
    II. how much a government can spend.
    A. I only   B. II only   C. Both I and II   D. Neither I nor II

30. Special assessments of property tax are made for improvements which benefit
    I. a limited number of property owners.
    II. all property owners for a limited time.
    A. I only   B. II only   C. Both I and II   D. Neither I nor II

31. The cost of which of the following could be met by means of a special assessment?
    A. Improvements to a municipal golf course.
    B. Extension of sewer lines to a privately owned industrial park.
    C. Construction of a fire station located in a new residential area of the city.
    D. Construction of a new school to serve a growing residential area.

32. An improvement district may be created as a result of action originated by
    I. a group of concerned citizens.
    II. local governing bodies.
    A. I only   B. II only   C. Both I and II   D. Neither I nor II

33. When an improvement district is created, the costs of the improvements are paid from
    I. general revenues.
    II. assessments on properties within the district.
    A. I only   B. II only   C. Both I and II   D. Neither I nor II

34. A property owner whose land is assessed for improvements in an improved district may pay his share by
    I. cash, directy to the contractor.
    II. letting it go to bond.
    A. I only   B. II only   C. Both I and II   D. Neither I nor II

35. Special assessments are apportioned according to
    A. the value of the land being assessed.
    B. the value of the buildings being assessed.
    C. the benefits received.
    D. the value of the land and buildings being assessed.

36. The city of Metroville is going to install curbs and gutters in one of its neighborhoods that does not presently have them. The special assessment for these curbs and gutters will be levied against individual properties according to
    I. the benefits received.
    II. the assessed value of the properties.
    A. I only   B. II only   C. Both I and II   D. Neither I nor II

37. Special assessments are superior in lien priority to all of the following EXCEPT:
    A. first mortgages.   C. federal income tax liens.
    B. mechanic's liens.   D. ad valorem tax liens.

38. The Ross family purchased their home for $65,000. The only improvements added were landscaping and fencing which cost $2,500. They later sold the home for $90,000 and paid a 6 per cent sales commission. In order to make the sale, they took back a purchase money mortgage of $10,000 which they sold to an investor for $7,500. For income tax purposes, the gain realized by the Ross family would be:
    A. $17,100.   C. $14,600.
    B. $4,600.   D. $7,100.

39. When a person sells land for more than he paid for it
     I.   there is no federal tax applicable to the gain.
     II. the gain is taxed by all state governments.
     A. I only   B. II only   C. Both I and II   D. Neither I nor II

40. Which of the following may be included in determining the cost basis of
     a home in determining income tax liability?
     I.   Cost of legal services in acquiring the home.
     II. Fees or commissions paid to help find the property.
     A. I only   B. II only   C. Both I and II   D. Neither I nor II

41. If you add an improvement to a home, which of the following can be
     included in determining the cost basis for income tax purposes?
     I.   The cost of materials used in the improvement.
     II. The value of your own services in erecting or installing the
          improvement.
     A. I only   B. II only   C. Both I and II   D. Neither I nor II

42. Which of the following would be considered an improvement to a home in
     determining its cost basis?
     I.   Repairs to a leaky roof.
     II.   Construction of a new fence.
     III. Repairs done as part of an extensive remodeling project.
     A. I and II only   C. II and III only
     B. I and III only   D. I, II and III

43. In order to qualify for inclusion in a home's adjusted sales price,
     fix-up expenses
     I.   must be done within 90 days prior to the time a contract to
          sell is signed.
     II. must be paid for within 30 days after the signing of a contract
          to sell.
     A. I only   B. II only   C. Both I and II   D. Neither I nor II

44. In order to postpone payment of income taxes on a gain from the sale of
     a residence, the owner may
     I.   purchase a more expensive home within 24 months.
     II.   begin construction of a more expensive new home and occupy it
           within 24 months.
     III. purchase a new home costing less and add improvements which bring
           the cost up to the sales price of the old home within 24 months.
     A. I or II only   C. I or III only
     B. II or III only   D. I, II or III

45. The Craigs, who are 65 years old, want to sell their home and move to a
     retirement community. They are eligible for their once-in-a-lifetime
     exclusion from capital gains tax on the sale provided
     A. the home does not sell for more than $125,000.
     B. they purchase a new home within 24 months for at least $125,000.
     C. they purchase a new home at a price at least equal to the sale
         price of the present home.
     D. they have occupied the home for at least 3 of the 5 years preceding
         the sale.

46. Fritz realized a capital gain of $40,000 on the sale of an investment property which he sold for $100,000. He received a $35,000 cash down payment and carried back a $65,000 mortgage. Which of the following statements are correct?
    I.   Taxes on the entire gain are due in the year of sale.
    II. Taxes on the gain are due on the portion of gain received in any given year.
    III. Interest earned on the mortgage is taxed as ordinary income.
    A. I and II only   C. II and III only
    B. I and III only   D. I, II and III

47. Deductions for a capital loss may NOT be taken on which of the following?
    I.   A rented condominium unit held as an investment.
    II. A private home occupied by the owner.
    A. I only   B. II only   C. Both I and II   D. Neither I nor II

48. Which of the following may be claimed as a personal deduction when a homeowner itemizes on his or her tax return?
    I.   Property tax on a personal residence.
    II. Mortgage interest on a personal residence.
    A. I only   B. II only   C. Both I and II   D. Neither I nor II

49. Under income tax laws passed in 1984 and 1985, a seller who takes a carryback mortgage
    I.   must charge 10 per cent interest or be penalized 9 per cent by the IRS.
    II. is NOT subject to penalties if the rate charged is at least equal to the rate on federal securities of similar maturity.
    III. is discouraged from charging a below-market rate.
    A. I and II only   C. II and III only
    B. I and III only   D. I, II and III

50. If a seller is willing to carry back financing at below-market interest rates, the seller
    I.   can expect to receive an above-market price for the property.
    II. must be careful of the minimum interest rate rules of the IRS.
    A. I only   B. II only   C. Both I and II   D. Neither I nor II

51. Sources of information on income tax laws and rules include
    I.   tax guides published by the Internal Revenue Service.
    II. privately published tax guides sold in bookstores.
    III. privately published tax newsletters.
    A. I and II only   C. II and III only
    B. I and III only   D. I, II and III

52. Because of the complexity of income tax laws and their impact on real estate, a real estate licensee should
    I.   have knowledge of tax laws at the level of an accountant.
    II. avoid knowledge of tax laws so as to avoid responsibility for providing tax information.
    III. know when to warn clients that a tax problem may exist or result.
    IV. have enough general knowledge of tax laws pertaining to real estate so as to be able to answer basic questions.
    A. I only   C. II only
    B. I, III and IV only   D. III and IV only

53. A real estate agent has a responsibility
    I.   to alert clients to seek tax counsel.
    II. for the quality and accuracy of tax information given by the agent to clients.
    A. I only   B. II only   C. Both I and II   D. Neither I nor II

54. Conveyance taxes on the transfer of title to real property are levied by
    I.   the federal government.
    II. some state governments.
    A. I only   B. II only   C. Both I and II   D. Neither I nor II

55. The conveyance tax on deeds is $.55 per $100 on the "new money." A property sells for $100,000 subject to an existing $30,000 loan. What is the amount of tax?
    A. $715.   C. $385.
    B. $550.   D. $165.

Property Tax Problems

1. In the city of Broadview, the total assessed value of all real estate
    is $240 million. The share of the city budget to be paid by ad valorem
    taxes is $6 million. Your property in that city is assessed at $40,000.

    A. What will be the tax rate, expressed in mills?

    _____

    B. What will be the annual taxes on your property?

    $_____

2. If a property has a market value of $240,000 and is assessed at $100,800,
    what is the assessment ratio?

    _____%

3. In the city of Eastville, the millage rate is 20 mills for the school
    budget, 10 mills for city services, and 5 mills for county services. If
    a property having a market value of $70,000 is assessed at a 50% ratio,
    what would be the annual taxes on the property?

    $_____

4. You own property in a city where the tax rate is $3.50 per $100 of
    assessed valuation. Your taxes are $1,365 annually on a property
    which has a market value of $60,000. What is the assessment
    ratio?

    _____%

5. You own property assessed at $65,000 in a community where the assessment ratio is 52% of value. Based on this, what is the market value of the property?

$_____

6. Sally buys a lot by paying the back taxes for the past 4 years. The tax rate is $21.00 per $1,000 of the assessed value. What did she pay for the lot if the assessed value of the lot was $12,000?

$_____

7. Mr. and Mrs. Jourdan bought property ten years ago to use as a second home on their weekends. This second home is taxed on the basis of 60% of assessed value, at the rate of $2.50 per hundred. This has been the case for the last five years. Since they bought, however, their yearly taxes have increased by $450. In the eyes of the tax assessor, how much has the property increased in value?

$_____

8. A 100-foot-by-100-foot lot was assessed at $150 per front foot and the house was assessed at $32,000. What was the total yearly tax if the rate was $4.00 per $100?

$_____

9. A house assessed at $102,000 was taxed at 2.2%. Taxes have just increased by 30%. What is the amount of the tax increase?

$_____

10. The assessed value of all property in the city of Blissville is
$120 million. The city budget is $5,040,000. Your property is assessed
at $350,000. What taxes will you pay?

$_____

11. A lender requires that the monthly mortgage payment include one-twelfth
of the annual taxes. Property value is $100,000. Assessment ratio is
30%. School tax rate is 12 mills; county tax rate is 25 mills. What is
the tax payment per month?

$_____

12. A property is assessed at $80,000. The tax rate is $26 per $1,000 with
a 2% discount for promptness and an 18% per annum charge for delinquency.

A. Determine the amount owed if the taxes are paid before the due
date.

$_____

B. Determine the amount owed if the taxes are paid 2 months after the
due date.

$_____

C. What is the difference to the property owner between paying on
time and paying 2 months late?

$_____

Gain on Sale Problem

This problem follows the saga of Don and Marg Green through their ownership of a home, the sale of the home, and the purchase of another home. Use the data given to calculate their gain and tax liability following the purchase of the second home.

April 1, 1959	Purchase home for $18,500. Closing costs $500.	Basis: $_____
May 1, 1960	Fence rear yard at a cost of $350.	Basis: $_____
July 1, 1962	Paint interior and exterior at a cost of $600.	Basis: $_____
June 1, 1964	Add screened porch at a cost of $1,500.	Basis: $_____
Sept. 1, 1968	Connect to public sewer at a cost of $800.	Basis: $_____
April 1, 1972	Add central air conditioning at a cost of $1,000.	Basis: $_____
June 1, 1980	Remodel bathroom at a cost of $5,000.	Basis: $_____
July 10, 1986	Sell home for $149,500.	
Aug. 10, 1986	Closing Date; sales commission and closing costs are $10,500.	Amount Realized: $_____

Calculation of gain:

Amount Realized	$_____
Less Basis	$_____
Equals Gain	$_____

Assume that the Greens owned their home free and clear of any debts at the time of the sale. Use the data given below to determine their tax liability in each of the following situations.

Situation No. 1

Aug. 1, 1986	Settlement date on the purchase of a new home at a price of $150,000. Closing costs are $1,000.	Cost of New Home:	$_____
Aug. 10, 1986	Settlement date on previous home.	Subtract Postponed Gain:	$_____
		Basis for New Home:	$_____

Situation No. 2

Suppose that on August 10, 1986, the Greens had sold their home and did not purchase another home on the basis stated in Situation No. 1 above. The purchaser made a down payment of $24,500 and agreed to pay $12,500 plus interest in each of the next ten years. The Greens are both 54 years of age.

1. What per cent of each dollar of sale price would be reported as gain each year in which payment is received?   _____%

2. What amount would be reported as gain in the year of the sale?   (Nearest whole dollar) $_____

3. What amount would be reported as gain in each of the following ten years?   (Nearest whole dollar) $_____

Situation No. 3

Same as in Situation No. 2 above except the down payment is $49,500 followed by $20,000 per year plus interest for 5 years, and the Greens are 55 years old.

1. What per cent of each dollar of sale price would be reported as gain each year in which payment is received?   _____%

2. What amount of sale would be reported as gain in the year of the sale?   (Nearest whole dollar) $_____

3. What amount would be reported as gain in each of the following five years?   (Nearest whole dollar) $_____

Answers—Chapter 13

Multiple Choice Questions

1. A   Real property taxes are the principal source of revenue for local governments.

2. C   The term "ad valorem" is Latin for "according to value."

3. C   Local services are paid for by real property taxes, but interstate highways are not paid for from local revenues.

4. B   The appropriation process, that of allocating to each property the taxes to be levied on that property, is done in the order shown by response B.

5. A   An increase in the tax rate, assessment ratio, or assessed value will increase the taxes to be levied on a property.

6. B   The assessment ratio may be equal to, or less than, the property value, but not greater than its value.

7. A $75,000 x .75 = $56,250
         $50,000 x 1.00 = $50,000
         $90,000 x .50 = $45,000
         $130,000 x .35 = $45,500

8. D   Taxes may be expressed as a millage rate, dollars of tax per $100 of assessed value, or dollars of tax per $1,000 of assessed value.

9. D $600,000 taxes divided by $24,000,000 total assessed value of all property = .025 = 25 mills. Therefore 2.5 mills is wrong.

10. D   All of the stated tax rates will result in equal amounts of taxes on a given property.

11. B   Failure to pay real property taxes will result in the loss of the property, but the owner's other assets will not be attached.

12. D   Property named in a tax certificate may be redeemed by the owner or by a lienholder, but not by anyone willing to pay the taxes and interest.

13. B   Tax deeds are issued following the expiration of the redemption period.

14. C   Tax deeds are issued upon the sale of the property in those states wherein the sale of the property for delinquent taxes follows the expiration of the redemption period.

15. A   Before bidding on a parcel of real estate being offered at a tax sale, a bidder should do a title search to determine what, if any, other encumbrances exist against the property.

16. C   The holder of a tax deed can enhance the marketability of the property by purchasing title insurance or conducting a quiet title suit.

17. C   Ad valorem taxes have lien priority over all other liens against a property.

18. A   The assessment of land and buildings in a community is a matter of public record.

19. D   The assessment rolls are public records of the assessed valuations of all properties in a jurisdiction.

20. B   A property owner may demand a review of the assessed value of his property through the appeals process.

21. C   The Board of Equalization's functions include the equalization of assessments between counties and also between individual property owners.

22. C   Assessment procedures between counties may be equalized by requiring all to use the same appraisal procedure and assessment ratio, or by allowing different methods and applying a correction factor.

23. A   City officials may offer property tax exemptions to business on the basis that the cost to the public is outweighed by the economic benefits.

24. C   Land and buildings may be exempt from taxation as a means of attracting industry to a community, or if they are used for religious or educational purposes.

25. B   Residences owned by elderly homeowners may get certain benefits but are not exempt from taxation. Government-owned utilities, property owned by charitable organizations, and hospitals are usually exempt.

26. C   Homes of the same value may bear different tax burdens because of delays in reassessment or because of different governmental services provided in different neighborhoods.

27. C   Varying sources of revenue from city to city or varying services provided by different cities may result in different tax burdens in different cities.

28. B   The ability of the owner to pay taxes does not influence the taxes levied on the property.

29. C   Both the amount of taxes that can be collected and the amount that a government can spend may be limited by statute.

30. A   Improvements which benefit a limited number of property owners are paid for by a special assessment on the properties which benefit from the improvements.

31. B   Extension of sewer lines to a privately owned industrial park would benefit a limited number of property owners and would likely be paid for by a special assessment.

32. C   An improvement district could result from action initiated by a group of concerned citizens or by local governing bodies.

33. B   The cost of improvements in an improvement district are met by assessments on properties within the district.

34. C   An owner may pay his share of the costs of improvements in an improvement district in cash to the contractor, or by letting it go to bond.

35. C   Special assessments are apportioned according to the value of the benefits received.

36. A   Special assessments for the cost of improvements are levied against individual properties according to the benefits received.

37. D   Special assessment liens are superior in lien priority to all liens but ad valorem tax liens.

38. C
```
    $90,000 sale price            $65,000 purchase price
  -  5,400 commission          +  2,500 improvements
  -  2,500 loan discount          $67,500 cost basis
    $82,100 amount realized

                                  $82,100 amount realized
                                -  67,500 cost basis
                                  $14,600 gain
```

39. D   Federal capital gains tax would apply to profit from the sale of land, but this gain is not taxed by all state governments.

40. C   Both the cost of legal services and fees or commissions paid to help find the property may be included in determining the cost basis of a home.

41. A   The value of personal services in erecting or installing improvements may not be included in determining the cost basis, but the cost of materials may be included.

42. C   The cost of construction of a new fence and repairs done as a part of an extensive remodeling project may be included in determining its cost basis. Repairs to a leaky roof may not be considered.

43. C   In order to qualify for inclusion in the adjusted sales price, fix-up expenses must be done within 90 days prior to sale, and paid for within 30 days after the signing of a contract of sale.

44.   D   To qualify for deferment of taxes on a gain from the sale of a residence, the owner may purchase a more expensive home within 24 months, construct and occupy a more expensive new home within 24 months, or purchase a new home costing less and add improvements which increase the cost up to the sales price of the old home within 24 months.

45.   D   Persons over 55 years of age may qualify for the once-in-a-lifetime exclusion from capital gains tax on the sale of their residence provided they occupied the home for at least 3 of the 5 years preceding the sale.

46.   C   Taxes on capital gains are due on the portion of the gains received in any given year, and interest on mortgages is taxed as ordinary income.

47.   B   Deductions for capital losses may not be taken on a private home occupied by the owner, but may be taken on property rented as an investment.

48.   C   Deductions may be taken for both property taxes and mortgage interest on a personal residence by a homeowner who files an itemized income tax return.

49.   C   The income tax laws of 1984 and 1985 discourage the charging of below-market rates on carryback mortgages. A seller is not subject to penalties if the rate charged is at least equal to the rate on federal securities of similar maturity.

50.   C   A seller who is willing to carry back financing at below market rates can expect to receive an above-market price, but must be careful of the minimum interest rate rules of the IRS.

51.   D   Information on income tax laws include IRS tax guides and privately published tax guides and newsletters.

52.   D   A real estate licensee should have enough general knowledge of tax laws to be able to answer basic questions, and should know when to warn clients that a tax problem could exist or result.

53.   C   A real estate agent has a responsibility to alert clients to seek tax counsel and for the quality and accuracy of any information given by the agent to clients.

54.   B   Conveyance taxes on real property title transfers are levied by certain state and local governments, but not by the federal government.

55.   C $100,000 price - $30,000 assumed loan = $70,000 taxable
$70,000 divided by $100 = 700 x $.55 = $385.

Property Tax Problems

1A. $6,000,000 ÷ $240,000,000 = .025 = 25 mills

1B. $40,000 x .025 = $1,000

2. $100,800 ÷ $240,000 = .42 = 42%

3. $70,000 x .50 x (.020 + .010 + .005) = $1,225

4. $1,365 ÷ ($3.50 per $100) = $1,365 ÷ .035 = $39,000 assessed value
      $39,000 ÷ $60,000 = 65% answer

5. $65,000 ÷ .52 = $125,000

6. $21.00 x 12 x 4 = $1,008

7. $450 ÷ .025 ÷ .60 = $30,000

8.   100' x $150 + $32,000 = $47,000 assessed value
      $47,000 x .04 = $1,880 answer

9. $102,000 x .022 = $2,244 taxes before increase.
      $2,244 x .30 = $673.20 amount of tax increase.

10. $5,040,000 ÷ $120,000,000 x $350,000 = $14,700

11. $100,000 x .30 x (.012 + .025) ÷ 12 = $92.50

12A. $80,000 x .026 x .98 = $2,038.40 if paid on time.

12B. $80,000 x .026 x .18 ÷ 12 = $31.20 monthly delinquency charge.
      $80,000 x .026 + 2 x $31.20 = $2,142.40 if paid late.

12C. $2,142.40 - $2,038.40 = $104.00 difference.

Gain on Sale Problem

April 1, 1959	Basis:	$ 19,000
May 1, 1960	Basis:	$ 19,350
July 1, 1962	Basis:	$ 19,350
June 1, 1964	Basis:	$ 20,850
September 1, 1968	Basis:	$ 21,650
April 1, 1972	Basis:	$ 22,650
June 1, 1980	Basis:	$ 27,650
August 10, 1986	Amount Realized:	$139,000
Calculation of gain:	Amount realized	$139,000
	Less basis	27,650
	Gain	$111,350

$151,000
$111,350
$ 39,650

price of $149,500 = 74.48%

248

10

ns elect to use their once-in-a-lifetime

0%.

868. Or, zero if they use their election.

896. Or, zero if they use their election.

Title Closing and Escrow

Chapter 14

1. The moment in time when a seller conveys title to a purchaser, and when the purchaser fulfills all his obligations pertinent to the sale may be referred to by any of the following terms EXCEPT:
   A. close of escrow.   C. closing date.
   B. settlement date.   D. completion date.

2. Details that must be handled between the time a purchase contract is signed and the closing typically include
   I. title search.   III. loan arrangements.
   II. deed preparation.   IV. checking the property taxes.
   A. I, II and III only   C. I, III and IV only
   B. II, III and IV only   D. I, II, III and IV

3. A buyer's walkthrough is conducted for the purpose of
   A. appraising the property in order to get a loan on it.
   B. inspecting the property for major structural defects.
   C. meeting the seller and obtaining the keys to the property.
   D. making a final inspection just prior to closing.

4. During the walkthrough, the buyer should
   I. test heating and air conditioning systems.
   II. test appliances that are NOT included in the sale.
   III. test the plumbing.
   IV. test the title to the property for defects.
   A. I, II and III only   C. I and III only
   B. I, III and IV only   D. I, II, III and IV

5. At which of the following are the buyer and seller more likely to shake hands upon completing the real estate transaction?
   A. Escrow closing.
   B. Settlement meeting.

Note: There are no deleted questions in this chapter for readers of
        Real Estate; An Introduction to the Profession.

6. A settlement meeting may take place in the offices of
   I. the real estate agent.   III. a title company.
   II. an attorney.   IV. a lender's office.
   A. I and II only   C. III and IV only
   B. II and III only   D. I, II, III and IV

7. When a real estate settlement is held in escrow,
   I. there is no closing meeting.
   II. the closing process may be conducted by mail.
   A. I only   B. II only   C. Both I and II   D. Neither I nor II

8. At a closing meeting for a real estate sale, which of the following would NOT normally be present?
   A. The purchaser and seller.
   B. The real estate agent who listed the property.
   C. Attorneys for purchaser and seller.
   D. The agent for the casualty insurance company which insures the property.

9. As part of a closing, which of the following documents would be used by a lienholder to indicate the unpaid balance?
   I. Bill of sale.   III. Offset statement.
   II. Title policy.   IV. Beneficiary statement.
   A. I only   C. III and IV only
   B. II only   D. II, III and IV only

10. At a settlement meeting, the buyer would sign which of the following instruments?
    I. The deed to the property.
    II. The mortgage on the property.
    III. The promissory note.
    A. I and II only   C. II and III only
    B. I and III only   D. I, II and III

11. In the course of a settlement meeting, the seller should deliver the deed to the purchaser before the purchaser signs the mortgage note and mortgage. Is this statement correct?
    A. Yes, because the purchaser should not pay for the property until he receives a deed.
    B. Yes, because the purchaser cannot mortgage property which he does not own.
    C. No, because the seller should not convey title until he receives payment.
    D. No, because delivery of the deed should be the last step in the transaction.

12. The purpose of a settlement statement is to
    I. provide an accounting of all funds involved in the transaction.
    II. identify all parties who receive funds from the transaction.
    A. I only   B. II only   C. Both I and II   D. Neither I nor II

13. The final action to be taken to complete a real estate transaction is to
    A. hold a settlement meeting.   C. acknowledge appropriate instruments.
    B. sign all instruments.   D. record appropriate instruments.

14. Which of the following are disbursed at a "dry closing?"
    I. The deed to the buyer.
    II. The money due the seller.
    A. I only   B. II only   C. Both I and II   D. Neither I nor II

15. When a real estate sale is closed through escrow, which of the following
    statements would NOT be correct?
    A. The seller delivers the deed to the escrow agent.
    B. Buyer and seller meet for the closing.
    C. The escrow agent is a neutral third party.
    D. Funds due from the buyer are paid to the escrow agent.

16. Which of the following may serve as an escrow agent?
    A. A title company.   C. An independent escrow company.
    B. A bank.   D. All of the above.

17. Barnes sold his home to Hyatt through broker Quinn. The sale is to be
    settled through escrow. The escrow agent would be selected by
    A. Barnes.   C. Quinn.
    B. Hyatt.   D. Mutual agreement between Barnes and
                                      Hyatt.

18. In most states in which title transfers are handled in escrow, the escrow
    agent must be
    I. bonded.
    II. licensed.
    A. I only   B. II only   C. Both I and II   D. Neither I nor II

19. While a buyer's funds are held by the escrow agent, they are kept
    A. in a trust account.
    B. in a safe deposit vault in cash.
    C. uncashed in a safe deposit vault.
    D. uncashed under lock and key in the escrow office.

20. The instructions to the escrow agent
    I. detail each party's obligations in the transaction.
    II. must be signed by both buyer and seller.
    A. I only   B. II only   C. Both I and II   D. Neither I nor II

21. Settlement of the sale of Reina's home to Hill is being handled by the
    Guaranty Escrow Company. Which of the following duties would the escrow
    agent NOT perform?
    A. Preparation of escrow instructions.
    B. Ordering of a title search.
    C. Preparation of the purchase agreement.
    D. Obtaining title insurance.

22. When a real estate transaction is handled in escrow, the need for which of the following is eliminated?
    I. Buyer and/or seller to employ an attorney.
    II. Either party to engage a real estate broker.
    A. I only   B. II only   C. Both I and II   D. Neither I nor II

23. In an escrow closing, funds are disbursed
    I.   when all escrow papers have been signed.
    II. as soon as the buyer brings his money in.
    III. after necessary recordings take place.
    IV. by the escrow agent.
    A. II only   C. II and IV only
    B. I and IV only   D. III and IV only

24. In the escrow closing method, the closing, delivery of title and recordation take place
    A. at separate times.   C. as each document is signed.
    B. at the same time.   D. as each document is received into escrow.

25. In an escrow closing, the escrow agent serves as agent for
    I. the buyer.
    II. the seller.
    A. I only   B. II only   C. Both I and II   D. Neither I nor II

26. One advantage of the escrow closing method is that it can eliminate
    I. personal confrontation between buyer and seller.
    II. the need for an attorney.
    A. I only   B. II only   C. Both I and II   D. Neither I nor II

27. In addition to the closing of sales of real property through standard purchase agreements, escrows can be used when a
    I.   property is being refinanced.
    II. mortgage loan is being paid off.
    III. property is being sold under an installment contract.
    A. I and III only   C. I and II only
    B. II and III only   D. I, II and III

28. What is the proper sequence for carrying out the following steps in completing the settlement of a sale of real property?
    I.   Purchaser pays in funds needed to close the sale.
    II. Seller delivers a deed to the property.
    III. Purchaser signs mortgage note and mortgage.
    IV. Deed and mortgage are recorded.
    V.   Purchaser and seller are given settlement statements.
    A. III, II, I, IV, V   C. I, III, II, V, IV
    B. II, III, I, V, IV   D. II, I, III, V, IV

29. Farah sells her home to Rossi through broker Timms. The settlement date will be chosen by
    A. Farah.   C. Timms.
    B. Rossi.   D. Mutual agreement between Farah and Rossi.

30. When a home is sold and a new loan by an institutional lender is required to complete the transaction, the typical time between purchase contract signing and settlement will most likely be
    A. 0--29 days.   C. 61--120 days.
    B. 30--60 days.   D. over 120 days.

31. By itself and without supporting language, the inclusion of the phrase "Time is of the essence" in a real estate purchase contract most nearly means the
    A. sale must settle on time or it is automatically void.
    B. buyer can rescind the deal if the closing does not take place on time.
    C. seller can rescind the deal if the closing does not take place on time.
    D. parties are expected to close on time but that reasonable delays for reasonable reasons will probably be tolerated.

32. If the parties to a real estate purchase contract find that it cannot be accomplished and agree orally to simply drop it with no further liability to either party, should they also sign mutual release papers?
    A. Yes, because the contract must be rescinded in writing.
    B. Yes, but only one party need sign.
    C. No, because it can be rescinded orally.
    D. No, because inaction is enough to rescind it.

33. Owner Adam and buyer Baker sign a real estate purchase contract with the closing to take place in 45 days. Before the closing Adam gets a better offer on the property. Can Adam accept the better offer?
      I. Yes, because property can always be sold to the highest bidder.
     II. Yes, if Adam and Baker rescind their contract.
    III. No, because Adam is committed to Baker.
     IV. No, because the closing has not taken place.
    A. I only   B. III only   C. IV only   D. II and III only

34. Among the items to be prorated at a settlement or escrow closing are
      I. taxes.
     II. rents from income producing properties.
    A. I only   B. II only   C. Both I and II   D. Neither I nor II

35. Prorations of items in a real estate closing are made usually as of the date of
      I. signing of the sales contract.
     II. title transfer.
    A. I only   B. II only   C. Both I and II   D. Neither I nor II

36. In a typical closing, insurance prorations will usually be
    A. a credit to the seller and an expense to the buyer.
    B. a credit to the buyer and an expense to the seller.
    C. a credit to the seller and a credit to the buyer.
    D. an expense to the buyer and an expense to the seller.

37. Brown sold his home to Green, and closing took place on June 18. Green agreed to assume Brown's hazard insurance policy, which was effective as of November 13 of the previous year. The premium had been paid in advance for one year from the effective date of the policy. Prorations are made on the basis of 30 day months, with the buyer responsible for the day of closing. Which of the following statements is true? The annual premium on the policy was $194.40.
    A. Green would be charged $78.30.
    B. Brown would be credited $116.10.
    C. Green would be credited $78.30.
    D. Green would be charged $194.40.

38. In the above transaction, Green agreed to assume Brown's 8% loan, having a balance of $36,720 as of June 1. Interest on this loan would be prorated as follows:
    A. Interest of $138.72 would be charged to Green.
    B. Interest of $106.08 would be charged to Green.
    C. Interest of $138.72 would be charged to Brown.
    D. Interest of $106.08 would be charged to Brown.

39. Rents are customarily prorated on the basis of
     I. 30-day months.
    II. the actual number of days in the month.
   III. a 360-day year.
    A. I only   C. I and III only
    B. II only   D. Neither I, II nor III

40. A property on which the annual taxes are $662.40 was sold and settlement will take place on April 14. The taxes in this community are on a calendar year basis and not yet paid. Based on 30-day months and charging the buyer with the day of closing, the proration will be as follows:
    A. Charge buyer $472.88.   C. Credit buyer $472.88.
    B. Charge seller $189.52.   D. Credit seller $189.52.

41. Taxes of $1,320 were paid in advance for the full calendar year. The property was sold and closing took place on August 16. Purchaser was responsible for the day of closing. Taxes would be prorated as follows:
    A. Debit purchaser $495, credit seller $825.
    B. Debit seller $825, credit purchaser $495.
    C. Debit seller $495, credit purchaser $825.
    D. Debit purchaser $495, credit seller $495.

42. Marquez is obtaining a new loan to buy a home. Closing will take place on December 5, and loan payments are to fall on the first of each month. To accomplish this, the interest proration on this loan will be a
    A. charge to the lender and a credit to Marquez, prorated forward.
    B. charge to Marquez and a credit to the lender, prorated forward.
    C. charge to the lender and a credit to Marquez, prorated backward.
    D. charge to Marquez and a credit to the lender, prorated backward.

43. Prorated items at a closing may be prorated as of
     I. the closing date.
    II. any date agreed upon by purchaser and seller.
    A. I only   B. II only   C. Both I and II   D. Neither I nor II

44. There is a street improvement assessment currently against Pickett's house. If Pickett sells
    A. by law Pickett must pay the assessment in full as part of the settlement.
    B. by law the buyer must pay the assessment in full at settlement.
    C. by law the buyer must assume the assessment.
    D. Pickett and the buyer can negotiate as to which of them will pay the assessment.

45. All of the following must comply with the provisions of the Real Estate Settlement Practices Act EXCEPT:
    A. sales financed by means of an FHA-insured loan.
    B. sales financed by an installment contract.
    C. a sale financed by means of a VA-guaranteed loan.
    D. all home financing through a lender who invests more than a million dollars a year in residential loans.

46. The Browns sold their home, which they owned free and clear. They accepted a down payment of 25% of the purchase price, and carried back a note and mortgage for the remainder. Would the provisions of RESPA apply to the Browns?
    A. Yes, because they carried back a mortgage.
    B. Yes, because they took less than 30% down.
    C. No, because no federally-related lender was involved.
    D. No, because this was the sale of a home by its owners.

47. RESPA prohibits, among other things,
    I. kickbacks and/or fees for services not actually performed during the closing process.
    II. the buyer from selecting his own title insurance company.
    A. I only   B. II only   C. Both I and II   D. Neither I nor II

48. RESPA
    I. prohibits the seller from requiring that the buyer purchase title insurance from a particular title company.
    II. requires that each settlement fee charged be for a justifiable service rendered.
    A. I only   B. II only   C. Both I and II   D. Neither I nor II

49. The amount of advance tax and insurance payments collected at closing by a lender for deposit in an impound or escrow account
    I. is regulated by RESPA.
    II. is limited to the owner's share of accrued taxes prior to closing, plus one-sixth of the next year's estimated tax and insurance payments.
    A. I only   B. II only   C. Both I and II   D. Neither I nor II

50. Under the provisions of RESPA,
    I. the buyer must be given an estimate of closing charges and costs in advance of closing.
    II. payments outside of escrow are prohibited.
    A. I only.   B. II only.   C. Both I and II.   D. Neither I nor II.

Settlement Problems

1. The seller pays 70% of closing costs and the buyer pays the balance. If closing costs are $540, how much more does the seller pay than the buyer?

$ _____

2. A two-family flat rented for $300 for one unit and $450 for the other. Both rentals were due on the first of each month. Property was to be closed on November 15 with the seller responsible for the day of closing. Both units were paid up. Would the seller be debited or credited?

_____ How much? $ _____

3. Taxes of $500 per year are on a calendar basis and are paid for the current year. The property is sold for $35,000. Settlement will be on May 1. Your commission is 6%. The mortgage balance is $22,790 and interest has been paid to May 1. Disregarding miscellaneous charges, how much will the owner receive at the settlement?

$ _____

4. An insurance policy was written on July 10, 1986, for a three-year term. The owner saved 30% of a year's premium by buying it for a three-year term. The amount of the policy was $96,000 and was written based upon an annual premium of 21 cents per $100. What proration of the premium would be due the seller if settlement was held on October 20, 1987?

$_____

5. There is a principal balance of $9,000 on a mortgage. The interest rate is 7 1/2% per annum. The taxes and insurance total $540 per year. The monthly payment is $130, covering interest, taxes and insurance and the balance is applied to reduce the principal. What is the principal balance after the monthly payment is made?

$_____

6. At closing, on November 18, a buyer assumes the existing second mortgage of $12,000. Interest at 10% per annum has been paid up to and including October 31st. Prorate the amount of interest that will be credited to the buyer. (Use a 30-day month and charge the buyer with the day of closing.)

$_____

7. County taxes of $300 have been paid through the end of the year. School taxes of $540 have been paid through next June 30. Settlement is held on November 1 and belongs to the buyer. How much proration credit is due the seller?

$_____

8. June 11 is settlement day on a 10-unit apartment building. Each unit rents for $600 per month, and all but one tenant has paid for June. If the buyer is responsible for the day of settlement, who would be debited and who would be credited, and how much?

Buyer _____ $_____

Seller _____ $_____

Settlement Worksheet

Use the data given below to prepare the settlement statement worksheet on the opposite page. Follow the instructions given in the problem, regardless of the law or custom in your state. You are to determine the dollar amounts of prorated items, and certain other items where the dollar amount is not stated in the problem. Calculate all prorations on the basis of 30-day months, and 360-day years, with the day of settlement accruing to and/or being the responsibility of the purchaser.

Date of settlement: July 16, 19__.

DATA:

1.	Purchase price	$62,500
2.	New first mortgage loan	80% of purchase price
3.	Hazard insurance, new policy	$148
4.	Earnest money deposit with contract of sale	$3,000
5.	Mortgage loan payoff, seller's existing loan	$31,211
6.	Taxes, Jan. 1--Dec. 31, not yet paid	$775, to be prorated
7.	Agent's commission	6% of purchase price
8.	Preparation of deed	$25, paid by seller
9.	Title examination (charge seller)	1/2 of 1% of purchase price
10.	Title insurance, owner's and mortgagee's policy (charge buyer)	$2.00/$1,000 of purchase price
11.	Preparation of carryback mortgage	$25, charge buyer
12.	Loan origination fee on first mtg.	1 1/4% of loan amount
13.	Survey, required by lender	$150, charge buyer
14.	Carryback mortgage given to seller	10% of purchase price
15.	Mortgage insurance premium	$156.25, charge buyer
16.	State transfer tax (buyer pays)	$.20/$100 of purchase price
17.	Recording fees: deed and first mortgage paid by buyer, carryback mortgage and mortgage release paid by seller	$6 each item

	BUYER'S STATEMENT		SELLER'S STATEMENT	
	DEBIT	CREDIT	DEBIT	CREDIT
Debit/Credit totals				
Balance due from buyer				
Balance due to seller				
Totals				

Answers—Chapter 14

Multiple Choice Questions

1. D   Local custom determines whether the day a sale is finalized is referred to as the settlement date, closing date or close of escrow.
   It is never referred to as the completion date.

2. D   Title search, deed preparation, loan arrangements and a check of the
   property taxes must all be completed between the signing of the purchase contract and closing of the sale.

3. D   The buyer's walkthrough is made as a final inspection just prior to
   the closing of a sale.

4. C   During the walkthrough, the buyer should test the heating and air
   conditioning systems, and the plumbing.

5. B   The buyer and seller do not meet during an escrow closing, so could
   not shake hands. They usually do meet at a settlement meeting.

6. D   A settlement meeting may take place at any location that is acceptable to all parties.

7. C   An escrow closing may be conducted by mail, and there is no closing
   meeting.

8. D   The casualty insurance agent will not normally attend a settlement
   meeting, but the purchaser, seller, real estate agent and attorneys
   for both parties will normally attend.

9. C   An offset statement or a beneficiary statement will often be used by
   a lienholder to indicate the unpaid balance. Unpaid liens will not
   be disclosed by a bill of sale. Title insurance will indicate unpaid
   liens, but not the unpaid balance.

10. C   The buyer will sign the mortgage and the promissory note. The deed
    is signed by the seller.

11. B   The purchaser must hold title to the property before he can mortgage
    it, so the deed must be delivered before the mortgage is signed.

12. C   A settlement statement provides an accounting of all funds and iden-
    tifies the parties who are to receive funds from the transaction.

13. D   Recordation of appropriate instruments is the final step in a real
    estate transaction.

14. D   Neither the deed to the buyer nor the funds to the seller are dis-
    bursed at a dry closing.

15. B   The buyer and seller do not meet for settlement when a sale is closed through escrow.

16. D   A title company, bank or an independent escrow company may all serve as an escrow agent.

17. D   The selection of an escrow agent is made by mutual agreement between the buyer and seller. The agent is not a party to this selection.

18. C   Escrow agents must be licensed and bonded in most states where real estate sales are closed through escrow.

19. A   Funds being held by an escrow agent are deposited in a trust account.

20. C   Instructions to the escrow agent detail each party's obligations and must be signed by both buyer and seller.

21. C   The purchase agreement will have been completed before the escrow is opened.

22. D   Settlement by an escrow agent does not eliminate the need for a real estate broker or an attorney.

23. D   In an escrow closing, funds are disbursed by the escrow agent after all necessary recordings have taken place.

24. B   The closing, delivery of title and recordation take place at the same time in an escrow closing.

25. C   The escrow agent serves as an agent for both buyer and seller.

26. A   Escrow closings can eliminate personal confrontations between buyer and seller, but do not eliminate the need for an attorney.

27. D   Escrows can be used when a property is being refinanced, a mortgage loan is being paid off or when a sale is being made by means of an installment contract.

28. B   Step   I.   Seller delivers the deed.
                  II.   Purchaser signs the note and mortgage.
                 III.   Purchaser pays funds needed to close.
                  IV.   Purchaser and seller are given settlement statements.
                   V.   Deed and mortgage are recorded.

29. D   The settlement date is chosen by mutual agreement between purchaser and seller.

30. B   Typically, the settlement will be scheduled for between 30 and 60 days after the signing of a purchase agreement.

31. D   The law will usually tolerate reasonable delays for reasonable reasons, even though the contract contains a "time is of the essence" clause.

32. A   The contract must be rescinded in writing in order to relieve the parties from potential future liability.

33. D   The original contract is legally enforceable. However, the better offer could be accepted if both parties agree to rescind the original contract.

34. C   Taxes and rents from income producing properties are among items prorated at the settlement or escrow closing.

35. B   Prorations are usually made as of the date of title transfer.

36. A   Since the seller has previously paid the insurance premium to a date beyond the closing, the proration will be a credit to the seller and an expense to the buyer.

37. A   The proration would be a charge to the purchaser and a credit to the seller, computed as follows:
Premium of $194.50 divided by 12 months = $16.20/month
$16.20/month divided by 30 days = $.54 per day
June 18 to November 13 = 4 months, 25 days
4 x $16.20 = $64.80
25 x $.54 = $13.50
$64.80 + $13.50 = $78.30 charged to the buyer.

38. C   On July 1 the buyer will pay interest for the entire month of June. However, the seller owned the home the first 17 days of June and therefore owes the buyer 17 days of interest, computed as follows:
$36,720 x .08 ÷ 360 = $8.16 interest per day.
$8.16 x 17 days = $138.72 interest for 17 days.

39. B   Rents are usually prorated on the basis of the actual number of days in the month in which the closing takes place.

40. B   Since the taxes have not been paid, the prorated amount would be a charge to the seller and computed as follows:
Annual taxes of $662.40 divided by 12 months = $55.20 per month
$55.20 per month divided by 30 days = $1.84 per day
January 1 to April 13 = 3 months, 13 days (the day of closing is charged to the buyer)
3 x $55.20 = $165.60; 13 x $1.84 = $23.92
$165.60 + $23.92 = $189.52 charge to seller.

41. D   Prepaid taxes will result in a credit to the seller and a debit to the purchaser. The computation is as follows:
Annual taxes of $1,320 divided by 12 months = $110 per month
August 16 to December 31 = 4.5 months taxes prepaid by the seller
$110 x 4.5 = $495 credit to the seller and debit to the purchaser.

42. B   To accomplish this, Marquez will be charged interest for the remainder of December at the time of closing. The first monthly payment will be due on February 1 for the month of January.

43.   C   Prorated items may be prorated as of the date of closing or any other date agreed upon by the purchaser and seller.

44.   D   Payment for the street assessment can be negotiated by the parties to the contract.

45.   B   Sales financed by means of an installment contract are not covered by the provisions of RESPA.

46.   C   Since no federally-related lender was involved, this sale is not covered by the provisions of RESPA.

47.   A   RESPA prohibits kickbacks or fees for services not actually performed during the closing process, but does not prohibit the buyer from selecting the title insurance company.

48.   C   RESPA prohibits the seller from requiring that the buyer purchase title insurance from a particular title company. RESPA requires that each settlement fee charged be for a justifiable service rendered.

49.   C   RESPA limits tax and insurance escrows required by a lender at closing to the owner's share of accrued taxes prior to closing, plus 1/6th of the next year's estimated tax and insurance payments.

50.   A   RESPA requires that the buyer be given an estimate of closing charges and costs in advance of closing, but does not prohibit payments outside of escrow.

Settlement Problems

1.   70% x $540 = $378   (seller pays)
      30% x $540 = $162   (buyer pays)
                   $216   answer

2. $450 + $300 = $750 total rent paid on November 1 for the month of November
      $750 ÷ 30 = $25 per day
      $25 x 15 days = $375 debit seller, credit buyer

3. $500 ÷ 12 x 8 (remaining months after settlement) = $333.33
      $35,000 x .06 = $2,100 commission
      $35,000 - $22,790 - $2,100 + $333.33 = $10,443.33 answer

4.   1988 yr.   18 mo.   40 day
      1987 yr.   10 mo.   20 day
         1   8   20   = 20.67 mo. remaining after settlement

      $96,000 x $.21/$100 x 2.7 ÷ 36 months x 20.67 months = $312.53 answer.
      (Note that 2.7 is the price of a three-year policy compared to a one-year policy.)

5. $540 ÷ 12 months = $45 monthly payment for taxes and insurance
    $9,000 x .075 ÷ 12 = $56.25 interest this month on the loan
    $130 - $56.25 - $45 = $28.75 principal reduction this month
    $9,000 - $28.75 = $8,971.25 answer

6. Seller owes buyer for the first 17 days of November.
    $12,000 x .10 interest ÷ 360 days per year x 17 days = $56.67 answer

7. County taxes for Nov. and Dec., credit seller 2 months,
    $300 ÷ 12 x 2 = $50
    School taxes for Nov. through June, credit seller 8 months,
    $540 ÷ 12 x 8 = $360
    $50 + $360 = $410 answer

8. There are 20 days in June for which the seller has collected rent on 9
    units that now belongs to the buyer.
    $600 ÷ 30 days = $20 per day per unit.
    20 days x $20 per day x 9 units = $3,600
    Credit the buyer $3,600 and debit the seller $3,600.

		BUYER'S STATEMENT		SELLER'S STATEMENT	
		DEBIT	CREDIT	DEBIT	CREDIT
1.	Purchase price	$62500.00			$62500.00
2.	New first loan proceeds		$50000.00		
3.	Hazard insurance	148.00			
4.	Earnest money deposit		3000.00		
5.	Seller's mtg. loan payoff			$31211.00	
6.	Taxes, prorated		419.79	419.79	
7.	Agent's commission			3750.00	
8.	Preparation of deed			25.00	
9.	Title examination			312.50	
10.	Title insurance	125.00			
11.	Preparation of mortgage	25.00			
12.	Loan origination fee	625.00			
13.	Survey	150.00			
14.	Carryback mtg. to seller		6250.00	6250.00	
15.	Mortgage ins. premium	156.25			
16.	Transfer tax	125.00			
17.	Recording fees	12.00		12.00	
Debit/Credit totals		$63866.25	$59669.79	$41980.29	$62500.00
Balance due from buyer			4196.46		
Balance due to seller				20519.71	
Totals		$63866.25	$63866.25	$62500.00	$62500.00

Real Estate Leases

Chapter 15

1. Which of the following statements regarding a leasehold estate is/are true?
   A. The tenant is known as the lessee.
   B. The landlord holds a reversion during the term of the lease.
   C. The landlord is known as the lessor.
   D. All of the above.

2. A lease for a definite period of time, which terminates when that time has expired, is an estate
   A. for years.   C. at will.
   B. periodic estate.   D. at sufferance.

3. A lease of fixed length that continually renews itself for like periods of time until the lessor or lessee acts to terminate it is
   A. a holdover estate.   C. an estate at will.
   B. a periodic estate.   D. an estate at sufferance.

4. A lease is a
   I. conveyance.
   II. contract.
   A. I only   B. II only   C. Both I and II   D. Neither I nor II

5. Which of the following leases could be enforceable in court, even though it was not in writing?
   I. A two-week lease of a vacation cottage.
   II. A month-to-month lease.
   III. A three-year commercial lease.
   IV. A one year lease on an apartment.
   A. I only   C. II and III only
   B. II only   D. I, II and IV only

Note: If you are reading <u>Real Estate: An Introduction to the Profession</u> you may omit the following questions: 30-32 and 42-56.

6. Flint leased a building to Newton under an agreement which gave Newton the right to occupy the premises for two years, with an option to renew for an additional one-year period. In order to be enforceable, must this lease be in writing and signed by both Flint and Newton?
    A. Yes, because all contracts dealing with real property must be in writing in order to be enforceable.
    B. Yes, because the lease is for a period of time in excess of one year.
    C. No, because oral leases for five years or less are enforceable.
    D. No, because a 2-year oral lease is enforceable.

7. To be valid, which of the following must be in writing and signed?
     I. A month-to-month lease.
    II. A 14 month lease.
    A. I only   B. II only   C. Both I and II   D. Neither I nor II

8. The right of the lessee to uninterrupted use of the leased premises is called
     I. quiet possession.
    II. quiet enjoyment.
    A. I only   B. II only   C. Both I and II   D. Neither I nor II

9. Under the terms of a one-year lease,
     I. the tenant commits to pay a full year's rent, even if he vacates the premises before the year expires.
    II. the landlord commits the property to the tenant for the year of the lease.
    A. I only   B. II only   C. Both I and II   D. Neither I nor II

10. A written lease agreement is still legal even though it fails to include
     I. the terms of the lease.
    II. a property description.
    A. I only   B. II only   C. Both I and II   D. Neither I nor II

11. A written lease agreement is still legal even though it fails to include
     I. the amount of rent to be paid.
    II. a security deposit.
    A. I only   B. II only   C. Both I and II   D. Neither I nor II

12. As compared to a lease for years, a month-to-month lease gives flexibility to the
     I. landlord.
    II. tenant.
    A. I only   B. II only   C. Both I and II   D. Neither I nor II

13. Jack leased an apartment from Bunny under a lease which calls for a total rent of six thousand dollars for the year, but is silent as to when or in what installments the rent is to be paid. Under common law the rent will be due
    A. when Jack takes possession of the premises.
    B. in equal installments on the first day of each month.
    C. when the lease is signed.
    D. at the end of the year.

14. A landlord can charge and a tenant can expect to pay for
    I. damages to the premises by the tenant.
   II. normal wear and tear to the premises by the tenant.
  A. I only   B. II only   C. Both I and II   D. Neither I nor II

15. Bob Short and Bill Tall rent an apartment unit from owner Haf High. Bill dies during the lease term. The lease is still binding upon
    I. Bob.
   II. Haf.
  III. Bill's estate.
  A. I only   C. II only
  B. I and II only   D. I, II and III

16. The word "waive" means to
  A. say "goodbye".   C. surrender.
  B. demand.   D. die naturally.

17. Consumer protection laws and courts place the burden of upkeep and repairs of rented premises on the tenant in
    I. commercial leases.
   II. residential leases.
  A. I only   B. II only   C. Both I and II   D. Neither I nor II

18. Charles installed built-in bookcases in his rented apartment without the landlord's permission. Which of the following statements is NOT true?
  A. The bookcases became fixtures when installed by Charles.
  B. Charles can be held responsible for expenses incurred by the landlord in removing the bookcases upon expiration of the lease.
  C. Charles forfeited his security deposit by installing the bookcases without the landlord's permission.
  D. The bookcases become the property of the landlord upon expiration of the lease.

19. State-enacted landlord-tenant laws tend to
    I. favor the tenant.
   II. strike a reasonable balance between the rights and responsibilities of both parties.
  A. I only   B. II only   C. Both I and II   D. Neither I nor II

20. A lease under which the tenant pays a fixed rent and the landlord pays all the operating expenses is a
  A. net lease.   C. term lease.
  B. fixed lease.   D. gross lease.

21. A lease which calls for specified rental increases at predetermined intervals is known as a
    I. step-up lease.
   II. graduated lease.
  A. I only   B. II only   C. Both I and II   D. Neither I nor II

22. The clause in a lease which allows the landlord to pass along to the tenant certain increases in operating expenses is called
    I. an escalator clause.
    II. a participation clause.
    A. I only   B. II only   C. Both I and II   D. Neither I nor II

23. When the tenant pays a base rent plus some or all of the operating expenses of a property, the result is a
    A. gross lease.   C. percentage lease.
    B. net lease.   D. graduated lease.

24. A lease in which the tenant pays a rent based upon the gross sales made from the rented premises is known as a
    I. percentage lease.
    II. participation lease.
    A. I only   B. II only   C. Both I and II   D. Neither I nor II

25. Which of the following is NOT specifically designed to protect against rising operating costs?
    A. A net lease.   C. An index clause.
    B. An escalator clause.   D. A gross lease.

26. In Barbara's one-year apartment lease, she has a clause that allows her to renew the lease for an additional year at a predetermined rent. This is called
    A. a refusal clause.   C. an assignment clause.
    B. an option clause.   D. a sublease clause.

27. Jane's lease of her apartment is silent as to her right to sublet. May Jane sublet without the landlord's permission?
    A. Yes, because executory contracts may be assigned unless they contain a nonassignment clause.
    B. Yes, because Jane would remain responsible to the landlord under the terms of the lease.
    C. No, because the landlord would have the right to veto any assignment.
    D. No, because landlord-tenants laws prohibit the assignment of a lease without the landlord's permission.

28. Karl signed a one-year lease on an apartment with a rental agency. He sublet the apartment to Kurt, who defaulted on the sublease. Any action entered by the landlord would be against
    I. Karl.   III. both Karl and Kurt.
    II. Kurt.   IV. the rental agent.
    A. I only   B. II only   C. III only   D. I and IV only

29. A sublease constitutes
    I. a novation.
    II. an assignment of rights held under contract.
    A. I only   B. II only   C. Both I and II   D. Neither I nor II

30. Under the terms of a typical ground lease,
    I. the lessor is the fee simple owner of the land.
    II. the lessee pays for and owns the improvements.
    A. I only   B. II only   C. Both I and II   D. Neither I nor II

31. Weldon owns a tract of land on which there is a commercial building and a parking lot. Which of the following may be leased as separate entities?
    I. The commercial building.
    II. The parking lot to a church for use on Sundays only.
    III. The air space above the parking lot.
    IV. The rights to subsurface minerals.
    A. I, II, III and IV   C. I and IV only
    B. I and II only   D. I, III and IV only

32. Which of the following statements is NOT correct with regard to the contract rent and economic rent of a property?
    A. The rent that a tenant must pay the landlord is its contract rent.
    B. At the beginning of the lease, the contract rent is usually the same as the economic rent.
    C. The rent which a property can command in the open market is its economic rent.
    D. The contract rent and the economic rent will remain the same throughout the term of the lease.

33. Nancy's business has prospered and she needs an additional warehouse. She wants a five-year lease with an escape available at the end of two years, and she wants to be able to stay in the building for an additional five years if her business continues to need the space. Additionally, she wants protection against unexpected rent increases. Her real estate agent would look for warehouses whose owners would offer:
    I. gross rent fixed for the life of the lease.
    II. indexed rent.
    III. a two-year lease with an option to renew for three years and an option for five more years.
    IV. a two-year lease with an option to renew for three years followed by an option to buy.
    A. I, III and IV only   C. II and III only
    B. II, III and IV only   D. III and IV only

34. A lease for years may be terminated by
    I. constructive eviction.   III. mutual agreement.
    II. eminent domain.   IV. actual eviction.
    A. II and IV only   C. I, III and IV only
    B. I and III only   D. I, II, III and IV

35. Galvan had a five year lease on a store building which called for the landlord to provide maintenance on the property. Although he notified the landlord on several occasions of a badly leaking roof, the landlord failed to make the necessary repairs. At his option, Galvan could
    I. stop paying rent until the roof was repaired.
    II. terminate the lease by claiming constructive eviction.
    A. I only   B. II only   C. Both I and II   D. Neither I nor II

36. Fred's landlord served Fred with an eviction notice because of his complaints to the housing authority regarding lack of maintenance for his apartment. This eviction was
    I. a retaliatory eviction.
    II. illegal.
    A. I only   B. II only   C. Both I and II   D. Neither I nor II

37. Shawn has a lease on a service station which is being taken by the state highway department under eminent domain for the purpose of widening the highway. The state must pay compensation to
    I. Shawn.
    II. the landlord.
    A. I only   B. II only   C. Both I and II   D. Neither I nor II

38. Enrico has a five-year lease on space in an office building. After this lease was recorded in the public records, the landlord secured a new mortgage on the property, on which he later defaulted. When the lender foreclosed on the property, could Enrico's lease be terminated by the purchaser at foreclosure?
    A. Yes, because the foreclosure of a mortgage terminates any leases on the property.
    B. Yes, because the purchaser at foreclosure would have the option of honoring the lease or not doing so.
    C. No, because mortgage foreclosure has no effect on a valid lease.
    D. No, because the lease was recorded prior to the mortgage.

39. Discrimination in the availability of housing on the basis of race is prohibited by the
    I. Civil Rights Act of 1866.
    II. Fair Housing Act of 1968.
    A. I only   B. II only   C. Both I and II   D. Neither I nor II

40. Vera, a real estate broker, was offered a rental listing by a homeowner who stated that he would not rent the property to a person of certain religious beliefs. Vera should
    A. refuse to accept the listing on these terms.
    B. accept the listing and leave it up to the owner to refuse any offers received from persons of that religion.
    C. accept the listing and steer persons of that religion to other properties.
    D. file a complaint of discrimination against the owner.

41. Under federal law, the owner of one single-family dwelling in which he has resided for ten years, who does not employ an agent and does not use discriminatory advertising, may discriminate in the sale or rental of the property on any of the following bases EXCEPT:
    A. religion.   C. color.
    B. race.   D. national origin.

42. Experience with rent controls generally indicates that rent control
    A. solves more problems than it creates.
    B. creates more problems than it solves.

43. A side effect of rent control has been
    I. black markets in rent-controlled apartments.
    II. conversion of rental units to condominium units.
    A. I only   B. II only   C. Both I and II   D. Neither I nor II

44. An investor who is contemplating building or buying rental housing will
    I. compare market rents with operating costs.
    II. capitalize the net income to determine how much to pay for the building.
    A. I only   B. II only   C. Both I and II   D. Neither I nor II

45. Advertising money for rental housing is best spent on
    I. newspaper classified advertising.
    II. signs and arrows on and near the property.
    III. radio advertising.
    IV. television advertising.
    A. I and III only   C. III only
    B. I and II only   D. I and IV only

46. A lengthy tenant application form
    I. tends to discourage marginally qualified applicants.
    II. provides a basis for checking the applicant's references.
    A. I only   B. II only   C. Both I and II   D. Neither I nor II

47. State and local laws which restrict or prohibit discrimination in the availability of rental housing may
    I. be more restrictive than federal statutes.
    II. prohibit additional forms of discrimination.
    A. I only   B. II only   C. Both I and II   D. Neither I nor II

48. Property owners can attract tenants in a soft rental market by
    I. reductions in rent.
    II. rent concessions.
    A. I only   B. II only   C. Both I and II   D. Neither I nor II

49. To retain tenants, a property manager should think of them as
    A. permanent residents, even though turnover is expected.
    B. temporary residents who will leave at the expiration of their lease.

50. A property manager can do much to establish and maintain good relations with tenants through
    I. prompt attention to repairs and maintenance.
    II. good communications with the tenants.
    A. I only   B. II only   C. Both I and II   D. Neither I nor II

51. Before sending a tenant a notice when his rent payment is not received on time, a property manager will usually wait
    A. five days.   C. fifteen days.
    B. ten days.   D. thirty days.

52. Generally, today's laws regarding eviction of a tenant for non-payment of rents, as compared to those in the past, favor the
    A. tenant.
    B. landlord.

53. The best defense against losses from uncollected rent is
    A. a threat of legal action against the delinquent tenant.
    B. careful tenant selection, good service and a businesslike policy on rent collection.

54. An on-site resident manager serves as
    I. general superintendent of the property.
    II. the eyes and ears of the property management company.
    A. I only   B. II only   C. Both I and II   D. Neither I nor II

55. Generally, one on-site property manager can handle
    A. approximately 200 units.   C. approximately 100 units.
    B. approximately 150 units.   D. approximately 50-60 units.

56. Which of the following would be classified as off-site management?
    A. Accounting.
    B. Handling tenant complaints.
    C. Showing vacant space to prospective tenants.
    D. Maintenance work.

57. A successful apartment manager needs to be
    I. experienced in managing people and money.
    II. handy with tools.
    A. I only   B. II only   C. Both I and II   D. Neither I nor II

58. The Institute of Real Estate Management is a
    I. government agency.
    II. professional property management organization.
    A. I only   B. II only   C. Both I and II   D. Neither I nor II

59. The Institute of Real Estate Management awards the designation
    I. REM.
    II. CPM.
    A. I only   B. II only   C. Both I and II   D. Neither I nor II

60. A person who holds the designation Systems Maintenance Administrator has
    completed required courses offered by the
    A. Building Owners and Managers Institute.
    B. Institute of Real Estate Management.

Property Management Problems

1. Pat leased a retail store to Mike on a percentage basis. The lease calls for a minimum monthly rental of $5,000 plus 4% of the gross yearly business over $600,000. How much rent would Pat receive yearly from Mike, if Mike did a gross yearly business of $1,100,000?

$_____

2. A broker and a condominium unit owner enter into a property management agreement under which the broker is to receive as commission 1/3 of the first month's rent of $600 to find a tenant plus 4% of monthly gross rent in subsequent months. How much has the broker earned in total commissions after a period of 14 months, if he rents the unit and it remains occupied?

$_____

3. A city has a rent control law that says that rents may only be increased monthly by 2 1/4% of the cost of improvements. One landlord made improvements of $2,000 and raised the rent from $405 to $455. How much over the rent control did he go?

$_____

4. You have the management contract on a three-unit apartment house building
    and are to receive 6% of the gross rentals as commission. You collect
    for one month as follows: $500 for each of two units; $400 for one unit;
    with $140 paid out in repairs. How much was the net amount paid to the
    owner's account that month?

$_____

5. Broker Bahn has just negotiated a lease with options on a warehouse. The
    lease rent is $8,000 per month for the first two years; followed by an
    option to renew at $9,000 per month for three years; followed by an
    option to buy the property for $1,200,000. Broker Bahn charges 3% of the
    gross rent for negotiating leases and 3% on sales. If the tenant rents
    for five years and then buys, what is the total commission earned by
    Broker Bahn?

$_____

Answers—Chapter 15

Multiple Choice Questions

1. D   The landlord is the lessor and the tenant is the lessee. The land-
          lord's right to regain control and possession of the premises upon
          termination of the lease is known as a reversion.

2. A   Any lease which contains a definite termination date is classified as
          an estate for years.

3. B   A periodic estate continually renews itself until terminated by
          either lessee or lessor.

4. C   A lease conveys certain rights in the leased premises to the lessor
          and contains all the elements of a contract.

5. D   A lease of more than one year must be in writing in order to be
          enforceable. As a rule, a two-week lease, a month-to-month lease
          and a lease for one year are enforceable even though not in writing.

6. B   In order to be enforceable, a lease for more than one year must be
          in writing.

7. B   A month-to-month lease is enforceable even though not in writing, but
          a lease for more than one year must be in writing in order to be
          enforceable.

8. B   A tenant's right to uninterrupted use of the leased premises is known
          as quiet enjoyment.

9. C   A lease for one year commits the tenant to a full year's rent and the
          landlord to granting the tenant occupancy for the full year.

10. D   A lease must contain the terms of the agreement between landlord and
          tenant and a description of the property in order to be legal.

11. B   A lease must contain a statement of the amount of rent to be paid but
          a security deposit is not essential.

12. C   A month-to-month lease gives flexibility to both landlord and tenant.

13. D   Unless the lease calls for rent to be paid in advance, it is not due
          until the end of the lease.

14. A   A tenant is held responsible for damage to the premises, but not for
          normal wear and tear.

15. D   The death of either party does not terminate a lease; it remains binding upon the estate of the deceased and all other parties to the lease.

16. C   The term "waive" means to surrender, abandon or relinquish.

17. A   The burden of upkeep and repairs of rented premises falls upon the tenant in commercial leases but not in residential leases.

18. C   The bookcases became fixtures when installed in a permanent manner and became the property of the landlord. The tenant can be held responsible for expenses incurred in their removal, but their installation would not automatically cause forfeiture of the tenant's security deposit.

19. B   State-enacted landlord-tenant laws tend to strike a reasonable balance between the rights and responsibilities of both parties.

20. D   A gross lease is one in which the tenant pays a fixed rent and the landlord pays all the operating expenses.

21. C   The terms "step-up lease" and "graduated lease" are both used to denote a lease which calls for specified rental increases at predetermined intervals.

22. C   The terms "escalator clause" or "participation clause" refer to contract language whereby the landlord may pass along to the tenant increases in operating expenses.

23. B   Under a net lease, the tenant agrees to pay some or all of the operating expenses of the property in addition to a base rent.

24. A   A percentage lease calls for rent to be paid all or in part in the form of a percentage of the gross sales made from the premises.

25. D   Under the terms of a gross lease the landlord has no automatic protection against rising operating costs, but could be so protected by the terms of a net lease, an escalator clause or an index clause.

26. B   An option clause permits the tenant to renew the lease for an additional period at a predetermined rent.

27. A   A lease is an executory contract and may be assigned unless it contains a nonassignment clause.

28. A   When a contract is assigned, the assignor remains solely liable for its terms and obligations. The assignee is liable to the assignor.

29. B   The substitution of new parties to an existing contract is novation; a sublease is an assignment of contract rights.

30. C   Typically, under a ground lease, the lessor holds fee simple title to the land and the lessee pays for and owns the improvements.

31. A   Any of the entities may be leased separately, or in combination with one another.

32. D   The contract rent and the economic rent are usually the same at the beginning of a lease, but the economic rent may increase or decrease during the term of the lease.

33. A   A gross rent lease for two years with an option to renew at the end of two years followed by an option to either renew or buy the property best fulfills Nancy's objective. She would want to avoid an indexed lease.

34. D   A lease for years may be terminated by constructive eviction, actual eviction, mutual agreement of the parties or by eminent domain.

35. B   The landlord's inaction constituted constructive eviction and makes the lease terminable at the tenant's option. The tenant is not relieved of the obligation to pay rent if he continues to remain in possession of the premises.

36. C   The landlord's actions constituted a retaliatory eviction and are illegal.

37. C   The government's exercise of its power of eminent domain brought damage to both the landlord and the tenant and both are entitled to compensation.

38. D   Because the lease was recorded prior to the mortgage, it is not affected by foreclosure of the mortgage, but remains binding upon the purchaser at foreclosure.

39. C   Both the Civil Rights Act of 1866 and the Fair Housing Act of 1968 prohibit discrimination in housing on the basis of race.

40. A   An agent who accepted a listing on these terms would be in violation of the Fair Housing Act of 1968.

41. B   The Fair Housing Act of 1968 makes an exception for an owner who meets these tests, but the Civil Rights Act of 1866 prohibits racial discrimination without any exceptions.

42. B   Rent controls tend to create more problems than they solve.

43. C   Rent controls have tended to create black markets in rent-controlled apartments, and conversion of rental properties into condominiums.

44. C   Comparison of market rents with operating costs and capitalization of net income to determine value are fundamental investment decisions in the purchase of income-producing properties.

45. B   In promoting rental housing, newspaper advertising and signs and arrows on and near the property are more cost-efficient forms of advertising than radio or television advertising.

46. C   A lengthy tenant application form tends to discourage marginally qualified tenants and also provides a basis for checking references.

47. C   State and local fair housing laws tend to be more restrictive than federal laws by containing prohibitions not included in the federal statutes.

48. C   Rent reductions and/or concessions are used to attract tenants in a soft rental market.

49. A   The treatment of tenants as permanent residents, even though turnover is expected, tends to increase tenant retention.

50. C   Good communication with tenants and prompt attention to repairs and maintenance are fundamental to good tenant relations.

51. A   Five days prior to notification of delinquent rents is the accepted waiting period.

52. A   Consumer protection laws in recent years have tended to favor the tenant over the landlord.

53. B   Careful tenant selection, good service and a businesslike policy of rent collection are more effective than threats of legal action in reducing losses from uncollected rents.

54. C   An on-site resident manager serves both as a general superintendent of the property and as the eyes and ears of the property management company.

55. D   As a rule of thumb, one on-site manager can handle 50-60 units without assistance.

56. A   Accounting is usually handled off-site; handling tenant complaints, showing vacancies to prospective tenants and maintenance are handled on-site.

57. C   Successful property managers tend to be experienced in handling people and money and handy with tools.

58. B   The Institute of Real Estate Management is a professional property management organization within the National Association of Realtors.

59. B   The designation CPM is an abbreviation for Certified Property Manager, and is awarded by the IREM.

60. A   The Building Owners and Managers Institute confers the designation Systems Maintenance Administrator upon members who have completed required courses offered by the institute.

Property Management Problems

1. ($1,100,000 - $600,000) x .04 = $20,000 rent on the overage
    $5,000 x 12 months = $60,000 base rent
    $60,000 + $20,000 = $80,000 rent for the year

2. ($600 ÷ 3) + ($600 x .04 x 13 months) = $512 answer

3. $2,000 x .0225 = $45.00 allowed rental increase
    $405 + $45 = $450 allowed new rent
    $455 - $450 = $5 over what law allows

4. (2 x $500 + $400) x .06 = $84 commission
    2 x $500 + $400 - $84 - $140 = $1,176 answer

5. $8,000 x 12 months x 2 years x .03 = $ 5,760 first 2 years
    $9,000 x 12 months x 3 years x .03 = $ 9,720 next 3 years
    $1,200,000 x .03 = $36,000 sale
    Total = $51,480 commission

Real Estate Appraisal

Chapter 16

1. Which of the following is NOT one of the three standard approaches to the appraisal of real property?
   A. Income approach.
   B. Cost approach.
   C. Assessment approach.
   D. Market approach.

2. In order to determine the market value of a parcel of real property, the appraiser assumes that
   I. payment will be made in cash or its equivalent.
   II. a reasonable time will be allowed for market exposure.
   III. both buyer and seller will be fully informed.
   IV. neither buyer nor seller are under any abnormal pressure to buy or or sell.
   V. the title to the property is marketable.
   A. II, III, IV and V only
   B. I, II, III and IV only
   C. I, II, IV and V only
   D. I, II, III, IV and V

3. Generally, in the application of the market comparison approach to value determination, a real estate appraiser looks for data on sales of comparable properties which have occurred within the last
   A. six months.
   B. ten days.
   C. year.
   D. thirty days.

4. To apply the market data approach, a real estate appraiser must collect all the following data on each comparable sale EXCEPT:
   A. date of sale.
   B. marketability of title.
   C. financing terms.
   D. sale price.

Note: If you are reading <u>Real Estate: An Introduction to the Profession</u> you may omit the following questions: 63-66.

5. Should an appraiser personally inspect each property used as a comparable sale in making an appraisal by the market comparison approach?
   A. Yes, because physical changes may have occurred since the time of the sale of the comparable.
   B. Yes, to avoid errors in making his appraisal.
   C. No, because the present physical condition of the comparable property is irrelevant to the appraisal.
   D. No, because a physical inspection of the property is not relevant to the appraisal of the subject property.

6. In making an appraisal by the market approach, an appraiser would choose which of the following as a comparable?
   A. A similar home with equal amenities which was listed for sale by a real estate broker but not yet sold.
   B. A nearly identical home with equal amenities which was sold last week at mortgage foreclosure.
   C. A similar home with equal amenities which was sold under market conditions six months ago.
   D. A similar home donated last week to a charitable organization with a life estate retained by the donor.

7. In checking the price for which a property was sold as a basis for establishing comparables in an appraisal, you receive the following information: from conveyance tax paid on the deed, an indicated price of $48,500; from a title insurance company's records, a sale price of $47,500; from a neighbor who was a friend of the seller, a sale price of $49,500; and from an in-law visiting the buyer, a sale price of $45,000. To which of the above sources would you give more credence?
   A. The neighbor.
   B. Tax records.
   C. The title insurance company's records.
   D. The in-law.

8. In making an appraisal by the market approach, you find two comparable sales. One was sold eight months ago and the sale was settled 30 days ago. The other was sold three months ago and the sale was settled two months ago. All other things being equal, to which would you give the most weight in making your appraisal?
   A. The most recent sale.
   B. The most recent settlement.

9. When the supply of comparable properties exceeds an appraiser's needs, he should
   A. choose those that require the most adjustments.
   B. choose those that require the fewest adjustments.
   C. utilize all comparables he can find.
   D. choose the one best comparable and discard all the others.

10. Able listed his home for sale at a price of $100,000 and received an offer to purchase at a price of $95,000 from a qualified prospect. Which of the following statements are correct?
    I.   The probable upper limit of value on this property is approximately $100,000.
    II. The lower limit of value for this property is probably about $95,000.
    III. The market value of the property is probably between $95,000 and $100,000.
    IV. Neither the listed price nor the offered price can be used as an indication of value for the property.
    A. III only   B. II only   C. I, II and III only   D. IV only

11. Adjustments for differences between the subject property and the comparable property are made to
    A. the subject property.
    B. the comparable property.
    C. either property as indicated by the appraiser's findings.
    D. the appraiser's final estimate of the value of the subject property.

12. In making a market comparison approach appraisal of a residence, the appraiser would NOT make any adjustments for
    A. date of sale of the comparable.
    B. terms of sale of the comparable.
    C. improvements made to a comparable after it was sold.
    D. amenities.

13. In making an appraisal of a single family residence in a neighborhood where values have risen at an average rate of 6 per cent per year over the past two years, what amount would be added to the value of a comparable which was sold six months ago for $80,000?
    A. $240.   C. $480.
    B. $4,800.   D. $2,400.

14. In the process of appraising an office building, an appraiser has located a comparable office building which is 240 square feet larger than the subject property. The appraiser estimates construction costs to be $80 per square foot, and depreciation to be approximately 10 per cent. Which of the following adjustments would be made based on this information?
    A. The value of the comparable would be reduced by $17,280.
    B. The value of the subject property would be increased by $19,200.
    C. The value of the comparable would be reduced by $19,200.
    D. The value of the subject property would be increased by $17,280.

15. In the market comparison approach to appraisal, adjustments must be made for differences in
    I.   building age, condition and quality.
    II. landscaping, lot features and location.
    III. terms and conditions of sale.
    IV. acquisition costs to the present owner.
    A. I, II, III and IV   C. II and III only
    B. I and II only   D. I, II and III only

16. In a temperate climate not subject to extreme weather conditions, is any adjustment necessary in appraising a house which has a two-car garage as compared to a similar house with a two-car carport?
   A. No, as long as they both accommodate two cars.
   B. No, because both provide adequate shelter for cars.
   C. Yes, if buyers will pay more for a garage.
   D. Yes, because a garage costs more to build than a carport.

17. Two comparables are identical tract type homes in the same subdivision, built in the same year and both sold on resale within 30 days of one another. Lots are of identical value. Comparable #1 was equipped with standard builder's model range and refrigerator, while Comparable #2 had deluxe appliances which cost $1,000 extra when the homes were new. The home with the deluxe appliances was sold for $500 more than the other. The subject property has the standard builder's models.
   I. No adjustments would be made to Comparable #1.
   II. A $500 adjustment would be made to Comparable #2.
   A. I only   B. II only   C. Both I and II   D. Neither I nor II

18. Adjustments for advantageous financing would be made in the
   I. market comparison approach to appraisal.
   II. cost approach to appraisal.
   A. I only   B. II only   C. Both I and II   D. Neither I nor II

19. After all adjustments are made to a comparable property, its comparative value for appraisal purposes is known as its
   A. adjusted market price.   C. amended market price.
   B. indicated market value.   D. revised market price.

20. In completing an appraisal by the market comparison approach, the process by which comparables are weighted according to similarity to the subject property is known as the
   A. adjustment process.   C. reconciliation process.
   B. correlation process.   D. weighting process.

21. The value of vacant land is commonly stated in any of the following terms EXCEPT value per
   A. square foot.   C. front foot.
   B. acre.   D. square yard.

22. Two vacant lots adjacent to one another are being appraised. They each have the same street frontage, but one is twice the depth of the other. The lot with the greater depth will be appraised at
   I.   twice the value of the other.
   II. the same value as the other.
   III. half the value of the other.
   A. I only   B. II only   C. III only   D. Neither I nor II nor III

23. In making a market comparison appraisal of vacant lots,
   A. only lots of similar zoning should be employed.
   B. zoning is not important, since zoning laws allow for change in zoning.
   C. lots with different zoning may be used in a pinch.
   D. lots with different zoning should be used.

24. A competitive market analysis provides a listing agent with
    I. a guide to the probable sale price of a property.
   II. an effective tool for listing a property at a price that will bring about a sale.
 III. a basis for determining whether to accept a listing.
  A. I, II and III
  B. II only
  C. I and III only
  D. I and II only

25. Sales information from a real estate agent's multiple listing book would be used with
    I. the standard market comparison method.
   II. the competitive market analysis method.
  A. I only   B. II only   C. Both I and II   D. Neither I nor II

26. To evaluate a home in order to list it for sale, a real estate agent could use the
    I. standard market comparison method.
   II. competitive market analysis method.
  A. I only   B. II only   C. Both I and II   D. Neither I nor II

27. Seller motivation is considered most in the
  A. income approach.
  B. cost approach.
  C. gross rent multiplier method.
  D. competitive market analysis method.

28. Which of the following approaches is most likely to provide only a rough estimate of the value of a rental property?
  A. Cost approach.
  B. Income approach.
  C. Market comparison approach.
  D. Gross rent multiplier.

29. You are appraising a ten-unit apartment building where each unit rents for $450 per month. Three similar apartment buildings have recently sold at the following prices and with the monthly total building rents as shown. Using the gross rent multiplier method, what gross rent multiplier should you apply to the ten-unit building you are appraising?

Sales price	Total monthly rent
$450,000	$5,000
$382,500	$4,250
$427,500	$4,750

  A. 0.0111
  B. 7.5
  C. 9.0
  D. 90.0

30. Same facts as in question 29 above. Using the gross rent multiplier method, what is the value of the ten-unit building you are appraising?
  A. $33,750
  B. $337,500
  C. $405,000
  D. $486,000

31. An appraisal by the cost approach will include all of the following EXCEPT:
  A. an estimate of the value of the land as if it were vacant.
  B. reproduction or replacement cost of the buildings.
  C. depreciation on the land.
  D. depreciation on the improvements.

32. In appraising an historically significant residence built in the Victorian era using the cost approach, an appraiser will probably appraise it on the basis of its
   A. reproduction cost.   C. replacement cost.
   B. restoration cost.   D. reconstruction cost.

33. What would be the indicated value of a new residence rectangular in shape, which measured 40 feet by 45 feet, with an attached garage which measured 20 feet by 20 feet, if construction costs for the dwelling were $60 per square foot and for the garage $30 per square foot?
   A. $108,000.   C. $112,000.
   B. $120,000.   D. $118,000.

34. An appraiser is valuing a residence located in an industrial neighborhood. The residence contains four bedrooms, one bath, and is presently in need of a new roof. The property exhibits all the following EXCEPT:
   A. physical deterioration.
   B. economic obsolescence on the building.
   C. functional obsolescence on the building.
   D. economic obsolescence on the land.

35. A residence which is in need of painting, and which has a poorly designed floor plan suffers from
    I. curable depreciation.
   II. incurable depreciation.
   A. I only   B. II only   C. Both I and II   D. Neither I nor II

36. Which of the following results from factors outside the property?
   A. Functional obsolescence.   C. Economic obsolescence.
   B. Physical deterioration.   D. None of the above.

37. In applying the income approach to real property, the appraiser considers which of the following?
   A. The amount of income produced by the property.
   B. The rate of return demanded by investors.
   C. How long the investment will produce income.
   D. All of the above.

38. The conversion of future income into present value is known as
   A. capitalization.   C. hypothecation.
   B. amortization.   D. appreciation.

39. Arthur, Bruce, Charles and David are students in an appraisal course. In completing a problem using the income approach, Arthur uses a capitalization rate of 8.5 per cent, Bruce 9.0 per cent, Charles 9.5 per cent, and David 10.0 per cent. Which person will produce the highest indicated value for the property?
   A. Arthur.   C. Charles.
   B. Bruce.   D. David.

40. What would be the indicated value of a property having an income of $1,200 per month, using a capitalization rate of 11 per cent, and rounded to the nearest $100 increment?
    A. $10,900   C. $130,900
    B. $15,400   D. $109,900

41. The rents that a property can be expected to produce on an annual basis may be referred to as the
    I. projected gross income.
    II. scheduled gross income.
    A. I only   B. II only   C. Both I and II   D. Neither I nor II

42. In projecting the gross income and expenses of a building, the best starting point is
    A. its projected income and expenses for the current year.
    B. the actual record of income and expenses for the past three to five years.
    C. the projected income for the next three to five years.
    D. the projected income for the remaining economic life of the building.

43. In income and expense forecasting, a small error in income projections results in
    A. a larger error in the market value of the property.
    B. an equal error in the market value of the property.
    C. a smaller error in the market value of the property.
    D. no error in the market value of the property.

44. A projected annual operating statement for a rented building would NOT include
    A. property taxes.   C. capital improvements.
    B. insurance premiums.   D. utilities.

45. Reserves for replacement are established for items in a building that must be replaced
    A. annually.
    B. more than once in the building's life, but not annually.
    C. only once during the life of the building.
    D. at unpredictable intervals during the building's life.

46. The operating expense ratio of a building is determined by dividing the total operating expenses by the
    A. effective net income.   C. effective gross income.
    B. net operating income.   D. actual gross income.

47. From the net operating income of a property, the owner receives
    I. a return on his investment.
    II. a return of his investment.
    A. I only   B. II only   C. Both I and II   D. Neither I nor II

48. Using the mortgage-equity table in Chapter 16 of the text as a guide,
    what would be the effect of a 2 per cent increase in mortgage interest
    rates?
    A. There would be no change since appraisals are made on the basis of
        a cash purchase.
    B. An increase of 1.4 to 1.5 per cent in the overall rate.
    C. a decrease in the capitalization rate.
    D. an automatic increase in the appraised value of the property.

49. All of the following statements are correct EXCEPT:
    A. all appraisal approaches are suitable for any type of real property.
    B. the income approach is usually the best method of appraising an
        apartment building.
    C. special-purpose buildings are usually best appraised by the cost
        approach.
    D. the market comparison approach is usually the best method for
        residential properties.

50. An appraisal report may be made in the form of
      I. an oral report.   III. a form report.
     II. a letter.   IV. a narrative report.
    A. I, II, III and IV   C. III and IV only
    B. II, III and IV only   D. III only

51. The actual selling price of a property is determined by the
      I. buyer.
     II. seller.
    III. appraiser.
    A. I only   B. II only   C. III only   D. I and II only

52. Standardized appraisal forms have been a major step in
      I. facilitating a large secondary mortgage market.
     II. computerizing appraisal report preparation.
    A. I only   B. II only   C. Both I and II   D. Neither I nor II

53. Which of the following would probably cost the most?
    A. Oral report.   C. Form appraisal.
    B. Appraisal letter.   D. Narrative appraisal.

54. Which of the following will most likely require a full narrative
    appraisal report?
    A. An owner who wishes to sell his home.
    B. A prospective purchaser of an apartment building.
    C. A lender who is considering an application for a home loan.
    D. A government agency purchasing under eminent domain.

55. A real estate salesperson gave an owner an off-hand estimate of the value
    of his home. Relying on this information, the owner listed with the
    salesperson's broker and contracted to sell the home at the salesperson's
    estimated value. The property was later appraised by a qualified ap-
    praiser for a substantially larger amount. The broker could be
      I. subject to disciplinary action by the real estate department.
     II. liable for civil damages to the property owner.
    A. I only   B. II only   C. Both I and II   D. Neither I nor II

56. A properly-prepared appraisal report contains which of the following?
    I. A guarantee that the roof won't leak.
    II. A certificate of value.
    A. I only   B. II only   C. Both I and II   D. Neither I nor II

57. From the viewpoint of a qualified real estate appraiser, the value of the subject property is NOT affected by
    A. demand.   C. sentiment of the seller.
    B. scarcity.   D. transferability.

58. The principle which states that the maximum value of a property tends to be set by the cost of acquiring another equally desirable property is known as the principle of
    A. anticipation.   C. highest and best use.
    B. subrogation.   D. substitution.

59. The use of a property which will give it its greatest current value is its
    A. highest use.   C. highest and best use.
    B. best use.   D. maximum use.

60. The principle which refers to the ability of people to pay for land coupled with the relative scarcity of land is known as the principle of
    A. substitution.   C. competition.
    B. supply and demand.   D. diminishing returns.

61. The relationship between added cost and the value it returns is known as the principle of
    I. diminishing marginal returns.
    II. contribution.
    A. I only   B. II only   C. Both I and II   D. Neither I nor II

62. The principle which holds that maximum value is realized when a reasonable degree of homogeniety is present in a neighborhood is known as the principle of
    A. harmony.   C. similarity.
    B. homogeneity.   D. conformity.

63. May a property have different values if the purposes of two or more appraisals are not the same?
    A. Yes, because value is affected by the purpose of the appraisal.
    B. Yes, because not all appraisers see the property in the same light.
    C. No, because a property has only one value at any given time.
    D. No, because the purpose of the appraisal does not affect its value.

64. The insurance value of a property differs from its market value because
    I. the value of the land is not included.
    II. the amount of coverage is based on the replacement cost of the structures.
    A. I only   B. II only   C. Both I and II   D. Neither I nor II

65. The process of combining two or more parcels of land into one larger parcel is called
    A. assemblage.   C. salvage.
    B. plottage.   D. reproduction.

66. If two parcels are combined into one larger parcel that is worth more than the total value of the individual parcels, that added value is called
    A. addage.   C. rentage.
    B. estatage.   D. plottage.

67. A market where there is an excess of supply over demand is known as a
    A. buyer's market.   C. seller's market.
    B. broad market.   D. thin market.

68. The City of Plainview, population 100,000, has one small lake on which 12 people have houses. Turnover of these houses averages less than one house per year. Can the market for these lakefront houses be described as thin?
    A. Yes, because there will be much demand for so few houses.
    B. Yes, because there are few houses and little turnover each year.
    C. No, because this situation describes a broad market.
    D. No, because this situation describes a buyer's market.

69. The Society of Real Estate Appraisers offers all of the following professional designations EXCEPT:
    A. SREA.   C. SRA.
    B. SRPA.   D. RM.

70. The appraisal designation MAI stands for
    A. Master Appraisal Instructor.
    B. Master Appraisal Institute.
    C. Member of the Appraisal Institute.
    D. None of the above.

Appraisal Problems

1. It cost a builder $80,000 to build a house several years ago. Since then, building costs have risen 45% and then decreased 12% below this high point. How much would it cost him to build this same house today?

$_____

2. An appraiser determines the replacement cost of a house to be $76,000 at today's prices. He has estimated its present value to be $63,080. What was the per cent of depreciation determined by the apppraiser?

_____%

3. A man has 117 acres of soybeans that net him $29,250 per year. If land like this is capitalized at 10%, what is his land worth per acre?

$_____

4. In the illustration below, what per cent of the area of the lot is covered by the house?

_____%

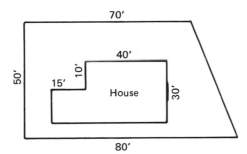

5. A builder buys land for $90,000, spends $150,000 for a street, $1,935,000 for a 25-unit condominium structure, and $135,000 for miscellaneous. He borrowed all the money at 12% per annum for ten months. If he wants to make a 15% profit, how much must he sell each unit for?

$_____

6. A home is presently valued at $112,000. What was its previous sales price if it has appreciated 12% since then?

$_____

7. On a 110-foot by 200-foot lot a two-story building will be built. Each floor will be 80 feet by 95 feet and will cost $38 per square foot. Landscaping will cost $5.00 per square foot exclusive of the building. The land costs $430 per front foot. What will be the total cost of the project?

$_____

8. An investor wants to purchase a 10-unit apartment building where 5 units rent for $350 per month and 5 units rent for $400 per month. How much should he pay for the building if monthly operating expenses amount to $1,250 and he wants to earn 8.0% on his investment?

$_____

9. A property earns $900,000 per year and has expenses of 45% of that amount. If the property is capitalized at 12%, what is its value?

$_____

10. A family built this house for $63 per square foot. The land cost $29,000 an acre. How much did they spend?

$_____

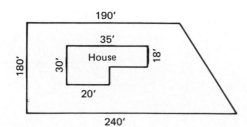

Answers—Chapter 16

Multiple Choice Questions

1. C   There is no recognized approach to appraisal which is identified as the assessment approach.

2. D   All five of these assumptions are made by the appraiser in determining the market value of a property.

3. A   A comparable property sale which has occurred within the past six months is usually valid and useful for estimating current market values.

4. B   The appraiser is not responsible for determining the marketability of title and assumes that it will be marketable.

5. B   Comparables should be inspected personally by the appraiser in order to avoid errors in making the appraisal.

6. C   A similar home with equal amenities which was sold under market conditions six months ago would be more indicative of current values than any of the other choices given.

7. C   The title insurance company's records are more likely to reflect the true sale price than any of the other sources.

8. A   The most recent sale would more likely reflect current market conditions. Settlement dates are not always indicative of current market values, especially when they lag the sale agreement by more than two months.

9. B   Comparables with fewer adjustments are of greater usefulness than those with many adjustments; several comparables are desirable, but the number must be weighed against the effort involved.

10. C   The owner's asking price probably sets the upper limit of the property's value, and the prospect's offer the lower limit of value.

11. B   Adjustments are made to the comparable property because the appraiser cannot adjust the value of something for which he does not yet know the value.

12. C   The value of improvements made after the property was sold would not be reflected in the sale price of a comparable. Therefore no adjustments for them are made.

13. D $80,000 value x 3% (one-half the annual rate of 6%) = $2,400.

14. A   240 sq. ft. x $80/sq. ft. - 10% depreciation = $17,280. This would
         be deducted from the comparable.

15. D   Acquisition cost to the present owner is not considered by an
         appraiser.

16. C   If buyers will pay more for a garage, this must be considered by the
         appraiser.

17. C   Comparable number 1 is equivalent to the subject property. A $500
         adjustment to comparable number 2 is made to reflect the current
         value of the custom appliances.

18. A   Adjustments for advantageous financing would be made in the market
         comparison approach, but not in the cost approach.

19. A   A comparable's adjusted market price reflects all adjustments made
         and is its comparative value for appraisal purposes.

20. B   The process of weighting each of the comparables is known as the
         correlation process.

21. D   Land is seldom valued on a square yard basis, but is commonly valued
         on a square foot, acreage or front foot basis.

22. D   The lot with the greater depth is worth more than the other, but less
         than twice as much.

23. A   Only lots of similar zoning should be employed when making an
         appraisal.

24. A   Responses I, II and III are all correct.

25. C   Sales information from a real estate agent's multiple listing book
         would be used with either the standard market comparison method or
         the competitive market analysis.

26. C   A real estate agent may use either the standard market comparison
         method or the competitive market analysis method, or both methods in
         evaluating a home in order to list it for sale.

27. D   Seller motivation is considered most in the competitive market
         analysis method.

28. D   A gross rent multiplier is more likely to produce only a rough esti-
         mate of a property's value because it considers only the gross income
         without considering other variables.

29. B
Sales prices	Monthly rents	Annual rents
$ 450,000	$ 5,000	$ 60,000
382,500	4,250	51,000
427,500	4,750	57,000
$1,260,000 Total	$14,000 Total	$168,000 Total

$1,260,000 divided by $168,000 = 7.5 GRM.

30. C $450 monthly rent x 10 units x 12 months x 7.5 GRM = $405,000 value.

31. C   Land is not depreciated in making an appraisal.

32. A   Because the building is historically significant, reproduction cost would be appropriate.

33. B   40 ft x 45 ft x $60/sq. ft. = $108,000 residence
20 ft x 20 ft x $30/sq. ft. = $ 12,000 garage
$120,000 total value

34. D   The building exhibits physical deterioration, economic obsolescence, and functional obsolescence. The land (which is probably useful for industry) is not obsolete.

35. C   The building suffers from curable depreciation in its need for painting, and incurable depreciation from its poorly designed floor plan.

36. C   Economic obsolescence results from factors outside the property; functional obsolescence and physical deterioration result from factors inside the property.

37. D   The amount of income produced, the rate of return demanded by investors, and the length of the investment period are all considered in the income approach to appraisal.

38. A   Capitalization is the conversion of future income into present value.

39. A   The lower the capitalization rate used by the appraiser, the higher the indicated value of the property.

40. C $1,200 income x 12 months divided by 11% = $130,909, round to $130,900.

41. C   Anticipated annual rents from a property on an annual basis are identified as either projected gross income or scheduled gross income.

42. B   Actual income and expenses for the past three to five years will provide the best starting point for projecting future gross income and expenses.

43. A   A small error in income projection is magnified into a larger error in the indicated value of a property.

44. C   Capital improvements would not be included in a projected annual operating statement.

45. B   Reserves for improvement are established for items that must be replaced more than once in a building's life, but not annually.

46. C   Total operating expense divided by the effective gross income equals the operating expense ratio.

47. C   Both a return on investment and a return of investment are received from the net operating income of a property.

48. B   The table indicates an increase of 1.4 to 1.5 per cent in the overall rate as the result of a 2 per cent increase in mortgage interest rates. All other things being constant, this will reduce the value of property.

49. A   Not all appraisal approaches are suitable for all properties.

50. A   An appraisal report may be in the form of an oral report, a letter, a form report or a narrative report.

51. D   The actual selling price of a property is determined by agreement between the buyer and the seller.

52. C   Standardized appraisal forms facilitate a large secondary mortgage market and lend themselves to computerization.

53. D   A narrative report would probably cost the most because of the extra time and effort required in its preparation.

54. D   A government agency purchasing under eminent domain will usually require a full narrative appraisal report; owners wishing to sell, prospective purchasers and/or lenders considering loan applications are not as demanding.

55. C   The broker could be held liable for civil damages and would be subject to disciplinary action by the real estate department for unprofessional conduct.

56. D   A properly-prepared appraisal report will contain neither a structural guarantee nor a certificate of value.

57. C   An appraiser makes no allowances for sentiment, but does consider demand, scarcity and transferability.

58. D   The principle of substitution holds that the maximum value of a property tends to be set by the cost of acquiring another equally desirable property.

59. C   A property's highest and best use is that which will give its greatest current value.

60. B   The ability of people to pay for land coupled with the relative
          scarcity of land is known as the principle of supply and demand.

61. C   The relationship between added cost and the value it returns is known
          as either the principle of diminishing marginal returns or the prin-
          ciple of contribution.

62. D   The principle of conformity holds that maximum value is realized when
          a reasonable degree of homogeneity is present in a neighborhood.

63. A   A property may have more than one value, depending upon the purpose
          for which the valuation was performed.

64. C   The insurance value of a property is based on the replacement cost of
          the structures and excludes land value; therefore, it differs from
          the property's market value.

65. A   Assemblage is the process of combining two or more parcels of land
          into one larger parcel.

66. D   Plottage value results from assemblage and is the added value over
          and above the sum of the smaller parcels.

67. A   A buyer's market results from an excess of supply over demand.

68. B   This is a thin market because of so few properties and slow turnover.

69. D   The designation RM is offered by the American Institute of Real
          Estate Appraisers, not by the Society of Real Estate Appraisers.

70. C.   The designation MAI stands for Member of the Appraisal Institute.

Appraisal Problems

1. $80,000 x 1.45 x .88 = $102,080

2. $76,000 - $63,080 = $12,920 dollar amount of depreciation
    $12,920 ÷ $76,000 = .17 = 17% answer

3. $29,250 ÷ 117 acres ÷ .10 = $2,500 per acre

4. (70' + 80') ÷ 2 x 50' = 3,750 sqft area of lot
    (30' x 40') + (15' x 20') = 1,500 sqft area of house
    1,500 ÷ 3,750 = .4 = 40% answer

5. $90,000 + $150,000 + $1,935,000 + $135,000 = $2,310,000 loan
    $2,310,000 x 12% ÷ 12 months x 10 months = $231,000 interest
    $2,310,000 + $231,000 x 1.15 ÷ 25 units = $116,886 per unit, answer

6. $112,000 is 112% of what price?
   $112,000 = 1.12 x price
   price = $112,000 ÷ 1.12 = $100,000 answer

7. (110' x 200' - 80' x 95') x $5.00 = $72,000 landscaping
   80' x 95' x 2 stories x $38.00 = $557,600 building
   110' x $430 = $47,300 land
   $72,000 + $577,600 + $47,300 = $696,900 answer

8. ($400 x 5 units + $350 x 5 units) x 12 months ÷ .08 = $375,000

9. $900,000 x .55 ÷ .12 = $4,125,000
   (Note that .55 is what remains of each dollar after deducting $.45 of
   expenses.)

10. (30' x 20' + 15' x 18') x $63 = $54,810 cost of house
    (190' + 240') ÷ 2 x 180' ÷ 43,560 x $29,000 = $25,764 cost of land
    $54,810 + $25,764 = $80,574 answer

The Owner–Broker Relationship

Chapter 17

1. A real estate listing
     I. is an employment contract between a property owner and a real
         estate broker.
    II. authorizes a real estate broker to sell and convey title to an
         owner's real property.
    A. I only   B. II only   C. Both I and II   D. Neither I nor II

2. All of the following statements are true EXCEPT:
    A. a listing is a contract between an owner and the listing salesperson.
    B. the broker is legally liable for the proper execution of a listing
       contract.
    C. sales associates are licensed salespersons or brokers who work for
       a broker.
    D. sales associates operate under the authority of an employing broker's
       license.

3. Sales associate Lee secured a written listing on a property for sale,
   signed by the owner and the employing broker. Is this an enforceable
   listing contract?
    A. Yes, because the broker is a licensed agent.
    B. Yes, because all essential elements of a listing contract are
       present.
    C. No, because no contract exists until the property is sold.
    D. No, because no consideration will be paid until the property is sold.

4. A listing to find a buyer for each of the following types of properties
   will usually be for a period of time ranging from six months to one year
   EXCEPT:
    A. farms.   C. residential properties.
    B. commercial properties.   D. industrial properties.

Note: There are no deleted questions in this chapter for readers of
       <u>Real Estate: An Introduction to the Profession.</u>

5. A typical exclusive right to sell listing requires the owner to
    I. exclude other brokers from advertising or placing a sign on the property.
    II. pay a commission if a purchaser is found who agrees to buy at the price and terms stipulated in the listing.
    A. I only   B. II only   C. Both I and II   D. Neither I nor II

6. The amount of commission to be paid the broker for selling a property is
    A. set by state law.
    B. negotiated at the time a buyer is found.
    C. set forth in the rules of the state real estate commission.
    D. stated in the listing contract.

7. Under the terms of an exclusive right to sell listing, a commission is due the listing broker if a buyer is found by
    I. the listing broker.
    II. a sales associate employed by the listing broker.
    III. the owner, through his own efforts.
    IV. another broker.
    A. I and II only   C. I, II, III and IV
    B. I, II and IV only   D. I, II and III only

8. Broker Kim secured a written listing on a property. Kim later located a buyer who was ready, willing and able to buy at the price and terms stated in the listing contract, but the owner refused to sign a sales agreement because of animosity toward the buyer. Is Kim entitled to a commission even though no sale was consummated?
    A. Yes, because a commission was earned when the listing was signed.
    B. Yes, because Kim produced a ready, willing and able buyer at the price and terms requested in the listing.
    C. No, because no sales contract was signed by the owner.
    D. No, because there was not an offer and acceptance.

9. Which of the following is NOT true of an exclusive right to sell listing?
    A. Brokers will usually exert their maximum sales effort under this type of listing.
    B. The broker will receive a commission regardless of whether the property is sold.
    C. The owner may not sell of his own efforts without liability for a commission to the broker.
    D. The property may not be listed with another broker during the listing period.

10. An exclusive agency listing
    I. permits the owner to sell of his own efforts without liability to pay a commission to the listing broker.
    II. allows the owner to list concurrently with other brokers.
    A. I only   B. II only   C. Both I and II   D. Neither I nor II

11. An owner gave an open listing to brokers Smith, Jones and Miller. Smith
    advertised the property for sale. Jones showed it to several prospects.
    Miller secured an acceptable offer from the only person to whom he showed
    the property. Which of the following statements are correct?
    A. The commission would be divided between Smith, Jones and Miller.
    B. The owner is liable to broker Smith for the advertising expense.
    C. If the owner had found a buyer through his own efforts, he would be
       liable for a commission to each broker.
    D. Miller is due a commission if the owner accepts the offer to
       purchase.

12. All of the following are true of net listings EXCEPT:
    A. many states prohibit a broker from accepting a net listing.
    B. most brokers are reluctant to accept them, even when permitted to
       do so.
    C. all net listings are open listings.
    D. the commission is the excess above the seller's net price.

13. Owner Cage wants to list his home for $100,000 with a broker at 6%
    commission and at the same time advertise it himself for $96,000. He
    feels that if he can sell it himself he will be money ahead even though
    the price is lower. Legally Cage can do this if he signs an
      I. exclusive right to sell listing.
     II. exclusive agency listing.
    III. open listing.
    A. I only   B. II only   C. III only   D. II or III only

14. Under the terms of an advance fee listing, the listing broker receives
      I. an hourly fee for time spent in selling the property.
     II. compensation for out-of-pocket expenses.
    A. I only   B. II only   C. Both I and II   D. Neither I nor II

15. An advance cost listing differs from an advance fee listing in that
      I. the broker receives compensation for out-of-pocket expenses, but
          no hourly fee.
     II. the commission will not be based on the sales price.
    A. I only   B. II only   C. Both I and II   D. Neither I nor II

16. Under the terms of a multiple listing agreement, if a broker other than
    the listing broker sells the property, the owner
      I. may be liable for two commissions on the sale.
     II. may sell of his own efforts without any obligation to pay a
          commission.
    A. I only   B. II only   C. Both I and II   D. Neither I nor II

17. The advantages of a multiple listing arrangement include
      I. greater market exposure of the property.
     II. the possibility of a higher sales price.
    III. quicker sale.
    A. I only   B. I and II only   C. I, II and III   D. III only

18. Recent innovations for marketing properties through multiple listing services include
    I. computerized listings.
    II. videodisc display of listings.
    A. I only   B. II only   C. Both I and II   D. Neither I nor II

19. Broker Lynch secured a "no sale, no commission" listing on a property, signed by the owner and broker Lynch. A buyer was found who was ready, willing and able to buy, and a sales agreement was signed by both buyer and seller. The sales agreement was later cancelled arbitrarily by the seller. Is the seller liable for a commission to broker Lynch?
    A. Yes, but only for half the commission.
    B. Yes, because the cancellation was arbitrary on his part.
    C. No, because the sale was not closed.
    D. No, because this type of contract is not enforceable.

20. Under the terms of an exclusive agency listing, broker David showed a property to a prospect and notified the seller of the showing. The prospect then approached the seller directly and bought the property at a lower price using a "straw-man" to hide the buyer's identity from the broker. Can broker David recover a commission on this sale?
    A. Yes, because he was the procuring cause of the sale.
    B. Yes, because he is entitled to a commission if the property was sold during the listing period.
    C. No, because the owner has the right to sell of his own efforts without payment of a commission.
    D. No, because he did not introduce the straw-man to the property.

21. When a property under an open listing is shown to a prospect by two different brokers and a sale results, the commission is
    A. payable to the broker who first showed the property to the buyer.
    B. divided between the two brokers.
    C. payable to the broker who made the sale.
    D. payable in full to each broker.

22. An exclusive listing contract with a definite termination date is NOT terminable by
    A. sale of the property.
    B. death of the listing salesperson.
    C. expiration.
    D. mutual agreement.

23. An open listing may be terminated by which of the following means?
    I.   Sale of the property.
    II. Abandonment by the broker.
    III. Destruction of the property by casualty.
    IV. Death of the owner.
    A. I, II, III and IV   C. III and IV only
    B. I and II only   D. I, II and IV only

24. If a purchaser arbitrarily defaults on a purchase contract, any earnest money previously paid, in the absence of an agreement to the contrary, will be
   A. paid to the broker as compensation for his efforts.
   B. divided between the broker and the owner/seller.
   C. returned to the purchaser.
   D. paid to the owner/seller.

25. Which of the following is most likely to accept only listings that he thinks will sell quickly?
   A. Flat-fee brokers.   C. Discount brokers.
   B. Full-service brokers.   D. Self-help brokers.

26. Sometimes homeowners attempt to sell their property themselves without the aid of a broker because
    I. of their perceived value of the services rendered by the broker.
   II. the sales commission would consume too much of their equity in the property.
   A. I only   B. II only   C. Both I and II   D. Neither I nor II

27. All of the following statements are true EXCEPT:
   A. the statute of frauds requires all agency agreements to be made in writing in order to be enforceable.
   B. a real estate listing is an agency contract.
   C. in a real estate listing, the property owner is the principal.
   D. a real estate broker is the agent under a real estate listing.

28. When an agent is given the right to transact all types of matters on behalf of the principal, he serves as a
   A. notary public.   C. universal agent.
   B. third party.   D. special agent.

29. An agent who is authorized to bind his employer in a trade or business is
   A. a special agent.   C. an exclusive agent.
   B. a general agent.   D. a principal agent.

30. The relationship of a real estate broker to the owner of property listed for sale with the broker is that of a
   A. general agent.   C. limited agent.
   B. universal agent.   D. special agent.

31. Which of the following is NOT true of a listing contract?
   A. A corporation may be a principal.
   B. A natural person may be an agent.
   C. A sales associate may be an agent.
   D. Purchasers are third parties to the contract.

32. An agent's authority may be granted by
    I. written agreement.
   II. custom in the industry.
   A. I only   B. II only   C. Both I and II   D. Neither I nor II

33. When an agent's authority arises from custom in the industry, it is
    identified as
    A. implied authority.   C. customary authority.
    B. ostensible authority.   D. conventional authority.

34. An agency may be created by
    I. ratification.
    II. estoppel.
    A. I only   B. II only   C. Both I and II   D. Neither I nor II

35. Broker Gomez was part owner of an apartment building along with two co-
    owners. When they decided to sell the building, broker Gomez was named
    as the agent in the listing agreement. Broker Gomez thus held an agency
    A. by ratification.   C. by estoppel.
    B. coupled with an interest.   D. by implication.

36. A broker has fiduciary responsibilities to
    I. the owner of property listed by him.
    II. third parties with whom he deals.
    A. I only   B. II only   C. Both I and II   D. Neither I nor II

37. Fiduciary responsibilities of an agent to his principal include all of
    the following EXCEPT:
    A. faithful performance.
    B. loyalty.
    C. accounting for funds or property received.
    D. provision of legal advice.

38. When a broker acts as an agent for both purchaser and seller in a trans-
    action, this is identified as
    A. an agency by estoppel.   C. an agency coupled with an interest.
    B. a dual agency.   D. an agency by ratification.

39. A broker may act as an agent for both parties in a transaction only with
    the permission of
    A. the property owner.   C. both parties.
    B. the real estate commission. D. the purchaser.

40. Isaacs introduced owner DiVita to prospect Park. DiVita and Park con-
    ducted negotiations among themselves without assistance from Isaacs.
    The role of Isaacs was that of a
    I. dual agent.
    II. middleman.
    A. I only   B. II only   C. Both I and II   D. Neither I nor II

41. Any earnest money deposits paid by the purchaser
    I. belong to the broker.
    II. must be placed in a proper trust account.
    A. I only   B. II only   C. Both I and II   D. Neither I nor II

42. The placing of funds belonging to others in a broker's personal bank account constitutes
    I. commingling.
    II. grounds for revocation of the broker's license.
    A. I only   B. II only   C. Both I and II   D. Neither I nor II

43. A broker who misrepresents a property to a prospect may be subject to all of the following EXCEPT:
    A. loss of his rights to a commission.
    B. revocation of his broker's license.
    C. criminal prosecution.
    D. civil action for damages.

44. An owner who gives false information regarding the listed property may be liable for
    I. a commission to the broker.
    II. cancellation of the sale.
    III. money damages to the purchaser.
    A. I, II and III   C. I only
    B. II only   D. I and III only

45. A broker who intentionally misleads a prospect by making an incorrect statement which he knows is not true is
    I. guilty of fraud.
    II. subject to license revocation.
    III. subject to litigation.
    A. I and II only   C. II and III only
    B. I, II and III   D. I and III only

46. An agent who fails to investigate the cause of an apparent underlying defect in a property which he is selling may be found
    I. criminally liable.
    II. liable for civil damages.
    A. I only   B. II only   C. Both I and II   D. Neither I nor II

47. When an agent engages someone to look into a question raised by a purchaser, he
    I. should make certain of the competency of the person so engaged.
    II. may be liable for civil damages if the person is not professionally competent.
    A. I only   B. II only   C. Both I and II   D. Neither I nor II

48. Can an agent protect himself from liability to disclose defects in a property by stating in writing that the property is being sold "as is"?
    A. Yes, because the statement makes it clear that the purchaser is aware of all problems that might arise.
    B. Yes, because of the rule of Caveat Emptor.
    C. No, because he may still be liable for having withheld material facts about the property.
    D. No, because the purchaser waives any right to future claims by accepting the property "as is."

49. If a principal asks an agent to participate in an illegal or unethical act in selling a property, the agent should do all the following EXCEPT:
A. advise against it.
B. have no part of it.
C. discourage the principal from doing it.
D. report the principal to the real estate department.

50. A broker can indemnify himself against legal actions by those with whom he deals by purchasing
    I. errors and omissions insurance.
    II. middleman insurance.
A. I only   B. II only   C. Both I and II   D. Neither I nor II

51. Nonfactual or extravagant statements which would be recognized by a reasonable person as exaggeration
    I. should be used with extreme care because of the potential liability for misrepresentation.
    II. are known as puffing or puffery.
A. I only   B. II only   C. Both I and II   D. Neither I nor II

52. Should a broker breach his fiduciary responsibility to his principal, he may find himself subject to
    I. disciplinary action by the real estate department.
    II. civil action by the principal.
    III. criminal prosecution.
A. I only   B. I and II only   C. III only   D. I, II and III

53. The obligations of a principal to an agent include
    I. compensation.   III. indemnification.
    II. reimbursement.   IV. performance.
A. I, II, III and IV   C. I only
B. I, II and IV only   D. I and II only

54. In dealing with third parties in a real estate transaction, a broker should be careful to avoid all the following EXCEPT:
A. giving misleading or incorrect information.
B. disclosing his loyalty to his principal.
C. giving or accepting undisclosed fees.
D. concealing his identity as an agent of the principal.

55. The relationship of a sales associate to the employing broker is
    I. that of a special agent.
    II. subject to all laws and rules of agency.
A. I only   B. II only   C. Both I and II   D. Neither I nor II

56. When acting as a cooperating broker, an agent should make it clear to all parties in the transaction
    I. that his legal responsibilities must be to the purchaser.
    II. whether he is acting in the interest of the purchaser or seller.
A. I only   B. II only   C. Both I and II   D. Neither I nor II

57. When a buyer employs a broker to represent him in negotiations for a property,
   I. the commission to the listing broker is eliminated.
   II. offers to purchase can be based on the net amount the seller will receive.
   III. the problem of divided broker loyalty is eliminated.
   A. I, II and III   B. II and III only   C. III only   D. I only

58. The requirement that prospective buyers be given a HUD property report applies to
   A. all interstate land sales.
   B. resales of subdivision lots being sold to residents of another state.
   C. all subdivision lots located in one state and sold to residents of another state.
   D. new subdivision lots being offered to residents of another state.

59. The property report required by federal or state law to be given to prospective purchasers
   I. indicates government approval of the property.
   II. must be given to the purchaser before a purchase agreement is signed.
   A. I only   B. II only   C. Both I and II   D. Neither I nor II

60. The Civil Rights Act of 1866 prohibits
   A. racial discrimination.   C. blockbusting.
   B. steering.   D. discrimination for any reason.

61. All of the following are prohibited by the Fair Housing ACT of 1968, as amended, EXCEPT:
   A. discrimination in advertising.
   B. denial of availability of housing on the basis of religion.
   C. discrimination in terms or conditions for sale or rent.
   D. discrimination on the basis of age.

62. Which of the following is NOT prohibited by the Fair Housing Act of 1968?
   A. Discrimination on the basis of physical handicap.
   B. The offering of different loan terms by commercial lenders based on race or religion of the loan applicant.
   C. Refusal to sell, rent or negotiate with any person.
   D. Steering and blockbusting.

63. The practice of directing homeseekers to particular neighborhoods based on race, color, religion, sex or national origin
   I. is known as steering.
   II. is prohibited by the Civil Rights Act of 1866.
   III. constitutes blockbusting.
   IV. is prohibited by the Fair Housing Act of 1968.
   A. I and II only   C. I and IV only
   B. II and III only   D. III and IV only

64. All of the following are true of the inducement of panic selling in a neighborhood for financial gain EXCEPT:
   A. it is prohibited by the Fair Housing Act of 1968.
   B. it is limited to fear of loss of value because of the changing of the racial composition of a neighborhood.
   C. it is known as blockbusting.
   D. the prohibition applies to licensed real estate agents.

65. The Fair Housing Act of 1968 applies to
   I. single-family housing.
   II. multiple dwellings.
   A. I only   B. II only   C. Both I and II   D. Neither I nor II

66. The owner of a single-family house in which he lives wants to sell. If he does not use discriminatory language in advertising, has not sold any other house within the past two years, and does not employ an agent, may he discriminate on the basis of race in selecting a purchaser?
   A. Yes, because the fair housing laws permit discrimination under these conditions.
   B. Yes, because the law applies only to sales made by licensed agents.
   C. No, because this would be prohibited by the Civil Rights Act of 1866.
   D. No, because this would be prohibited by the Fair Housing Act of 1968.

67. Bob and Sally, unmarried, want to purchase a condominium unit but have been refused because they are not married but living together. Can the developer be prosecuted in federal courts for refusing to sell to them?
   A. Yes, because this violates the federal fair housing laws.
   B. Yes, because this constitutes discrimination in housing as determined in the Jones vs. Mayer case.
   C. No, because discrimination on this basis is not prohibited by federal fair housing laws.
   D. No, because this violates the provisions of the Fair Housing Act of 1968.

68. A church which operates housing for the elderly may restrict occupancy to members of the church if
   I. membership in the church is open to all persons.
   II. the units are to be rented, but not if they are being offered for sale.
   A. I only   B. II only   C. Both I and II   D. Neither I nor II

69. The Sunset Hills Country Club has several guest bedrooms which are made available to members and guests for a nominal charge, but are not available to the general public. Does this constitute a violation of the federal fair housing laws?
   A. Yes, because rental housing of this nature must be open to the public.
   B. Yes, because the charging of a fee constitutes a commercial purpose.
   C. No, because the club is exempt under the provisions of the Fair Housing Act of 1968.
   D. No, because this does not constitute steering or blockbusting.

70. A victim of discrimination in housing may seek enforcement of the 1968 Fair Housing Act by any of the following means EXCEPT:
    A. filing a complaint with the Department of Housing and Urban Development.
    B. filing action in federal court.
    C. filing a complaint with the U. S. Attorney General.
    D. filing a complaint with the state real estate department.

71. A person seeking enforcement of the Civil Rights Act of 1866 may do so by filing
    I. an action in federal court.
    II. a complaint with the U. S. Attorney General.
    A. I only   B. II only   C. Both I and II   D. Neither I nor II

72. A licensed real estate agent is offered a listing by an owner who stipulates that he will not sell to any person of a certain national origin. The agent should
    A. accept the listing and leave it up to the owner to reject offers from these persons.
    B. refuse to accept the listing.
    C. report the owner to the real estate department.
    D. file a complaint against the owner with HUD.

Listing Problem

Use the data given below to complete the following listing form. When you have completed the listing form, answer the questions which follow.

Property description: Single-family residence at 123 West
                                            Maple St., Yourtown, Anystate. Legal-
                                            ly described as Lot 6, Block 3, Sec-
                                            tion 4, Sunset Hills Subdivision,
                                            Yourtown, Kings County, Anystate.

Listed Price: $94,500

Terms: Cash. Or purchaser may assume
                                            existing first mortgage loan having a
                                            balance of $57,150 as of July 1,
                                            19__, bearing interest at the rate
                                            of 9% per annum, and monthly payments
                                            of $495.08, principal and interest
                                            only, maturing July 1, 2008.

Owners: Craven A. Moove and Wanda Moove,
                                            husband and wife

Broker: Shirley Kandew Realty Co.

Listing Period: Listing to commence at Noon, June 10,
                                            19__, for a 90 day period (you de-
                                            termine expiration date).

Commission rate: 6 per cent

Broker to be protected for: 90 days following expiration, for
                                            prospects introduced during listing
                                            period.

Listing signed on: June 10, 19__

You are to sign the listing for the Shirley Kandew Realty Co. Use the current year for the date.

Exclusive Right to Sell Listing Contract

Property Description: _____

_____

_____

Price: _____   Terms: _____

_____

_____

_____

    In consideration of the services of _____
(herein called the "Broker"), to be rendered to _____
_____ (herein called the "Owner"), and the promise of
said Broker to make reasonable efforts to obtain a purchaser, therefore, the Owner hereby grants to the Broker for the period of time from
noon on _____, to noon on _____ (herein called
the "listing period") the exclusive and irrevocable right to advertise
and find a purchaser for the above described property at the price and
terms shown or for such sum and terms or exchange as the owner later
agrees to accept.

    Owner hereby agrees to pay Broker a cash fee of _____% of the
selling or exchange price

    (a) in case of any sale or exchange of the above property within
the listing period either by the Broker, the Owner, or any person, or

    (b) upon the Broker finding a purchaser who is ready, willing, and
able to complete the purchase as proposed by the owner, or

    (c) in the event of a sale or exchange within _____ days of the
expiration of the listing period to any party shown the above property
during the listing period by the Broker or his representative and where
the name was disclosed to the Owner.

    The Owner agrees to give the Broker access to the buildings on the
property for the purposes of showing them at reasonable hours
and the Owner agrees to refer to Broker all inquiries regarding this
property during the listing period.

Accepted: _____   Owner: _____

   By: _____   Owner: _____

              Date: _____

Commission Calculations .

Based on the listing contract on the previous page, answer the following seven questions.

1. If the property sells for the listed price and the buyer assumes the existing first mortgage loan, the commission to Kandew Realty will be how much?

    $_____

2. If a prospect is found who offers $93,000 and the owners accept, how much commission will Kandew Realty receive?

    $_____

3. If the sellers say they will take a net $88,000 after paying a 6% commission, for how much must the property sell?

    $_____

4. On properties that are listed and sold by Kandew Realty sales associates, Kandew deducts a $100 multiple listing fee from the commission received and then splits the balance 25% to the listing sales associate, 45% to the selling sales associate, and 30% to Kandew Realty. If the property sells for $94,000, how much does each of the following receive?

    Listing sales associate $_____

    Selling sales associate $_____

    Kandew Realty Company $_____

5. On properties that are listed by a Kandew Realty sales associate and sold by another broker, a $100 MLS fee is deducted from the commission and the balance is split 25% to the listing sales associate, 25% to Kandew Realty and 50% to the selling broker. If the property sells for $94,200, how much does each of the following receive?

   Listing sales associate $_____

   Kandew Realty Company $_____

   Selling broker $_____

6. Continuing question #5, at the selling broker's office, commissions from the sale of properties listed with other brokers results in a 50-50 split between the broker's office and the sales associate. How much does each receive?

   Broker $_____

   Sales associate $_____

7. If the salesperson who listed and sold this property at Kandew Realty received $3,927 and that represented 70% of the 6% commission collected by Kandew, how much did the property sell for?

   $_____

Answers—Chapter 17

Multiple Choice Questions

1. A   A real estate listing is an employment contract between a property owner and a real estate broker. It does not authorize the broker to sell and convey title to the property.

2. A   A listing is a contract between the owner and the listing salesperson's employing broker, not the owner and the listing salesperson.

3. B   The written listing agreement contains all the essential elements of a valid and enforceable listing contract.

4. C   Residential property listings are usually made for periods of three or four months; farm, commercial and industrial properties are normally listed for periods of six months or longer.

5. C   Typically, an exclusive right to sell listing requires the owner to exclude other brokers from advertising or placing a sign on the property, and to pay a commission if a buyer is found who is ready, willing and able to buy at the price and terms stipulated in the listing.

6. D   The amount of a broker's commission is negotiated at the time the listing is signed and is stated in the listing contract.

7. C   An exclusive right to sell listing requires the payment of a commission to the broker if a sale occurs during the listing period, regardless of who sells the property.

8. B   The listing broker is entitled to a commission because a ready, willing and able purchaser was found at the price and terms of the seller's offer to sell.

9. B   An exclusive right to sell listing entitles the broker to a commission if the property is sold, but not regardless of whether the property is sold.

10. A   An exclusive agency listing permits the owner to sell of his own efforts without liability for a commission to the listing broker, but does not allow the owner to list concurrently with other brokers.

11. D   Under the terms of an open listing, only the broker who produces a buyer is entitled to a commission, but the owner retains the right to sell of his own efforts without liability for a commission to anyone.

12. C   A net listing may be an open listing, exclusive right to sell or an exclusive agency.

13. D   Either an exclusive agency listing or an open listing permits the owner to sell of his own efforts without liability for a commission. An exclusive right to sell does not permit this.

14. C   An advance fee listing requires the payment of an hourly fee to the broker for time spent in selling the property plus reimbursement for out-of-pocket expenses.

15. A   Under the terms of an advance cost listing, the broker receives compensation for out-of-pocket expenses and may also charge a commission based on the sales price.

16. D   A multiple listing agreement requires the payment of only one commission which is divided between the listing and selling brokers. It does not permit the owner to sell of his own efforts without liability for a commission.

17. C   A multiple listing offers greater market exposure, and the possibility of a higher sales price and a quicker sale.

18. C   Computerized listings and videodisc display of listings are both recent innovations for marketing properties through multiple listing services.

19. B   The seller is liable for a commission because the cancellation was arbitrary on his part and violated the terms of a valid listing contract and a valid contract of sale.

20. A   Since broker David was the procuring cause of the sale, he is entitled to a commission.

21. C   Under the terms of an open listing, the commission is payable to the broker who made the sale.

22. B   An exclusive listing contract is a contract between the owner and the broker who employs the listing salesperson and is not terminable by the death of the listing salesperson.

23. A   An open listing may be terminated by sale of the property, abandonment by the broker, destruction of the property or the death of the owner or the broker.

24. D   Unless the purchase contract contains an agreement to the contrary, any forfeited earnest money deposits become the property of the owner/seller.

25. C   Discount brokers must sell more properties in less time in order to be successful, so they reject listings that will not sell quickly.

26. C   Homeowners sometimes attempt to sell their property without a broker's aid because of their perceived value of the broker's services or because the payment of a sales commission would consume too much of their equity.

27.   A   The statute of frauds does not require all agency agreements to be in writing in order to be enforceable.

28.   C   A universal agency authorizes the agent to transact all types of matters for the principal.

29.   B   A general agent is authorized to bind his employer in a trade or business.

30.   D   A real estate broker is a special agent of the owner of property listed for sale with the broker.

31.   C   A sales associate is a sub-agent of the employing broker, who is the agent for the principal under a listing contract.

32.   C   An agent's authority may be granted by written agreement or by custom in the industry.

33.   A   Agency authority which is derived from custom in the industry is identified as implied authority.

34.   C   An agency may be created by ratification or estoppel.

35.   B   A broker who lists a property in which he has an ownership interest holds an agency coupled with an interest.

36.   A   A broker's fiduciary responsibility is to his principal, not to third parties with whom he deals.

37.   D   An agent does not have the fiduciary responsibility of giving legal advice, and is prohibited from doing so unless the agent is a member of the bar.

38.   B   A dual agency exists when the broker acts as agent for both purchaser and seller in a transaction.

39.   C   For a broker to act as a dual agent in a transaction, both parties must agree to the dual agency.

40.   B   A middleman brings the parties to a transaction together but does not participate in negotiations.

41.   C   Earnest money deposits are not the property of the broker. State laws require that they be placed in the trust account of the broker, attorney, escrow company or title company pending the completion of the transaction.

42.   C   Commingling is the combining of the funds of others with those of the agent, and constitutes grounds for revocation of a broker's license.

43.   C   Misrepresentation by a broker can result in the loss of rights to a commission, revocation of license or civil action for damages, but not in criminal prosecution.

44. A An owner who gives false information may be liable for a commission to the broker, cancellation of the sale and money damages to the purchaser.

45. B The intentional misleading of a prospect through statements known not to be true makes a broker guilty of fraud and subject to license revocation and litigation.

46. B An agent's failure to investigate the cause of an apparent underlying defect can result in civil liability for damages to the injured party.

47. C An agent may be held responsible for the competency of persons engaged by the agent to investigate a question raised by a purchaser.

48. C An "as is" sale does not free the agent from liability for withholding material facts about a property.

49. D The real estate department lacks jurisdiction over this matter and could not take any action against the principal.

50. A The purpose of errors and omissions insurance is to indemnify an agent against legal actions brought by those with whom he deals.

51. C Puffing or puffery is the making of an extravagant or nonfactual statement which would be recognized by a reasonable person as an exaggeration. Puffery should be used with extreme care because of the potential liability for misrepresentation.

52. B A breach of fiduciary responsibility by a broker may lead to disciplinary action by the real estate department and civil action by the principal, but not to criminal prosecution.

53. A A principal owes the agent compensation, reimbursement, indemnification and performance.

54. B A broker should always make clear to third parties his obligation of loyalty to the principal.

55. B A sales associate is a general agent for the employing broker, not a special agent, and the relationship is subject to all laws and rules of agency.

56. B A cooperating broker must make clear to all parties whether he is acting in the interests of the purchaser or seller.

57. B A buyer who employs a broker to represent him eliminates the problem of divided broker loyalty and can base his offers on the net amount the seller will receive from the sale.

58. D HUD property reports are given to prospective purchasers of new subdivision lots that are offered to residents of another state.

59. B   Property reports required by state or federal law do not indicate governmental approval of the property. These reports must be given to the prospective purchaser before a purchase agreement is signed.

60. A   The Civil Rights Act of 1866 prohibits discrimination on the basis of race, but not on any other basis.

61. D   The Fair Housing Act of 1968 prohibits discrimination in housing on the basis of religion, in terms or conditions for sale or rent or in advertising, but not on the basis of age.

62. A   The Fair Housing Act of 1968 does not prohibit discrimination on the basis of physical handicap.

63. C   Steering is the practice of directing homeseekers to particular neighborhoods based on race, color, religion, sex or national origin and is prohibited by the Fair Housing Act of 1968.

64. B   Blockbusting is not limited to the fear of loss of value because of the changing racial composition of a neighborhood.

65. C   The Fair Housing Act of 1968 applies to single-family housing and to multiple dwellings.

66. C   The Civil Rights Act of 1866 prohibits racial discrimination without any exemptions.

67. C   The fair housing laws do not contain prohibitions against discrimination on the basis of marital status.

68. A   The Fair Housing Act of 1968 permits discrimination in church-operated housing if membership in the church is open to anyone.

69. C   The prohibitions of the Fair Housing Act of 1968 do not apply to housing operated by a private club if it is not operated for a commercial purpose.

70. D   State real estate departments do not enforce the federal fair housing laws.

71. A   The Civil Rights Act of 1866 is enforced by having the complainant file an action in federal court.

72. B   The agent should refuse to accept the listing because to do so would violate the federal fair housing laws.

Commission Calculations

1. $94,500 x .06 = $5,670

2. $93,000 x .06 = $5,580

3. $88,000 ÷ .94 = $93,617

4. $94,000 x .06 = $5,640 commission before MLS fee and splits
    $5,640 - $100 = $5,540 commission after MLS fee
    $5,540 x .25 = $1,385 for the listing sales associate
    $5,540 x .45 = $2,493 for the selling sales associate
    $5,540 x .30 = $1,662 for Kandew Realty Company

5. $94,200 x .06 = $5,652 commission before MLS fee and splits
    $5,652 - $100 = $5,552 commission after MLS fee
    $5,552 x .25 = $1,388 for the listing sales associate
    $5,552 x .25 = $1,388 for Kandew Realty Company
    $5,552 x .50 = $2,776 for the selling broker

6. $2,776 x .50 = $1,388 for the broker
    $2,776 x .50 = $1,388 for the sales associate

7. $3,927 = 70% x 6% x selling price
    $3,927 ÷ .7 ÷ .06 = selling price
    $93,500 = selling price

Licensing Laws and
Professional Affiliation
Chapter 18

1. Real estate licensing laws represent a government's effort to ascertain
   that real estate brokers and salespersons
      I. are persons of good reputation as to honesty and truthfulness.
     II. are competent.
   A. I only   B. II only   C. Both I and II   D. Neither I nor II

2. A person who sells real estate for others
      I. must be licensed in order to collect compensation.
     II. need not be licensed if no compensation is involved.
   A. I only   B. II only   C. Both I and II   D. Neither I nor II

3. All of the following are normally exempt from the requirement for licen-
   sure in order to sell real estate as an incidental part of their duties
   EXCEPT:
   A. an attorney at law.   C. a trustee under a deed of trust.
   B. the executor of an estate. D. a real estate appraiser.

4. Which of the following may conduct a real estate brokerage business
   without a proper license?
      I. Members of the state bar.
     II. Attorneys-in-fact.
   A. I only   B. II only   C. Both I and II   D. Neither I nor II

5. A real estate broker differs from a real estate salesperson under the law
   in that
      I. the broker may act independently in conducting a brokerage
         business.
     II. a salesperson may operate in the brokerage business only under the
         supervision of a real estate broker.
   A. I only   B. II only   C. Both I and II   D. Neither I nor II

Note: There are no deleted questions in this chapter for readers of
       <u>Real Estate: An Introduction to the Profession.</u>

6. Which of the following could be licensed as a real estate broker?
   - I. A corporation.
   - II. A partnership.
   - III. An actual person.
   - IV. A sole proprietorship.
   - A. III only
   - B. I, II, III and IV
   - C. I, II and III only
   - D. III and IV only

7. A person who holds a real estate license is a
   - A. licensor.
   - B. licensee.
   - C. vestee.
   - D. vestor.

8. Which of the following is NOT a real estate license category?
   - I. Salesperson.
   - II. Broker.
   - III. Attorney-in-fact
   - A. I only   B. II only   C. III only   D. Neither I, II nor III

9. Sally Ritz owns no real property other than her home and does not hold a real estate license. She told her friends she was planning to sell her home herself and they gave her the following advice. Which of these statements is/are true?
   - I. The law does NOT permit her to sell her home unless she first passes a state-administered real estate exam.
   - II. Sally can sell her home without a real estate license only if she first appoints herself as a trustee for her property.
   - A. I only   B. II only   C. Both I and II   D. Neither I nor II

10. A real estate listing is a contract between
    - A. the owner and the listing broker.
    - B. the owner, the broker and the listing salesperson.
    - C. the owner and the listing salesperson.
    - D. the broker and the listing salesperson.

11. The ultimate responsibility for a mistake in a document prepared by a real estate salesperson rests
    - I. equally upon the salesperson and the employing broker.
    - II. upon the employing broker.
    - A. I only   B. II only   C. Both I and II   D. Neither I nor II

12. The term "sales associate" may refer to
    - I. a licensed salesperson employed by a real estate broker.
    - II. a licensed real estate broker employed by another licensed broker.
    - A. I only   B. II only   C. Both I and II   D. Neither I nor II

13. In most states, in order for a person to be licensed as a real estate broker,
    - I. previous experience as a real estate salesperson is required.
    - II. formal education in real estate subjects is required.
    - A. I only   B. II only   C. Both I and II   D. Neither I nor II

14. The topics covered in broker license examinations differ from those in
    salesperson license examinations in that they
      I. are covered in more depth.
     II. place greater emphasis on the applicant's abilities in document
         preparation.
    A. I only   B. II only   C. Both I and II   D. Neither I nor II

15. Continuing education requirements exist for the purpose of
      I. assuring that only competent license applicants are granted real
         estate licenses.
     II. requiring licensees to stay up to date in their field.
    A. I only   B. II only   C. Both I and II   D. Neither I nor II

16. Before being granted an original salesperson's license, an applicant must
      I. pass the examination for salesperson licensure.
     II. name the broker with whom the applicant will be associated.
    III. complete any state-mandated education requirements.
    A. I only   C. I and III only
    B. I and II only   D. I, II and III

17. A person who has met all pre-license requirements for original licensure
    may operate as a real estate salesperson upon
    A. notification of having passed the examination.
    B. affiliation with a licensed real estate broker.
    C. filing an application for licensure.
    D. receipt of the license by the employing broker.

18. After licensure as a real estate broker or salesperson, a licensee must,
    in order to maintain the license, do all the following EXCEPT:
    A. meet any continuing education requirements.
    B. retake the original license examination and pass it.
    C. pay license renewal fees.
    D. renew the license prior to the expiration of any allowable grace
       period.

19. License examinations which are prepared and administered by the national
    testing services include questions based on
      I. general principles of real estate practice.
     II. real estate laws, regulations and practices of the jurisdiction
         where the exam is being given.
    A. I only   B. II only   C. Both I and II   D. Neither I nor II

20. As a general rule, a person who holds a real estate license in one state
    may negotiate sales of real property
      I. within the boundaries of the state.
     II. in any other state.
    III. in other states if negotiations are carried out within the boun-
         daries of the state of licensure.
    A. I, II and III   C. I and III only
    B. I and II only   D. I only

21. A real estate broker may share a commission on a real estate sale with any of the following EXCEPT:
    A. a salesperson licensed in his employ.
    B. a broker licensed in another state.
    C. another broker licensed in his state of licensure.
    D. a salesperson licensed with another broker in his state of licensure.

22. Broker Fasi maintains his office in a community near the border of his state of residency. He often has the opportunity to list or sell properties located in the adjacent state, which does not require residency for licensure. In order to deal with these properties, he may do any of the following EXCEPT:
    A. establish a branch office in the adjacent state, managed by a broker-associate licensed in that state.
    B. secure a nonresident license in the adjacent state.
    C. cooperate with another broker who is a licensed resident broker in the adjacent state.
    D. conduct all negotiations within the boundaries of his state of residency.

23. A broker who wishes to operate outside his home state will usually be required to file a notice of consent with the Secretary of State in
    I.   his home state.
    II. each state in which he wishes to operate.
    A. I only   B. II only   C. Both I and II   D. Neither I nor II

24. A real estate broker may operate his business as a sole proprietorship under
    I.   his own name.
    II. a fictitious name.
    A. I only   B. II only   C. Both I and II   D. Neither I nor II

25. Which of the following would NOT be classified as doing business under a fictitious name?
    I.   Victor Alcala, Real Estate Broker.
    II.   Victor Alcala, dba The Victor Alcala Real Estate Company.
    III. Victor Alcala, dba Alcala Realty.
    A. I, II and III   C. III only
    B. II only   D. I only

26. For a corporation to be granted a license as a real estate broker,
    A. all officers must be licensed as real estate brokers.
    B. all stockholders must be licensees.
    C. the chief executive officer must be a licensed broker.
    D. salespersons may NOT hold office in the corporation.

27. In most states, a branch office maintained by a licensed brokerage firm must
    I.   secure a branch office license in the firm's name.
    II. be managed by a licensed real estate broker.
    A. I only   B. II only   C. Both I and II   D. Neither I nor II

28. The requirement that a real estate agent hold a real estate license is set by the
    A. real estate commission. C. real estate director or commissioner.
    B. legislature. D. governor.

29. In most states, members of the real estate commission are
       I. full-time employees appointed by the governor.
      II. all licensed real estate agents.
    A. I only B. II only C. Both I and II D. Neither I nor II

30. The staff of the real estate department or real estate division of most states
       I. establishes regulations governing license applicants.
      II. are full-time civil servants.
     III. investigates complaints regarding licensees.
      IV. performs administrative functions of the department or division.
    A. I, II, III and IV C. II and IV only
    B. I, II and IV only D. II, III and IV only

31. Dibson was found guilty of a violation of the real estate license law at a formal hearing before the real estate commission. This could result in
       I. the revocation of Dibson's license.
      II. an appeal by Dibson before a court of competent jurisdiction.
    A. I only B. II only C. Both I and II D. Neither I nor II

32. Protection against financial losses suffered by a party who was the victim of a licensee's wrongful acts may be provided by
       I. bonding requirements for licensees.
      II. state-sponsored recovery funds.
    A. I only B. II only C. Both I and II D. Neither I nor II

33. Real estate agents who deal in real estate partnerships, timeshare units, rental pools, etc. may find that they will also be required to obtain
    A. an investment counselor's license.
    B. a securities license.
    C. a money manager's license.
    D. a social security license.

34. Among the considerations to be resolved before deciding to become a real estate agent are
       I. uncertain earnings from commission-only compensation plans.
      II. irregular working hours.
    A. I only B. II only C. Both I and II D. Neither I nor II

35. A real estate salesperson may reasonably expect to work
       I. for a salary.
      II. on his own.
     III. with people.
    A. I only B. II only C. III only D. II and III only

36. A new real estate salesperson will most effectively use his/her time looking for
    I. a broker that pays a salary or guarantee.
    II. a 100% commission office.
    A. I only   B. II only   C. Both I and II   D. Neither I nor II

37. Places to look for a broker with whom to affiliate include:
    I. real estate classified ads.
    II. Yellow Pages of phone book.
    III. state employment office.
    IV. private employment agencies.
    A. I only   C. I and II only
    B. II only   D. I, II, III and IV

38. For a real estate salesperson to be considered an independent contractor, all of the following conditions must be met EXCEPT:
    A. the associate must be a licensed real estate agent.
    B. compensation must be based on sales production.
    C. there must be a written agreement setting forth the associate's independent contractor status.
    D. the broker must withhold federal income taxes and social security contributions from the associate's earnings.

39. Affiliation with a national network of franchised real estate brokerage firms appeals to
    I. firms having from 10 to 50 employees.
    II. large national real estate firms.
    A. I only   B. II only   C. Both I and II   D. Neither I nor II

40. The term "Realtor" applies to any
    A. licensed real estate salesperson.
    B. licensed real estate broker.
    C. member of a state real estate commission.
    D. member of the National Association of Realtors.

41. The Realtors' Code of Ethics covers a Realtor's relations with
    A. his clients.   C. fellow Realtors.
    B. the general public.   D. All of the above.

42. Membership in institutes such as the Realtors' National Marketing Institute and the Farm and Land Institute is
    A. open to any licensed real estate broker or salesperson.
    B. requires membership in the National Association of Realtors.
    C. open to any person.
    D. automatically granted to any member of the National Association of Realtors.

The following questions will provide you with additional practice.

43. An agent received a 3% commission on one-fourth of her total sales. On the remainder she received a 6% comission. What was her average commission for all of her sales?
    A. 5.75%   C. 5.25%
    B. 4.25%   D. 4.5%

44. Three properties sold for a total of $120,000. The gross commission is 8%. Office policy is to give 10% of all commissions to the Office Manager. The balance is then divided, giving 45% to the office and the remainder to the salesperson who listed and sold the property. How much did the salesperson earn?
    A. $9,600
    B. $5,400
    C. $4,752
    D. $960

45. A rental agency receives one-third of the first month's rent and 3 1/2% of each month's rent after that. If the agency leases the apartment for one year at $360 per month, how much does the rental agent get?
    A. $271.20
    B. $258.60
    C. $138.60
    D. $12.60

46. A vacant lot was purchased three years ago for $35,000. It was recently listed for sale at a price 20% greater than that. If the seller accepts an offer that is $3,000 below list price, what would she receive after paying the 6% commission?
    A. $39,480
    B. $36,660
    C. $36,480
    D. $36,900

47. A broker charges 6% on the first $100,000, 5% on the next $100,000, 4% on the next $200,000 and 3% above that. On a $1,000,000 sale, what will the commission be?
    A. $30,000
    B. $37,000
    C. $60,000
    D. None of the above

48. Which of the following does not need a license?
    A. A person who offers to lease real estate for compensation.
    B. A person who offers to sell his own property.
    C. A person who offers to exchange real estate for compensation.
    D. A person who auctions real estate for compensation.

49. Bird passed the license examination for real estate salespersons. Which of the following statements are correct?
    I. He must be granted a license.
    II. He would be entitled to a hearing if refused a license.
    III. He must be advised of the reason for refusal if denied a license.
    A. I only   B. II only   C. I and II only   D. II and III only

50. A real estate broker violating a provision of the license law
    I. is not entitled to a commission if one is involved.
    II. could have his licensed revoked.
    A. I only   B. II only   C. Both I and II   D. Neither I nor II

51. The responsibilities of a state's real estate department, division or board include all the following EXCEPT:
    A. granting licenses to applicants.
    B. regulating brokerage fees.
    C. protecting the public interest.
    D. regulating the activities of licensees.

52. The state's real estate department, division or board is empowered to take legal action against all of the following EXCEPT:
   A. licensed real estate brokers.
   B. licensed real estate salespersons.
   C. an unlicensed person who violates the fair housing laws.
   D. a person who acts as a licensee without a license.

53. Wilson, who is not licensed to sell real estate, rented his neighbor's house to a friend. The neighbor bought Wilson a lobster dinner as promised. Did Wilson violate real estate licensing law?
   A. Yes, because there was compensation involved.
   B. No, because the compensation was minor.
   C. No, because the compensation was not money.
   D. No, because they were friends.

54. Which of the following could legally receive compensation for selling real estate for another person without a license as a broker or salesperson?
   A. A licensed real estate appraiser.
   B. The executor of an estate.
   C. The resident manager of an apartment house.
   D. A licensed auctioneer.

55. A telephone answering service for a broker's office may do which of the following?
    I. Give information to a caller about listings available.
   II. Take a listing by telephone.
   A. I only   B. II only   C. Both I and II   D. Neither I nor II

56. Any person who earns a real estate commission and is not licensed is guilty of
   A. duress.   C. breaking the law.
   B. an unethical act.   D. negligence.

57. A builder desires to employ a salesperson for commission to sell houses built by him; he must
   A. obtain a salesperson's license.
   B. notify the state of the contract between himself and the salesperson.
   C. obtain a broker's license.
   D. pay the salesperson less than the usual commission.

58. A real estate listing may be advertised only in the name of the
   A. cooperating broker.
   B. salesperson who obtains listing.
   C. principal licensed broker.
   D. real estate salesperson on the premises.

59. Which of the following persons are specifically exempt from holding a real estate license?
   A. War veterans.   C. Part-time salespersons.
   B. Executors of estates.   D. Listers of real estate.

60. A broker's license is revoked for one year. His two salespersons, who are not the cause of the revocation,
    A. must be placed on inactive status during that time.
    B. may, upon proper application, transfer to another broker.
    C. would lose their licenses for one year.
    D. may continue to operate the broker's business.

61. Real estate regulations set the minimum commission to be charged as
    A. three percent.   C. six percent.
    B. four percent.   D. No minimum is set.

62. A licensed broker may share a commission with
    A. the person who introduced the buyer to the broker.
    B. a salesperson of another broker who assisted in the sale.
    C. a licensed broker who assisted in the sale.
    D. an attorney at law who is a friend of the seller.

63. When a broker discharges a salesperson, he should
    A. give the salesperson his license.
    B. return the license to the real estate department, division or board.
    C. remove the license from the wall and keep it on file until all of the salesperson's deals have been closed out.
    D. instruct the salesperson to return license to real estate commission.

64. A license may be revoked upon proof of
    A. dispute between broker and salesperson as to a commission.
    B. violation of fair housing law.
    C. refusal to accept an overpriced listing.
    D. not selling enough real estate.

65. Mary Newcomer, who is studying for her real estate license, has taken a job as a receptionist at a real estate office. One afternoon, while all the sales personnel are out, a gentleman comes into the office and asks for the price of a property on which her company has a "For Sale" sign. Mary recognizes the value of a new client and wants to be as helpful as possible. By law, she can
    A. tell the gentleman the price and terms as listed, but not show the property or write up an offer.
    B. tell the gentleman the price only and ask him to come back.
    C. hand him a copy of the listing.
    D. say nothing about the price and terms and ask how he can be contacted by a salesperson.

66. Salesperson Quick works for Broker Sail and has just sold a property listed by Sail. Which of the following statements is true?
    I. Quick will receive a commission check from the buyer.
    II. Quick will receive a commission check from the seller.
    III. Quick is entitled to half of the commission and Sail the other half.
    IV. The commission will be collected by Sail and divided per previous agreement between Quick and Sail.
    A. I and III only   C. II and III only
    B. III only   D. IV only

67. Which of the following statements is/are true?
    I.   The laws of agency hold a broker responsible for the acts of his sales associates.
    II. Tax laws may treat a real estate sales associate as an independent contractor.
    A. I only   B. II only   C. Both I and II   D. Neither I nor II

68. Marian B. Greene secured a license as a real estate broker and opened a brokerage office. She would have to file a fictitious name statement if she operated the firm under the name of
    I.   Marian B. Greene, Real Estate Broker.
    II. The Marian B. Greene Real Estate Company.
    A. I only   B. II only   C. Both I and II   D. Neither I nor II

69. A property owner who wants to sell his home is interested in
    I.   how much he can get for it.
    II.   how much it will cost to sell.
    III. how much the listing salesperson will earn.
    A. I and II   B. II only   C. II and III   D. I, II and III

70. Which of the following is NOT required of an applicant for licensure as a real estate salesperson?
    A. An application for license.
    B. A passing grade on the license examination.
    C. A good reputation.
    D. A broker who has agreed to sponsorship.

Answers—Chapter 18

Multiple Choice Questions

1. C   Through real estate license laws, state governments try to assure that persons licensed to do business in real estate are competent and are of good reputation for honesty and truthfulness.

2. C   In order to collect a commission for selling real estate for others, one must be licensed. If no compensation is involved, one may sell real estate for others without a license.

3. D   Attorneys, executors and trustees are exempt from license requirements while acting as such. Appraisers are not exempt.

4. D   Members of the bar and attorneys-in-fact are exempt from license requirements while dealing in real estate as an incidental part of their duties, but may not operate a brokerage office without a license.

5. C   A real estate broker may operate independently. A real estate salesperson may operate only under the supervision of an employing broker.

6. B   Actual persons and any legally constituted form of business entity may be licensed as a real estate broker.

7. B   The holder of any form of license is referred to as a licensee.

8. C   There is no category of license for attorneys-in-fact.

9. D   As a rule, owners of real estate are exempt from license requirements in selling or otherwise dealing with their own property.

10. A   A real estate listing is a contract between the owner and the listing broker; salespersons act as sub-agents of the broker and are not principal parties to listing agreements.

11. B   The employing broker is ultimately responsible for the acts of salespersons in his employ.

12. C   The term "sales associate" refers to licensed salespersons and brokers who are employed by a broker.

13. C   Most states require a combination of formal education and experience for licensure as a real estate broker.

14. C   Broker license examinations tend to cover the topics in greater depth and place a greater emphasis on document preparation than do salesperson examinations.

15. B   The purpose of continuing education requirements is to require licensees to stay up to date in their field.

16. D   Requirements for licensure as a real estate salesperson include completion of education requirements, passing an examination and employment by a licensed real estate broker.

17. D   The employing broker must receive the salesperson's license before the salesperson may operate as a licensee.

18. B   Licensees are not required to retake original license examinations in order to maintain or renew their licenses.

19. C   License examinations given by the national testing services include questions on general real estate practices together with real estate laws, regulations and practices of the jurisdiction.

20. C   In addition to permitting licensees to deal in real estate in the state of licensure, most states also allow commissions on out-of-state transactions provided negotiations are carried out entirely within the boundaries of the state of licensure.

21. D   A real estate broker may share a commission with salespersons licensed in his employ or with other licensed brokers in any state, but not with salespersons licensed with other brokers.

22. A   In order to establish a branch office in another state, the broker must first secure a nonresident broker's license in that state.

23. B   A notice of consent must be filed in each state in which a broker maintains a nonresident license.

24. C   A sole proprietorship may be operated under the proprietor's own name or under a fictitious name.

25. D   A business operated under any name other than the proprietor's own name is considered to be operating under a fictitious name.

26. C   The chief executive officer of a corporation must hold a real estate broker's license in order for the corporation to be licensed as a real estate broker.

27. C   Most states require that a branch office hold a branch office license and be managed by a licensed real estate broker.

28. B   Licensing requirements are set by statutes which are enacted by the state legislature.

29. D   In most states, members of the real estate commission are part-time volunteers, some of whom are licensed real estate agents and some of whom are public members.

30. D   Regulations governing license applicants are established by the real estate commission and state legislature, not by staff members of the department or division.

31. C   The real estate commission is empowered to revoke a licensee's license, and the revocation may be appealed to a court of competent jurisdiction.

32. C   Many states protect the public against financial losses suffered by a victim of a licensee's wrongful acts by bonding requirements or through state-sponsored recovery funds.

33. B   A licensee who deals in investment contracts in real estate as opposed to the actual real estate itself may be required to secure a securities license in addition to a real estate license.

34. C   Persons who contemplate becoming real estate agents should be prepared to work irregular hours for uncertain earnings.

35. D   Real estate salespersons should expect to work on their own, with people, and be paid on a commission basis rather than a salary.

36. D   Neither response I nor II is the most effective way for a new real estate salesperson to utilize his/her time.

37. C   Real estate classified ads and the Yellow Pages of the telephone book are good places to look for a broker with whom to affiliate.

38. D   Independent contractors are responsible for their own income taxes and social security contributions.

39. A   Generally, affiliation with a national network of franchised real estate brokerage firms appeals to firms having from 10 to 50 employees.

40. D   In order to be identified as a Realtor, one must become a member of the National Association of Realtors.

41. D   The Realtors' Code of Ethics covers a Realtor's relations with his clients, the general public and with fellow Realtors.

42. B   Membership in Realtor institutes is restricted to members of the National Association of Realtors.

43. C   1/4 x 3% = 3/4%
        3/4 x 6% = 18/4%
        Total = 21/4% = 21% divided by 4 = 5.25% average

44. C $120,000 x 8% = $9,600 total commission
        $9,600 x 10% = $960 to manager
        $9,600 - $960 = $8,640 remainder
        $8,640 - 45% to office = $4,752 to salesperson

45.   B $360 x 1/3 = $120 first month's commission
            $360 x 3.5% x 11 months = $138.60 next 11 months
            $120 + $138.60 = $258.60 total commission

46.   B $35,000 x 1.20 = $42,000 list price
            $42,000 - $3,000 = $39,000 accepted by seller
            $39,000 x .94 = $36,660 after paying 6% commission

47.   B $100,000 x .06 = $6,000 on first $100,000
            $100,000 x .05 = $5,000 on next $100,000
            $200,000 x .04 = $8,000 on next $200,000
            $600,000 x .03 = $18,000 on remaining $600,000
            Total commission $37,000

48.   B   As a rule, a person who sells his/her own property does not need a
            license. (A few states require a license when an owner sells a
            substantial number of properties in a given year.)

49.   D   An applicant must be told the reason for license denial and can
            appeal.

50.   C   License law violations can result in both loss of commission and loss
            of license.

51.   B   The state does not get involved in regulating brokerage fees; that is
            left to negotiation between the broker and the client.

52.   C   A state's real estate department, division or board regulates
            licensees and license law application. As such, it has no jurisdic-
            tion over an unlicensed person who violates the fair housing laws.

53.   A   If there is compensation, or the promise of compensation, a license
            is required. The amount of compensation, or the fact that it was not
            in money or that they were friends is not the deciding factor.

54.   B   There is an exception to the license requirement for the executor of
            an estate.

55.   D   A telephone answering service cannot give information about listings
            or take a listing.

56.   C   It is against the law to earn a real estate commission without a real
            estate license.

57.   C   A real estate salesperson must have an employing broker; therefore,
            the builder would have to obtain a broker's license.

58.   C   Only the broker who takes the listing is authorized to advertise it.
            That is because only the broker has a contract with the property
            owner.

59.   B   Of this list, only executors of estates are exempt from holding a
            real estate license.

60. B The innocent salespersons will have to find another broker to work for if they wish to continue working as salespersons.

61. D The state sets no minimum commission rate, and to imply that it does is a violation of law.

62. C A broker may share a commission only with his sales associates and with other brokers.

63. B When a salesperson licensee no longer works for a broker, the broker must return that salesperson's license directly to the state.

64. B The state is not concerned with commission disputes between a broker and a salesperson, or whether a broker refuses to take an overpriced listing or whether a licensee doesn't sell any property. But the state is concerned if a licensee violates fair housing laws.

65. D No matter how tempting or pressing the situation, the law must be respected. Since she is not licensed, she cannot commit any act of selling, such as quote price and terms. She can, however, put the customer in contact with a licensee who can answer those questions.

66. D The seller pays the broker who, in turn, pays his sales associates and any cooperating brokers. Remember that everything flows through the broker.

67. C A broker is responsible for the acts of his/her sales associates. A sales associate can be treated as an independent contractor if certain conditions are met.

68. B The use of anything other than a person's full name requires a fictitious name statement. This is so clients and customers can identify the actual persons behind a company name.

69. A A property owner is primarily interested in how much the property will sell for and how much of that will be consumed by selling costs. The owner has little interest in, or need to know about, the salesperson's commission arrangement with the broker.

70. D A broker's sponsorship is not necessary to apply for a license and take the exam. It is, however, necessary before the license will be issued.

Condominiums, Cooperatives, PUDs and Timeshares

Chapter 19

1. The popularity of condominium ownership may be attributed in part to
     I.   scarcity of land in desirable areas.
    II.   rising construction costs.
   III.   the desire to own rather than rent.
    IV.   enactment of Section 234 of the National Housing Act.
   A. III only   C. II only
   B. I and IV only   D. I, II, III and IV

2. Section 234 of the National Housing Act
     I.   provides a legal model for condominium ownership.
    II.   makes available FHA insurance on mortgage loans on condominium
           units.
   A. I only   B. II only   C. Both I and II   D. Neither I nor II

3. State laws which provide the legal framework for condominium ownership
   may be identified by any of the following terms EXCEPT:
   A. strata titles act.   C. condominium act.
   B. cooperative housing act.   D. horizontal property act.

4. Condominium developments are restricted to
     I.   residential dwelling units.
    II.   multiple unit buildings.
   A. I only   B. II only   C. Both I and II   D. Neither I nor II

5. In order to create a condominium development, a developer may
     I.   construct a new building.
    II.   convert an existing building.
   A. I only   B. II only   C. Both I and II   D. Neither I nor II

6. Condominium developments are distinguished by the existence of
     I.   separate and common elements.
    II.   a system of self-government.
   A. I only   B. II only   C. Both I and II   D. Neither I nor II

Note: There are no deleted questions in this chapter for readers of
       Real Estate: An Introduction to the Profession.

7. Individual units in a condominium development are classed as
   A. separate property.
   B. common elements.
   C. cooperative elements.
   D. limited common elements.

8. Within a condominium development, common elements are owned by
   A. the owners' association.
   B. all unit owners, who hold undivided interests in the elements.
   C. the condominium developer.
   D. individual unit owners as community property.

9. Which of the following would be classified as limited common elements in a condominium development?
   A. Elevators.
   B. Hallways.
   C. Assigned parking spaces.
   D. The manager's apartment.

10. The plan for a condominium development which converts a single parcel of land into individual separate property estates and an estate composed of all common elements may be referred to as
    I. an enabling declaration.
    II. a master deed.
    A. I only   B. II only   C. Both I and II   D. Neither I nor II

11. A condominium owners' association is
    I. a mini-government by and for the condominium owners.
    II. provided for in the plan of condominium ownership.
    A. I only   B. II only   C. Both I and II   D. Neither I nor II

12. The rules by which an owners' association operates are known as
    A. bylaws.
    B. covenants, conditions and restrictions.
    C. house rules.
    D. ordinances.

13. Enabling declarations for condominium developments are usually filed by the
    A. property tax assessor.
    B. lender for the project.
    C. owners' association.
    D. condominium developer.

14. The purchaser of a condominium unit is obligated to abide by the development's
    I. covenants, conditions and restrictions.
    II. house rules.
    A. I only   B. II only   C. Both I and II   D. Neither I nor II

15. The purchaser of a condominium unit receives a
    A. deed from the seller.
    B. separate deed to the common elements.
    C. deed from the owner's association.
    D. shares of stock in the condominium.

16. Once the units in a condominium development have been sold and the association turned over to the unit owners, the association can change any of the following EXCEPT the:
    A. bylaws.   C. CC&Rs.
    B. enabling declaration.   D. house rules.

17. As compared to a local (city) government, the role of the board of directors of a condominium development approximates that of the
    A. mayor's office.   C. police department.
    B. city manager's office.   D. city council.

18. Day-to-day management of a condominium development may be provided by
    I.   an on-site manager.   III. the board of directors.
    II. a management company.   IV.   a management committee.
    A. I, II, III and IV   C. III only
    B. I and II only   D. I, II and III only

19. The funds for maintaining the annual budget of a condominium are obtained through
    A. association dues assessed upon each unit owner.
    B. taxes on the value of the units.
    C. liens on individual units.
    D. a mortgage on the common elements.

20. In a condominium, the authority to raise homeowner fees (association dues) rests with the
    A. board of directors.   C. condominium act.
    B. management company.   D. city and county.

21. An owners' association should set aside reserves for which of the following?
    I.   Painting of the building's exterior.
    II. Roof replacement.
    III. Driveway resurfacing.
    A. I and III only   C. I, II and III
    B. II and III only   D. None of the above.

22. The owners' association of a condominium is typically responsible for the payment of
    I. hazard insurance premiums on the common elements.
    II. maintenance within individual units.
    A. I only   B. II only   C. Both I and II   D. Neither I nor II

23. The guest of a unit owner was injured by stepping on broken glass in the swimming pool at the Sunset Hills condominium. Liability for this injury would probably fall upon
    I. the unit owner.
    II. the condominium association.
    A. I only   B. II only   C. Both I and II   D. Neither I nor II

24. Owner Goff defaulted on the mortgage loan on his condominium unit. At foreclosure, the high bid was not sufficient to satisfy the obligation, and the lender secured a deficiency judgment for the remainder of the amount due. This judgment would be entered against
   A. Goff's unit in the condominium.
   B. the condominium corporation.
   C. the condominium owners association.
   D. any other property, real or personal, owned by Goff.

25. Which of the following is (are) true?
   I. The condominium owners' association governs the type and amount of financing on individual units.
   II. The condominium owners' association may NOT control the uses to which an owner may put his unit.
   A. I only   B. II only   C. Both I and II   D. Neither I nor II

26. Failure to pay condominium association dues will result in a lien against the
   A. owners' association.
   B. delinquent owner's unit.
   C. city in which the condominium is located.
   D. enabling declaration.

27. In a condominium, property taxes are assessed against
   A. the owners' association for proration among unit owners.
   B. the master deed for proration by the association's board of directors.
   C. each individual unit with a bill sent to each unit's owner.
   D. the property management company which in turn collects from unit owners.

28. Condominium unit property taxes are a function of the
   I. market value of a unit.
   II. assessed value of a unit.
   A. I only   B. II only   C. Both I and II   D. Neither I nor II

29. The purchase of a condominium unit may be financed by means of
   I. an FHA-insured loan.
   II. an installment contract.
   III. a conventional loan.
   IV. seller carryback financing.
   A. I, II, III and IV   C. I, II and IV only
   B. I and III only   D. III only

30. Troy signed a contract for the purchase of a condominium unit and gave the developer an earnest money deposit, which was to be held by the developer until settlement. Before Troy's unit was built, the developer filed for bankruptcy. Troy would receive
   I. his deposit money back.
   II. a deed to a unit which had been completed.
   A. I only   B. II only   C. Both I and II   D. Neither I nor II

31. An existing building may be converted to a condominium by
    I. a condominium developer.
    II. the rental tenants who occupy the building.
    A. I only   B. II only   C. Both I and II   D. Neither I nor II

32. The purchaser of a condominium unit
    I. surrenders personal freedoms to community rule.
    II. exchanges freedom of choice for freedom from responsibility.
    A. I only   B. II only   C. Both I and II   D. Neither I nor II

33. Tom and Mary have owned at the Seaview Condominiums for two years. In order to enhance the view from their unit, they want to enlarge one of its windows. Which of the following statements is NOT true?
    A. They can do this as long as they don't injure adjoining units.
    B. To do this would violate the CC&Rs.
    C. Tom and Mary's windows do not belong to them; therefore they have no right to enlarge them.
    D. They can do this if given permission by the owners' association.

34. Ownership of the interior space of your home and garage and an undivided interest in the building structures, common areas and land area of the entire project describes a
    I. condominium.
    II. cooperative.
    A. I only   B. II only   C. Both I and II   D. Neither I nor II

35. Which of the following are characteristics of a cooperative housing development?
    I. Tenants do NOT hold fee title to their units.
    II. Cooperatives are NOT regulated by horizontal property acts.
    III. Tenants occupy their units under a proprietary lease.
    IV. Tenants are shareholders in a corporation which holds title to the property.
    A. I, III and IV only   C. III and IV only
    B. I, II, III and IV   D. II and IV only

36. Baker defaulted on his share of the monthly mortgage payments on the cooperative in which he lived. The cooperative corporation may NOT
    A. foreclose on his unit.
    B. terminate him as a shareholder.
    C. resell his shares to someone else.
    D. bring civil action in court to recover the delinquent amount.

37. Traditionally, the resale of cooperative shares have been financed by means of
    I. installment sales agreements.
    II. second mortgages on the seller's unit.
    A. I only   B. II only   C. Both I and II   D. Neither I nor II

38. Which of the following statements are correct?
    I. The government of a cooperative is very similar to that of a condominium.
    II. A condominium owner has no liability for the mortgage debt against his neighbor's unit.
    A. I only   B. II only   C. Both I and II   D. Neither I nor II

39. The governing body of a cooperative is called a
    A. cooperation.   C. CC&R.
    B. corporation.   D. board of directors.

40. Which is the oldest form of owner-occupied community housing in the United States?
    A. Condominium ownership.   C. Timeshared ownership.
    B. Planned unit development.   D. Cooperative ownership.

41. In some states, legislation makes it possible for a cooperative to be
    I. financed by the sale of stock which is pledged to a lender.
    II. assessed for property taxes on the basis of individual assessments to each cooperator.
    A. I only   B. II only   C. Both I and II   D. Neither I nor II

42. The owner of a unit in a planned unit development holds title to all of the following EXCEPT:
    A. the air above his unit.   C. a share of the common areas.
    B. the land beneath his unit.   D. fee simple title to his unit.

43. Which of the following is true of ownership in a planned unit development?
    I. Title to the common areas is held by the owners' association.
    II. There are no CC&Rs governing individual owners as with condominiums and cooperatives.
    A. I only   B. II only   C. Both I and II   D. Neither I nor II

44. In a planned unit development, the owners' association may have control over
    I. exterior paint colors.
    II. the number of persons who occupy a dwelling unit.
    A. I only   B. II only   C. Both I and II   D. Neither I nor II

45. Membership in the owners' association is automatic upon purchase of a
    I. unit in a condominium.
    II. house in a planned unit development.
    A. I only   B. II only   C. Both I and II   D. Neither I nor II

46. In a condominium, cooperative and planned unit development, rules governing the use of recreation facilities will be found in the
    A. deed to the property.   C. bylaws.
    B. enabling declaration.   D. CC&Rs and house rules.

47. In a planned unit development, the owners' association can dictate all of the following EXCEPT:
    A. exterior paint colors.   C. use of common areas.
    B. exterior landscaping.   D. interior paint colors.

48. The concept of dividing up and selling living units at a vacation
    facility for specified lengths of time each year is
      I. known as resort timesharing.
     II. a recent development in communal ownership of real estate.
    A. I only   B. II only   C. Both I and II   D. Neither I nor II

49. Of the two principal forms of timeshare formats, which comprises the
    larger percentage of the market?
    A. Right-to-use.
    B. Fee simple.
    C. Each holds an approximately equal market share.
    D. Statistics are not available.

50. Under the right-to-use plan of timesharing, the purchaser
      I. holds title to real property.
     II. is a tenant in common with other users of the unit.
    A. I only   B. II only   C. Both I and II   D. Neither I nor II

51. The purchaser of a timeshare unit under the fee simple format
      I. holds title in perpetuity.
     II. receives a deed to his share of ownership.
    A. I only   B. II only   C. Both I and II   D. Neither I nor II

52. Swenson is considering the purchase of a timeshare unit in a ski resort
    located in the Rocky Mountains. In terms of original cost the least ex-
    pensive purchase would be one week in a
    A. right-to-use development during the month of May.
    B. fee simple development during January.
    C. fee simple development during the month of June.
    D. right-to-use development during the month of December.

53. Among the more attractive features of timeshare ownership to a prospec-
    tive purchaser are
      I. the purchase of future vacations at a prepaid price.
     II. the ability to exchange one's timeshare among units at other
          resorts.
    A. I only   B. II only   C. Both I and II   D. Neither I nor II

54. In terms of investment possibilities, timeshares are generally regarded
    as
    A. low risk, high appreciation probability.
    B. high risk, low appreciation probability.
    C. high risk, high appreciation probability.
    D. about equal to other forms of real estate investment.

55. The sale of timeshares is regulated in about twenty-five states by
    A. the National Association of License Law Officials.
    B. the National TimeSharing Council.
    C. the National Association of Realtors.
    D. state legislation.

Answers—Chapter 19

Multiple Choice Questions

1. **D** Scarcity of land, rising construction costs, desire for ownership and enactment of Section 234 of the National Housing Act have all contributed to the popularity of condominium ownership.

2. **C** Section 234 of the National Housing Act provides a legal model for condominium ownership and makes availabe FHA insurance on mortgage loans on condominium units.

3. **B** Condominium housing is not covered by state laws governing cooperative ownership.

4. **D** Any multi-unit development may be organized as a condominium.

5. **C** Condominium developments may be created by constructing a new building or conversion of an existing building.

6. **C** A system of self-government and the existence of separate and common elements are distinguishing features of a condominium development.

7. **A** Individual units in a condominium are classed as separate property.

8. **B** Common elements in a condominium development are owned by all unit owners, who hold undivided interests in the elements.

9. **C** Limited common elements are those common elements the use of which is restricted to one unit owner.

10. **C** An enabling declaration or master deed is used to convert a single estate into separate property estates and an estate composed of the common elements.

11. **C** A condominium owners' association is a mini-government by and for the unit owners, and is provided for in the plan of condominium ownership.

12. **A** Bylaws provide the rules by which an owners' association operates.

13. **D** The condominium developer usually files the enabling declaration for a condominium development.

14. **C** The purchaser of a condominium development is obligated to abide by the development's covenants, conditions and restrictions as well as by any house rules.

15. **A** The purchaser of a condominium unit receives a deed from the seller.

16. B   The enabling declaration cannot be changed by an owners' association, but the bylaws, CC&Rs or house rules may be changed.

17. D   The role of the board of directors in a condominium compares to the city council in a local government.

18. B   Day-to-day management of a condominium development may be provided by an on-site manager or by a management company.

19. A   A condominium development secures its budgeted maintenance funds from association dues assessed upon each unit owner, usually monthly.

20. A   The board of directors of a condominium has the authority to raise association dues.

21. C   An owner's association should maintain reserves for maintenance of all the common elements listed here.

22. A   The owners' association of a condominium is responsible for hazard insurance on the common elements. Individual unit owners are responsible for maintenance within their units.

23. B   Liability arising from injuries received on any of the common elements belongs to the condominium association.

24. D   The deficiency judgment would be entered against any other property, real or personal, owned by Goff.

25. D   The condominium owners' association has no control over the financing of individual units, but may control the uses to which an owner may put his unit.

26. B   Failure to pay condominium association dues will result in a lien against the delinquent owner's unit.

27. C   In a condominium, taxes are assessed against each individual unit with a bill sent to each unit's owner.

28. C   The property taxes on a condominium unit are based on the assessed value of the unit which is based on its market value.

29. A   The purchase of a condominium unit may be financed by means of an FHA-insured loan, an installment contract, a conventional loan or by seller carryback financing.

30. D   Since the deposit was not held in escrow, the purchaser will receive neither a finished unit nor a refund of his deposit.

31. C   An existing building may be converted to a condominium by a condominium developer or by the rental tenants who occupy the building.

32. C   A condominium unit purchaser surrenders personal freedoms to community rule and exchanges freedom of choice for freedom from responsibility.

33.   A   Windows are common elements owned by all the unit owners. Any structural change is a violation of the CC&Rs; however, the owners' association can make an exception or change the CC&Rs.

34.   A   Condominium ownership consists of ownership of the interior space of a unit (sometimes including a garage) plus an interest in the building structures, common areas and land area of the entire project.

35.   B   All responses are characteristic of a cooperative development.

36.   A   A cooperative corporation does not foreclose on a delinquent cooperator but may terminate the cooperator as a shareholder, resell his shares, or bring civil action to recover the delinquent amount.

37.   A   Traditionally, the resale of cooperative shares has been financed by installment sales agreements because the underlying mortgage is a mortgage on the entire premises.

38.   C   Government of condominiums and cooperatives is very similar. A condominium owner has no liability for the mortgage debt against his neighbor's unit.

39.   D   A cooperative is governed by a board of directors elected by the cooperators.

40.   D   Cooperatives have been in existence in the United States for a much longer time than condominiums, PUDs or timeshared ownership.

41.   C   Some states allow a cooperative to be financed by the sale of stock which is pledged to a lender and property taxes to be assessed on the basis of individual assessments to each cooperator.

42.   C   In a planned unit development, title to the common areas is held by the owners' association, of which all unit owners are members.

43.   A   In a PUD, the title to common areas is held by the owners' association and there are CC&Rs governing individual owners.

44.   C   A PUD owner's association can control exterior paint colors and the number of persons who may occupy a dwelling unit.

45.   C   The purchase of a unit in a condominium or a house in a PUD includes membership in the owners' association.

46.   D   Rules governing the use of recreational facilities in a condominium, cooperative or planned unit development are found in the CC&Rs and house rules.

47.   D   The owners' association has no control over interior paint colors in a planned unit development.

48. C   Resort timesharing, the concept of selling divided shares in living units at a vacation facility, is a recent development in communal ownership of real estate.

49. B   Approximately 70 per cent of timeshared properties are owned in fee simple.

50. D   The purchaser in a right-to-use timeshared property does not hold title to the property and is not a tenant in common with other users of the unit.

51. C   The purchaser of a timeshare in a unit under the fee simple format holds a fee simple estate, and so holds title in perpetuity and receives a deed to his share in the property.

52. A   A right-to-use timeshare is usually less expensive than a similar fee simple timeshare, and an off-season week is less expensive than an in-season week.

53. C   The purchase of future vacations at a prepaid price and the ability to exchange are among the principal attractions of timeshare ownership.

54. B   As investments, timeshares are generally regarded as a high risk, low appreciation probability.

55. D   About 25 states have enacted legislation regulating timeshare sales.

Property Insurance

Chapter 20

1. As an owner of real estate, one is exposed to losses by
   I.   damage to the property.
   II. other persons being injured on the property.
   A. I only   B. II only   C. Both I and II   D. Neither I nor II

2. The concept of insurance is to
   I.   reimburse the insured for financial losses.
   II. insure that a loss-causing event will not occur.
   A. I only   B. II only   C. Both I and II   D. Neither I nor II

3. The New York Fire Insurance form
   I.   was originally enacted by the legislature of New York State.
   II. provides the foundation for most property damage insurance policies
        in this country.
   A. I only   B. II only   C. Both I and II   D. Neither I nor II

4. The New York Fire Insurance form does NOT provide coverage for losses
   A. by fire.
   B. by lightning.
   C. sustained while removing property from damaged premises.
   D. by flood.

5. Which of the following correspond?
   I.   insured---policyholder
   II. insurer---insurance company
   A. I only   B. II only   C. Both I and II   D. Neither I nor II

6. The money paid for insurance is called the insurance
   A. rider.   C. peril.
   B. endorsement.   D. premium.

Note: This chapter is deleted in its entirety for readers of <u>Real Estate:</u>
       <u>An Introduction to the Profession.</u>

7. An insurance endorsement is also known as
    I. a rider.
   II. an attachment.
  III. an assignment.
   A. I and II only   C. II and III only
   B. I and III only   D. I, II and III

8. Coverage for additional perils can be obtained by
    I. purchasing a separate policy.
   II. adding an endorsement to a regular fire insurance policy.
   A. I only   B. II only   C. Both I and II   D. Neither I nor II

9. The financial responsibility which one has to others as a result of one's
   actions or negligence is known as
    I. personal liability.
   II. public liability.
   A. I only   B. II only   C. Both I and II   D. Neither I nor II

10. A homeowner's insurance policy will NOT protect against which of the
    following?
    A. Public liability directly connected with the insured property.
    B. Damage to household goods contained in the insured premises.
    C. Flood damage to the insured premises.
    D. Theft of personal property.

11. In a typical homeowner's policy,
     I. section I deals with losses to the insured's property.
    II. section II covers liability of the insured and family.
    A. I only   B. II only   C. Both I and II   D. Neither I nor II

12. A typical homeowner insurance policy covers
     I. the dwelling house.
    II. other structures on the lot.
   III. living expenses while damage to the residence is being repaired.
    IV. personal property within the dwelling.
     V. automobiles in a garage on the premises.
    A. I, II, III, IV and V   C. I, III and IV only
    B. I, II, III and IV only   D. I, II and III only

13. Which of the following homeowner policy formats covers the most perils?
    A. Basic.   C. Special form.
    B. Broad form.   D. Comprehensive.

14. Coverage for the damage due to the weight of ice, snow and sleet would
    NOT be found in which of the following policies?
    A. HO-1.   C. HO-3.
    B. HO-2.   D. HO-5.

15. Which of the following homeowner policies is especially designed for
    older homes?
    A. HO-3.   C. HO-6.
    B. HO-5.   D. HO-8.

16. A typical HO-2 homeowner's policy covers damage caused by
    I. windstorm.   III. freezing water pipes.
    II. vandalism.   IV. earthquake.
    A. I, II, III and IV   C. I, III and IV only
    B. I, II and IV only   D. I, II and III only

17. An "all-risk" homeowner policy (HO-5) includes coverage for damage resulting from
    I. war.
    II. nuclear accident.
    A. I only   B. II only   C. Both I and II   D. Neither I nor II

18. A tenant in a rented dwelling who wants to insure against perils other than the dwelling itself should purchase which of the following policies?
    A. HO-2.   C. HO-4.
    B. HO-3.   D. HO-5.

19. John rents a dwelling unit in a condominium. To insure his home furnishings and his personal liability arising from this rental, he will ask his insurance agent for
    A. a condominium policy.   C. a tenant's policy.
    B. a landlord's policy.   D. an owner's policy.

20. An HO-6 policy provides a condominium unit owner with protection which covers
    I. personal property within the unit.
    II. the common elements.
    A. I only   B. II only   C. Both I and II   D. Neither I nor II

21. Section II of a homeowner insurance policy provides liability protection for
    I. the named insured.
    II. members of the named insured's family who live with the insured.
    A. I only   B. II only   C. Both I and II   D. Neither I nor II

22. The liability coverage of a homeowner policy
    I. applies only to the insured premises.
    II. provides protection away from the premises.
    A. I only   B. II only   C. Both I and II   D. Neither I nor II

23. Medical payments provided under a homeowner policy can be paid to
    I. the named insured and family members.
    II. guests of the insured on the premises.
    III. other persons away from the property who are injured by the insured.
    IV. claims arising from business pursuits.
    A. I, II and III only   C. I and II only
    B. II and III only   D. I, II, III and IV

24. Coverage under any homeowner policy can be extended by adding endorsements covering
    I. appreciation on the value of the property.
    II. worker's compensation.
    A. I only   B. II only   C. Both I and II   D. Neither I nor II

25. When a property is mortgaged to a lending institution, the lender will
    usually require the owner to provide
    A. fire and extended coverage on structures.
    B. personal property coverage.
    C. medical payments coverage.
    D. liability coverage.

26. The lender on a condominium unit will require proof that the
    I. unit owner carries liability insurance.
    II. condominium association carries insurance on the common elements.
    A. I only   B. II only   C. Both I and II   D. Neither I nor II

27. Mr. Green has a home which would cost $60,000 to replace. He carries
    $45,000 in insurance. A fire causes damage that will cost $20,000 to
    repair. Applying the 80% coinsurance calculation, how much would he
    receive to repair the damage?
    A. $20,000.   C. $16,000.
    B. $18,750.   D. $15,000.

28. Lenders on real estate mortgages may require that the borrower provide
    I.   a replacement cost policy.
    II. insurance on the full amount of the loan.
    III. insurance in an amount equal to the purchase price of the property.
    IV. inflation guard coverage.
    A. I and II only   C. II and IV only
    B. I, II and IV only   D. I, II, III and IV

29. An insurance policy which fixes the insurance company's liability to the
    insured to the actual cash value of the insured property is said to
    provide
    A. "old for new" coverage.   C. "old for old" coverage.
    B. "new for old" coverage.   D. "new for new" coverage.

30. A homeowner's policy in an amount equal to 80% of the replacement cost of
    the house would, in the event of a loss, pay
    A. actual cash value of the loss.
    B. less than actual cash value of the loss.
    C. replacement cost less depreciation.
    D. full replacement cost up to the face amount of the policy.

31. Flood insurance can be purchased for
    I. structures.
    II. contents.
    A. I only   B. II only   C. Both I and II   D. Neither I nor II

32. All of the following mortgages require either flood insurance or a cer-
    tificate that the mortgaged property is not in a flood zone EXCEPT:
    A. VA-guaranteed mortgages.
    B. FHA-insured mortgages.
    C. mortgages carried back by sellers.
    D. conventional mortgages secured from federally chartered savings
       and loans associations.

33. If an insurer cancels a policy that contains the New York Fire Form there must be a
    I. 5-day notice.
    II. prorated refund of the unused portion of the policy.
    A. I only   B. II only   C. Both I and II   D. Neither I nor II

34. The owner of a rented property may insure that property by obtaining
    I. an endorsement to an existing homeowner policy.
    II. a landlord package policy.
    A. I only   B. II only   C. Both I and II   D. Neither I nor II

35. A landlord package policy provides coverage for
    I. property damage.   III. medical expenses.
    II. liability.   IV. loss of rents.
    A. I, II, III and IV   C. II and III only
    B. I and IV only   D. I, II and IV only

36. If the insured wishes to cancel his New York Fire Form policy
    I. he must give a 5-day notice.
    II. he will receive a prorated refund.
    A. I only   B. II only   C. Both I and II   D. Neither I nor II

37. An insurer may suspend an insurance policy if
    I. the insured allows the hazard exposure to the insurer to increase beyond the risks contemplated when the policy was issued.
    II. the property is left vacant beyond a specified time.
    A. I only   B. II only   C. Both I and II   D. Neither I nor II

38. Roberta has recently secured a real estate broker's license and will use the den in her home as her real estate office. Which of the following statements is correct?
    I. Roberta should notify her insurance carrier of the business use of the property.
    II. Roberta's HO-3 policy provides adequate protection for this use of the property.
    A. I only   B. II only   C. Both I and II   D. Neither I nor II

39. Among the following, who holds an insurable interest?
    I. A property owner.
    II. A mortgage lender.
    A. I only   B. II only   C. Both I and II   D. Neither I nor II

40. The purchaser of a new home may protect himself against loss due to structural defects by
    I. having the home inspected before purchase.
    II. purchasing insurance under the Home Owners Warranty Program.
    A. I only   B. II only   C. Both I and II   D. Neither I nor II

Insurance Problems

1. Homer Knerr owns a home which would cost $80,000 to replace at present replacement costs. He reasons that any loss sustained would probably be less than this amount, as he is located near a fire department and someone is at home most of the time. In order to save money on his insurance premiums, he purchases a homeowner's policy in the amount of $40,000. Should the property suffer a loss costing $15,000 to repair, what would be the amount of recovery? Actual cash value of the loss is $10,000.

   $_____

2. The Greens have HO-2 coverage on their home in the amount of $130,000. Replacement cost is estimated at present at $135,000. The fireplace chimney becomes clogged with soot, resulting in smoke damage amounting to $800 from a fire in the fireplace. What amount will the Greens recover from the insurance company?

   $_____

3. Mr. Blue works in an office located in a high-rise office building. He parks his car in an assigned space adjacent to the building. High winds blow a sign off the roof of the building. The sign lands on Mr. Blue's car, resulting in several hundred dollars in damage. Who is responsible for paying to repair the damage?

   Mr. Blue _____   The building's owners _____

Answers—Chapter 20

Multiple Choice Questions

1. C The owner of real property is exposed to losses from casualty damage to the property and from personal liability to others who may be injured on the property.

2. A The concept of insurance is to reimburse the insured for financial losses. Insurance does not prevent loss-causing events from occurring.

3. C Originally enacted by the New York state legislature, the New York Fire Insurance Form has become the industry standard for property damage insurance policies in this country.

4. D Flood insurance is not among the coverages provided by the New York Fire Insurance Form.

5. C Both word pairs correspond.

6. D The premium is the money paid by the insured for insurance coverage.

7. A An endorsement to an insurance policy is also known as a rider or an attachment.

8. C Coverage for additional perils can be obtained by purchasing a separate policy or by adding an endorsement to an existing policy.

9. C Financial responsibility to others as a result of one's actions or negligence is known as personal liability or public liability.

10. C Flood damage is not covered by a homeowners' insurance policy; it is a separate coverage.

11. C In a typical homeowner's insurance policy, section I deals with losses to the insured's property and section II covers liability of the insured and family.

12. B A typical homeowner insurance policy will not cover automobiles kept in a garage on the premises, but does cover the dwelling house, other structures, living expenses while damage is being repaired and personal property within the dwelling.

13. D A comprehensive homeowner policy covers the most perils.

14. A An HO-1 policy will not cover damage caused by the weight of ice, snow and sleet. This would be covered by an HO-2, HO-3 or HO-5 policy.

15. D The HO-8 policy covers the same perils as an HO-1 policy and insures for actual cash value. It was designed especially for older homes.

16. D   A typical HO-2 policy does not cover earthquake damage, but does cover damage from windstorm, vandalism or freezing water pipes.

17. D   Damage from war or nuclear accident is not covered by an HO-5 policy, nor by any homeowner policy for that matter.

18. C   The HO-4 policy is especially designed to meet the needs of a tenant in a rented dwelling by duplicating the coverage of an HO-2 policy without insuring the dwelling itself.

19. C   A tenant's policy (HO-4) is designed to meet the needs of a tenant in a rented condominium unit.

20. A   An HO-6 policy insures a condominium unit owner's personal property within the unit. The association's policy covers the common elements.

21. C   Section II of a homeowner policy provides liability protection for the named insured and family members who live with the insured.

22. C   The liability coverage of a homeowner policy provides protection both on and away from the insured premises.

23. B   Medical payments can be paid only to guests of the insured on the premises or to others injured by the insured away from the property. The insured, family members, or claims arising from business pursuits are not eligible for medical payments.

24. C   Coverage for appreciation in property value and for worker's compensation can be added to a homeowner policy by endorsement.

25. A   Lenders will usually require the owner to provide fire and extended coverage on structures, but not personal property coverage.

26. B   The lender on a condominium unit will usually require proof that the condominium association carries insurance on the common elements, but will not require that the unit owner carry liability insurance.

27. B $$\frac{\$45,000 \text{ insurance carried}}{\$60,000 \text{ replacement cost x 80\%}} = .9375$$

$20,000 loss x .9375 = $18,750 recovery

28. A   Lenders typically require the borrower to carry a replacement cost policy equal to the full amount of the loan.

29. C   An "old for old" insurance policy fixes the insurance company's liability to the insured to the actual cash value of the insured property.

30. D   Homeowner's insurance in the amount of 80% of replacement cost will pay full replacement cost up to the face amount of the policy in the event of a loss.

31. C   Flood insurance can be purchased for both structures and contents.

32. C   Carryback financing does not normally require flood insurance or certification that a property is not in a flood zone. VA-guaranteed mortgages, FHA-insured mortgages and conventional mortgages from federally chartered S&Ls all require this.

33. C   An insurer who cancels a policy which contains the New York Fire Form must give the insured a 5-day notice and a prorated refund of unused premiums.

34. C   The owner of a rented property may insure the property by obtaining an endorsement to an existing homeowner policy or a landlord package policy.

35. A   A landlord package policy provides coverage for property damage, liability, medical expenses and loss of rents.

36. D   An insured may cancel a New York Fire Form policy without giving a 5 day notice. Any refunds will be based on short-rate premiums, which is less than a pro-rated refund.

37. C   An insurance policy may be suspended by the insurer if the hazard exposure is allowed to increase beyond the risks contemplated when the policy was issued or if the property is left vacant beyond a specified time.

38. A   The insured should be notified if any part of a residential property is used for business purposes.

39. C   Property owners and mortgage lenders hold an insurable interest in properties which they own or on which the lender holds a mortgage.

40. C   New home purchasers may protect against losses due to structural defects by having the home inspected before purchase and by purchasing insurance under the Home Owners Warranty Program.

INSURANCE PROBLEMS

1. $$\frac{\$40,000}{\$80,000 \times 80\%} \times \$15,000 = \$9,375$$

    But, this is less than the actual cash value of the loss. Therefore he will get $10,000 which represents the actual cash loss.

2. HO-2 coverage includes smoke damage and the Greens carry over 80% of replacement cost. Therefore they will recover the full $800.

3. The building's owners are responsible for damage caused by the sign falling off their building.

Land–Use Control

Chapter 21

1. Historically, early forms of land zoning can be traced to
   A. medieval towns and cities.
   B. colonial America.
   C. Boston, Baltimore and Indianapolis in the late 1800s.
   D. All of the above.

2. All of the following are examples of public land-use controls EXCEPT:
   A. zoning laws.   C. master plans.
   B. subdivision regulations.   D. deed restrictions.

3. Land-use controls may be imposed by
     I. state governments.
    II. local governments.
   III. subdivision developers.
   A. II only   C. III only
   B. II and III only   D. I, II and III

4. Land-use controls, when properly designed, consider
     I. the economic and social impact of development on the community.
    II. the right of the individual to develop his land.
   A. I only   B. II only   C. Both I and II   D. Neither I nor II

5. Zoning laws may NOT be used to regulate which of the following?
   A. The purpose for which a building may be constructed.
   B. The number of persons a building may accommodate.
   C. The placement of interior partitions.
   D. The height and bulk of a building.

Note: This chapter corresponds to Chapter 20 in Real Estate: An Intro-
      duction to the Profession and you may omit questions 31-33 and 37-40.

6. Through zoning, a community can protect existing land users from
   I. encroachment by undesirable uses.
   II. uncontrolled development.
   III. incompatible uses of land.
   IV. competitive business establishments.
   A. I, II, III and IV   C. II and III only
   B. I, II and III only   D. I and IV only

7. The basic authority for zoning laws is derived from a state's
   I. powers of eminent domain.
   II. right of taxation.
   A. I only   B. II only   C. Both I and II   D. Neither I nor II

8. Symbols or code abbreviations used to designate land-use zones such as
   agricultural, residential, commercial or industrial zones are
   A. uniform throughout the United States.
   B. the same for all counties within each state.
   C. not uniformly used throughout the United States.
   D. designated by state statute.

9. Zoning laws
   I. tell a landowner the use to which he may put his land.
   II. compensate an owner for loss of property value due to zoning.
   A. I only   B. II only   C. Both I and II   D. Neither I nor II

10. Checking the zoning on a parcel of land is a matter of
    I. going to the zoning office of the city or county where the parcel
       is located and inquiring as to its zoning.
    II. consulting the zoning ordinance as to permitted uses for that zone.
    A. I only   B. II only   C. Both I and II   D. Neither I nor II

11. Applied to land use, zoning laws may do all of the following EXCEPT:
    A. encourage uniformity in land usage.
    B. set minimum square footage requirements for buildings.
    C. determine the location of a building on a lot.
    D. dictate construction standards for buildings.

12. Should a landowner develop his land without first obtaining a building
    permit, he could
    I. be sent to jail.
    II. be forced to tear down the building.
    A. I only   B. II only   C. Both I and II   D. Neither I nor II

13. A use of property which is not in agreement with present zoning laws
    I. is called a nonconforming use.
    II. may be permitted under a so-called "grandfather clause."
    A. I only   B. II only   C. Both I and II   D. Neither I nor II

14. A grandfather clause in a zoning ordinance will permit the owner of a
    building which is in nonconforming use to do which of the following?
    A. Enlarge the building.   C. Extend its life.
    B. Remodel the exterior.   D. Perform all normal maintenance.

15. Permission to use a building for a nonconforming use may be accomplished by
    I.   amendment of the zoning ordinance.
    II. obtaining a zoning variance.
    A. I only   B. II only   C. Both I and II   D. Neither I nor II

16. A zoning variance
    I.   allows an owner to deviate from existing zoning law.
    II. involves a change in the zoning law.
    A. I only   B. II only   C. Both I and II   D. Neither I nor II

17. A convenience store was given a conditional use permit to operate in a residential subdivision for the sale of food items only. Later, the owners decided that they would like to add a line of hardware items. Could they do so under the provisions of their conditional use permit?
    A. Yes, because the conditional use permit allows them to do so.
    B. Yes, because once the conditional use permit has been granted, the items in their inventory cannot be restricted.
    C. No, because the conditional use permit restricts their inventory to food items.
    D. No, because the addition of hardware items would constitute a zoning variance.

18. When a small area of land in an existing neighborhood is rezoned, this is known as
    A. down zoning.   C. conditional zoning.
    B. spot zoning.   D. a zoning variance.

19. The zoning of a parcel of land was changed from apartment zoning to single-family residential use only. Which of the following statements is true?
    I.   The rezoning constituted downzoning.
    II. The owner would be compensated for the loss of land value.
    A. I only   B. II only   C. Both I and II   D. Neither I nor II

20. A garden apartment development is situated between an office park and a subdivision of single-family residences. These apartments are in a
    I.   buffer zone.
    II. down zone.
    A. I only   B. II only   C. Both I and II   D. Neither I nor II

21. Which of the following statements is/are true?
    I.   Zoning laws alone do not create land value.
    II. To the extent that they channel demand to certain parcels of land, zoning laws have an impact on property value.
    A. I only   B. II only   C. Both I and II   D. Neither I nor II

22. Before a subdivider can sell lots in a new subdivision,
    I.   all mapping requirements must be met.
    II. the subdivision plat must be recorded.
    A. I only   B. II only   C. Both I and II   D. Neither I nor II

23. Minimum standards for materials and construction of buildings are set by
    I. zoning laws.
    II. building codes.
    A. I only   B. II only   C. Both I and II   D. Neither I nor II

24. Building codes are employed to
    I. regulate the architectural style of buildings.
    II. establish acceptable material and construction standards for
        buildings.
    A. I only   B. II only   C. Both I and II   D. Neither I nor II

25. Before a newly constructed building may be utilized by tenants, the owner
    must secure a certificate of
    A. inspection.   C. approval.
    B. utilization.   D. occupancy.

26. Building codes may be enacted
    I. by local governments.
    II. at the state level of government.
    A. I only   B. II only   C. Both I and II   D. Neither I nor II

27. A deed given by grantor Able to grantee Baker contained a restriction
    prohibiting occupancy of the property by anyone other than persons of
    the Caucasian race. This restriction
    I. invalidated the deed.
    II. is unenforceable.
    A. I only   B. II only   C. Both I and II   D. Neither I nor II

28. A subdivider wants to limit the height to which trees can grow so as to
    preserve views. He would most likely do this with a
    A. zoning amendment.   C. buffer zone.
    B. conditional use permit.   D. deed restriction.

29. Future uses of land within a community may be regulated by all of the
    following EXCEPT:
    A. deed restrictions.   C. subdivision regulations.
    B. zoning laws.   D. building codes.

30. A master plan for land use within a community should
    I. provide for a balance between social and economic function within
       the community.
    II. include provisions for flexibility if future growth does not
        develop as expected.
    A. I only   B. II only   C. Both I and II   D. Neither I nor II

31. The effect of a proposed development on a community is determined by the
    preparation of
    A. a property disclosure report.
    B. an environmental impact statement.
    C. a prospectus.
    D. the community's master plan.

32. Environmental impact statements as a tool in land use planning provide
      I. a means of making better decisions regarding land uses.
     II. a means of estimating the impact of a proposed development on
          the environment.
     A. I only   B. II only   C. Both I and II   D. Neither I nor II

33. An environmental impact statement will NOT reveal the effect of a planned
    development on
     A. air quality.   C. property values.
     B. automobile traffic.   D. school enrollments.

34. Owner Mathis converted a single-family residence into two apartments. He
    now wants to list the property for sale with broker Meyer. Meyer should
      I. refuse to accept the listing.
     II. ascertain whether the conversion conforms to zoning requirements.
    III. determine if proper building permits were obtained.
     IV. advise all prospects of the legality of the conversion.
     A. I only   C. IV only
     B. II and III only   D. II, III and IV only

35. Deever is looking for acreage to develop into a residential subdivision.
    Broker Bruce shows Deever an attractive parcel at the edge of town that
    is currently zoned agricultural but looks ripe for development. Of the
    following choices, which would be the most rational for Deever?
     A. Make an extremely low offer so that if the zoning can't be changed
         to residential, Deever will not lose much.
     B. Pay the asking price and hope for the best.
     C. File for a zoning change on the property and, if it is approved,
         offer to buy the property.
     D. Make an offer on the property now with a contingency that zoning be
         changed to residential before settlement.

36. Owner Marvin has lived in a 40-year old house for the past three years.
    Marvin calls broker Bart to list the property for sale. Upon inspection
    of the house, Bart notices an extra bathroom that was added since the
    house was built; moreover, the bathroom has no means of ventilation to
    the outside. Bart asks Marvin if it was built with a permit and Marvin
    replies that he does not know as it was there when he bought the house.
    Marvin adds that all the fixtures work fine and for ventilation he leaves
    the bathroom door open to the hallway. If you were broker Bart would you
     A. refuse the listing on this point alone?
     B. refuse the listing until you talked to the building department?
     C. take the listing and not worry about the bathroom since the seller
         assured you that it is not a problem?
     D. take the listing, talk to the building department, and then advise
         Marvin as to his options?

37. A landowner who is denied a proposed development of his land by the com-
    munity's planning authorities
      I. can force the community to purchase the land under eminent domain.
     II. will receive payment for the loss in the land's value.
     A. I only   B. II only   C. Both I and II   D. Neither I nor II

38. Windfalls and wipeouts in land value which are brought about by land-use controls may sometimes be eliminated by creating
    I. an environmental impact statement.
    II. transferable development rights.
    A. I only   B. II only   C. Both I and II   D. Neither I nor II

39. Where they are in use, transferable development rights may be
    I. traded on the open market.
    II. purchased by the government and sold to other owners.
    A. I only   B. II only   C. Both I and II   D. Neither I nor II

40. To date, transferable development rights have been used to protect
    I. historical buildings.
    II. agricultural land.
    III. environmentally sensitive land.
    A. I and II only   C. II and III only
    B. I and III only   D. I, II and III

Answers—Chapter 21

Multiple Choice Questions

1. D   Early forms of land use controls were known in medieval towns and cities, colonial America, and the cities of Baltimore, Boston and Indianapolis in the late 1800s.

2. D   Deed restrictions are private land-use controls.

3. D   State governments, local governments and subdivision developers may all impose some form of land-use controls.

4. C   Properly designed land-use controls will consider both the social and economic impact of the controls upon the community, and an individual's right to develop his/her land.

5. C   The placement of interior partitions in a building is not regulated by zoning laws.

6. B   Zoning laws may not be used to protect an existing land user from competitive business establishments.

7. D   Authority to enact zoning laws is derived from a government's police powers.

8. C   Land-use designations are not uniformly used throughout the United States.

9. A   Zoning laws tell a landowner how land may be used, but do not provide compensation for loss of value due to zoning.

10. C   Checking the zoning on a parcel of land includes viewing the zoning maps and then consulting the zoning ordinances to see what is allowed.

11. D   Building codes dictate construction standards; zoning laws do not.

12. B   A landowner who developed land without first obtaining a building permit could be forced to tear down the building.

13. C   A nonconforming use is one not in accord with present zoning laws. It may sometimes be permitted under a grandfather clause.

14. D   Under the provisions of a grandfather clause, a building owner may perform all normal maintenance on the nonconforming building but may not remodel or enlarge the building or extend its life.

15. C   Permission to use a building for a nonconforming use may be accomplished by amendment of the zoning ordinance or by obtaining a zoning variance.

16. A   A zoning variance allows an owner to deviate from an existing zoning law without a change in the zoning law.

17. C   Because the use permit was granted conditionally, the inventory is restricted to those items permitted by the use permit.

18. B   Spot zoning is the rezoning of a small area of land in an existing neighborhood.

19. A   A change from apartment zoning to single-family residential zoning constitutes downzoning. The owners are not compensated for any loss of land value.

20. A   Land zoned for multi-family residential that is located between single-family residential zoning and commercial or industrial zoning would be a buffer zone.

21. C   While zoning laws do not alone create land value, their impact on property values is felt by the channeling of demand to certain parcels of land.

22. C   Before a subdivider can sell lots in a new subdivision, all mapping requirements must be met and the subdivision plat must be recorded.

23. B   Building codes set minimum standards of material and construction for buildings.

24. B   Building codes are employed to establish acceptable material and construction standards for buildings.

25. D   A certificate of occupancy must be obtained before a newly con-structed building may be utilized by tenants.

26. C   Buildings codes may be enacted at the local or state level of government.

27. B   A restriction which limits occupancy on racial grounds would be against public policy and would be unenforceable. The conveyance, however, would still be valid.

28. D   A deed restriction would be used to limit the height of trees in a subdivision.

29. D   Land uses may be regulated by deed restrictions, zoning laws or subdivision regulations, but not by building codes.

30. C   A master plan should provide for a balance between social and econo-mic functions and should include provisions for flexibility if future growth does not develop as expected.

31. B   An environmental impact statement sets forth the effect of a proposed development on the community.

32. C   Environmental impact statements provide a means of estimating the impact of a proposed development on the environment and provide a means of making better decisions regarding land uses.

33. C   An environmental impact statement will not reveal the effect of a planned development on property values.

34. D   Before accepting the listing, the broker should determine the conversion's conformity to zoning requirements and whether proper permits were obtained. He should also advise all prospects of the legality of the conversion.

35. D   The prospect should make the offer to purchase contingent upon the rezoning of the property for residential use.

36. D   The broker should accept the listing, check with the building department, and then advise the owner as to his options.

37. D   As a rule, landowners who are denied proposed development of their land cannot force purchase of the land by the community or payment for loss of land value.

38. B   Transferable development rights may be used to eliminate windfalls and wipeouts brought about by land-use controls.

39. C   Transferable development rights may be traded on the open market or purchased by the government and sold to others.

40. D   Transferable development rights have been used to protect historical buildings, agricultural land and environmentally sensitive land.

Real Estate and the Economy

Chapter 22

1. A community's economic base is determined by its ability to produce goods and/or services
   I. for consumption within the local area.
   II. that have exchange value outside the local area.
   A. I only   B. II only   C. Both I and II   D. Neither I nor II

2. Industries which produce goods and services for export are referred to by all the following terms EXCEPT:
   A. base industries.
   B. export industries.
   C. primary industries.
   D. backbone industries.

3. Which of the following terms would NOT apply to an industry which produces goods or services which are locally consumed?
   A. Service industry.
   B. Accessory industry.
   C. Secondary industry.
   D. Filler industry.

4. Which of the following would be an example of a base industry?
   I. The tourist industry in Florida.
   II. Oil wells on Alaska's North Slope.
   A. I only   B. II only   C. Both I and II   D. Neither I nor II

5. The real estate brokerage business is an example of a
   I. base industry.
   II. secondary industry.
   III. service industry.
   IV. primary industry.
   A. I and II only
   B. II and III only
   C. I and IV only
   D. III and IV only

Note: This chapter is deleted entirely for readers of <u>Real Estate: An Introduction to the Profession</u>.

6. The Hartford Manufacturing Company which was the largest employer in the city of Westview, recently closed its plant in that city. This will probably result in
    I.   declining real estate values.
    II. a slow-down in construction of new homes.
    III. a decline in the population of Westview.
    IV. the closing of some service industries.
    A. I, II and IV only   C. I, II, III and IV
    B. II, III and IV only   D. II, III and IV only

7. The existence of a base industry is essential to the
    I.   economic health of a community.
    II. maintenance of local real estate values.
    A. I only   B. II only   C. Both I and II   D. Neither I nor II

8. The extent to which regions and cities are vulnerable to changes in economic base depends on
    I.   the number and kinds of base industries which are present.
    II. the ability of base industries to consistently export their products.
    A. I only   B. II only   C. Both I and II   D. Neither I nor II

9. Communities which are suffering from an economic depression caused by a decline in demand for the products of a single base industry tend to
    I.   seek a diversification of their economic base.
    II. try to attract another single base industry to replace the failing industry.
    III. recover by increasing the number of service industries.
    A. I, II and III   C. I and III only
    B. II and III only   D. I and II only

10. Generally, for every job created by a base industry, there will be created in service industries approximately
    A. an equal number of jobs.
    B. two jobs.
    C. one job for every two persons employed in the base industry.
    D. four jobs.

11. When there is a sudden increase in the demand for housing in a community, the price of existing housing will
    A. rise slowly over the next 12 months.
    B. rise rapidly, then fall slightly as supply catches up with demand.
    C. not reflect the increased demand for approximately 12 months.

12. Over a period of years,
    I.   the supply of residential housing is one of temporary shortages and temporary excesses.
    II. there will be periods of rapid price changes mixed with periods of mild price changes.
    A. I only   B. II only   C. Both I and II   D. Neither I nor II

13. When the supply and demand relationship in a market is unbalanced because of excess supply, it is to the advantage of
    I. buyers.
    II. sellers.
    A. I only   B. II only   C. Both I and II   D. Neither I nor II

14. Generally, a person's peak earning years occur at ages
    A. 25-35 years.   C. 45-55 years.
    B. 35-45 years.   D. 60 years.

15. As young families mature, they tend to occupy the types of housing described below in what sequence?
    I.   Rental of a modest single-family home.
    II. Rental of an apartment.
    III. Ownership of a larger, more expensive single-family home.
    IV. Ownership of a modest single-family home.
    A. I, IV and III only   C. II, I, IV and III
    B. II, IV and III only   D. II, I, III and IV

16. Typically, most families acquire their largest and most expensive housing between ages
    A. 25 to 35.   C. 45 to 55.
    B. 35 to 45.   D. over age 60.

17. The post-World War II baby boom includes persons aged
    I. 30 to 40 in 1960.   III. 35 to 40 in 1985.
    II. 50 to 60 in 1980.   IV. 30 to 35 in 1990.
    A. I and II only   C. III only
    D. IV only   D. III and IV only

18. What is the effect upon the demand for housing of a dramatic increase in the birth rate?
    I. An immediate effect.
    II. A long-range effect.
    A. I only   B. II only   C. Both I and II   D. Neither I nor II

19. Real estate values are affected by the federal government's
    I. tax rules.   III. deficits.
    II. laws.   IV. monetary policies.
    A. I, II, III and IV   C. II and III only
    B. I and IV only   D. IV only

20. Under federal tax laws which allow homeowners to deduct mortgage loan interest when calculating federal income taxes, what would be the after-tax cost to a homeowner in the 30 per cent tax bracket of a home mortgage loan made at a 12 per cent rate of interest?
    A. 3.6 per cent   C. 9.5 per cent
    B. 8.4 per cent   D. 8.0 per cent

21. Federal tax laws have traditionally allowed owners of investment properties to deduct all of the following EXCEPT:
    A. operating costs.   C. depreciation on land.
    B. maintenance costs.   D. ad valorem taxes.

22. Between 1981 and 1985, depreciation allowances on real property for income tax purposes allowed
    A. depreciation of twice the value of a building.
    B. depreciation of land as well as buildings.
    C. an accounting life shorter than the useful life of a property.

23. From an investor's point of view, which is the most attractive allowable depreciation period for an investment property?
    A. 40 years   C. 20 years
    B. 30 years   D. 15 years

24. Federal tax treatment of the expenses and profits from real estate investments affect what a person
     I. can pay for a property.
    II. will pay for a property.
    A. I only   B. II only   C. Both I and II   D. Neither I nor II

25. Which has the greatest effect upon the interest rate an individual must pay for a real estate mortgage loan?
    A. Local governmental borrowing.
    B. State governmental borrowing.
    C. Federal governmental borrowing.
    D. Competition from commercial and industrial borrowers.

26. Through the Federal Reserve Banks, the Federal Reserve Board can
     I. create money.
    II. destroy money.
    A. I only   B. II only   C. Both I and II   D. Neither I nor II

27. In order to keep prices from falling in an economy that is growing at a 4 per cent annual rate, which of the following is necessary?
    A. A 4 per cent decrease in the money supply.
    B. A constant, unchanging money supply.
    C. A 2 per cent increase in the money supply.
    D. A 4 per cent increase in the money supply.

28. When a government prints more money than is needed for economic growth, the result is
     I. a short-term drop in interest rates.
    II. a long-term increase in inflation.
    A. I only   B. II only   C. Both I and II   D. Neither I nor II

29. All of the following have made home purchases by persons of modest income easier EXCEPT:
    A. FHA loan insurance programs.
    B. creation of extra money by the Federal Reserve.
    C. VA loan guaranty programs.
    D. income tax deductions for mortgage loan interest and taxes.

30. Prior to the enactment of the Equal Credit Opportunity Act, which of the following would have found it easier to qualify for a mortgage loan for the purchase of a residence if the total family income of all was identical?
    A. A married couple, each 30 years old, both employed, husband's salary equal to 70 per cent of family income.
    B. A divorced woman, 60 per cent of her income from employment and 40 per cent from alimony.
    C. A married couple, each 30 years old, all income from husband's employment.
    D. Two single women, each employed and each producing 50 per cent of the total household income.

31. The ECOA has contributed to greater numbers of homeowners among
    I. single persons.
    II. divorced persons.
    III. employed women.
    IV. employed couples.
    A. I, II, III and IV
    B. I and II only
    C. III only
    D. I and III only

32. The advent of the secondary mortgage market
    I. made available previously untapped sources of money for real estate mortgage loans.
    II. contributed to real estate speculation and inflation in the late 1970s.
    A. I only   B. II only   C. Both I and II   D. Neither I nor II

33. Cost-push inflation is the result of
    I. increased manufacturing costs.
    II. increased demand for a product.
    A. I only   B. II only   C. Both I and II   D. Neither I nor II

34. Demand-pull inflation has little to do with
    I. manufacturing costs.
    II. the availability of money.
    A. I only   B. II only   C. Both I and II   D. Neither I nor II

35. When too much money chases too few goods, it is known as
    A. cost-push inflation.
    B. demand-pull inflation.
    C. real-cost inflation.
    D. deflation.

36. Monetary inflation
    I. results from the creation of excessive amounts of money by government.
    II. can be controlled by keeping the growth in the monetary supply parallel to the growth in productivity.
    A. I only   B. II only   C. Both I and II   D. Neither I nor II

37. Inflation brought on by increased effort necessary to produce the same quantity of a good or service is known as
    A. demand-pull inflation.
    B. real-cost inflation.
    C. cost-push inflation.
    D. monetary inflation.

38. Real-cost inflation can be intensified by
    I. environmental controls.
    II. depletion of natural resources.
    A. I only   B. II only   C. Both I and II   D. Neither I nor II

39. Sales of residences to first-time purchasers were stimulated in the 1975-1980 period by the
    I. Equal Credit Opportunity Act.
    II. secondary mortgage market.
    A. I only   B. II only   C. Both I and II   D. Neither I nor II

40. The real cost of interest is the
    A. rate stated on the promissory note.
    B. inflation-adjusted cost.
    C. annual percentage rate.
    D. rate stated on the promissory note plus any discounts.

41. During the period from 1975 to 1980, the attractiveness of real estate as an investment was enhanced by
    I. tax deductions for interest on mortgage loans.
    II. rapidly appreciating property values.
    III. capital gains tax treatment of sales.
    IV. declining interest rates for mortgage loans.
    A. I, II, III and IV   C. II and IV only
    B. I and II only   D. I, II and III only

42. By the year 1980, in order to curb inflation, the policy of the Federal Reserve became one of
    A. generous monetary growth.   C. restrained monetary growth.
    B. negative monetary growth.   D. constant, no-growth monetary supply.

43. Expectations about inflation tend to
    A. lag actual changes.   C. precede actual changes.
    B. parallel actual changes.

44. Which of the following is more likely to be the LEAST demanding of appreciation potential in the ownership of real estate?
    A. The owner of a rental residence.
    B. An owner who occupies a property as a principal residence.
    C. A business which owns apartment buildings.
    D. A corporation which owns office buildings.

45. By 1985, the market for residential housing for first-time buyers was strongest for the sale of
    A. condominium units.
    B. large single-family houses of more than 1600 square feet.
    C. smaller single-family houses of approximately 1000 square feet.
    D. cooperative housing.

46. Ultimately, interest rates for real estate mortgage loans are determined by the
    A. marketplace.   C. nation's banking system.
    B. Federal Reserve Board.   D. savings and loan associations.

47. The Federal Reserve Board's objectives for the American economy include
    I.   high employment.
    II. stable prices.
    III. steady growth in productive capacity.
    IV. a stable foreign exchange rate for the dollar.
    A. III and IV only   C. I, II, III and IV
    B. II only   D. I, II and III only

48. The Federal Reserve Board influences the national economy by adjusting
    I.   interest rates.
    II. the money supply.
    A. I only   B. II only   C. Both I and II   D. Neither I nor II

49. An increase in the monetary base at a rate faster than that of the gross national product will lead to
    I.   a temporary fall in interest rates.
    II. temporary stimulation of economic growth.
    A. I only   B. II only   C. Both I and II   D. Neither I nor II

50. Failure of the government to balance its budget will likely lead to
    I.   higher interest rates.
    II. a recession.
    A. I only   B. II only   C. Both I and II   D. Neither I nor II

Answers—Chapter 22

Multiple Choice Questions

1. B A community's economic base depends upon its ability to produce goods and/or services that have exchange value outside the local area.

2. D Industries which produce goods and services for export are referred to as base industries, export industries or primary industries.

3. B Industries which produce goods and services for local consumption are known as service industries, secondary industries or filler industries.

4. C Florida's tourist industry and Alaska's oil industry are base industries because they bring in money from outside the area.

5. B The real estate brokerage business is an example of a secondary or service industry.

6. C The loss of a community's largest employer can result in declining real estate values, a slow-down in new construction, population decline and the closing of some service industries.

7. C Base industries are essential to a community's economic health and to the maintenance of real estate values.

8. C An area's vulnerability to change in its economic base depends on the number and kinds of base industries present and their ability to consistently export their products.

9. D Depressed communities which have depended upon a single base industry tend to seek diversification of their economic base or try to attract another single base industry to replace the lost industry.

10. B Generally, one job in a base industry generates two jobs in service industries.

11. B A sudden increase in demand will cause existing housing prices to rise rapidly, then fall slightly as supply catches up with demand.

12. C Over a period of years, the supply of residential housing is one of temporary shortages and temporary excesses, during which there will be periods of rapid price changes mixed with periods of mild price changes.

13. A An excess of supply works to the advantage of buyers.

14. C Most people's peak earning years occur between ages 45-55 years.

15. C   A family's housing pattern typically follows from apartment rental to single-family home rental to ownership of a modest single-family home to ownership of a more expensive single-family home.

16. C   Typically, the largest and most expensive housing is acquired between ages 45 and 55.

17. D   The post-World War II baby boom spanned a period of 15 years, from 1946 through 1960. This would include persons aged 35 to 40 in 1985 and persons aged 30 to 35 in 1990.

18. C   A dramatic increase in the birth rate creates an immediate demand for bedrooms and a long-range demand for houses.

19. A   Real estate values are affected by the federal government's tax rules, laws, deficits and monetary policies.

20. B   12 per cent interest minus 30 per cent tax rate = 8.4 per cent after-tax cost. (Or, 12% x .70 = 8.4%)

21. C   Federal tax laws do not allow an owner to depreciate land.

22. C   Accounting lives shorter than the actual useful lives of real property were allowed between 1981 and 1985.

23. D   From an investor's point of view, the shortest possible allowable depreciation period is the most attractive.

24. C   Federal tax treatment of the expenses and profits from real estate investments can affect what a person can pay and will pay for a property.

25. C   Federal governmental borrowing has the greatest effect upon what an individual must pay for a real estate mortgage loan.

26. C   The Federal Reserve Board, through the Federal Reserve Banks, can create or destroy money.

27. D   An increase in the money supply equal to the rate of growth is necessary to keep prices from falling in a growing economy.

28. C   The printing of more money than is needed for economic growth will lead to a short-term drop in interest rates and a long-term increase in inflation.

29. B   Creation of extra money by the Federal Reserve leads to inflation, which makes home purchases by persons of modest income more difficult.

30. C   Prior to the ECOA, lenders favored borrowers whose income was derived from the husband's employment over women or single persons.

31. A   The ECOA has contributed to greater numbers of homeowners among all categories of households.

32. C   The advent of the secondary mortgage market made available previously untapped sources of real estate mortgage loans and contributed to the real estate speculation and inflation of the late 1970s.

33. A   Cost-push inflation results from increased manufacturing costs.

34. A   Demand-pull inflation results from too much money chasing too few goods, and has little to do with manufacturing costs.

35. B   Demand-pull inflation results from too much money chasing too few goods.

36. C   Monetary inflation results from the creation of excessive amounts of money by the government and can be controlled by keeping monetary growth parallel to growth in productivity.

37. B   Real-cost inflation is brought on by increased effort necessary to produce the same quantity of goods or services.

38. C   Real cost inflation can be intensified by environmental controls or by depletion of natural resources.

39. C   The ECOA and the secondary mortgage market stimulated sales of residences to first-time purchasers during the period between 1975 and 1980.

40. B   The real cost of interest is the inflation-adjusted cost.

41. D   Between 1975 and 1980, tax deductions for interest on mortgage loans, rapidly appreciating property values and capital gains treatment of sales all contributed to the enhancement of real estate as an investment.

42. C   The Federal Reserve entered into a period of restrained monetary growth beginning in 1980 in order to curb inflation.

43. A   Expectations about inflation tend to lag actual changes. This is true whether inflation is heating up or cooling down.

44. B   An owner who occupies a property as a principal residence tends to be the least demanding of appreciation potential.

45. C   By 1985, the strongest residential real estate market for first-time buyers was smaller single-family houses.

46. A   Ultimately, the marketplace, through supply and demand, determines the interest rates for real estate mortgage loans.

47. C   The Federal Reserve Board's objectives for the American economy include high employment, stable prices, steady growth and a stable foreign exchange rate.

48.   B   The Federal Reserve Board influences the national economy by adjusting the money supply. This changes the supply-demand balance for money, and, in turn, interest rates. The Federal Reserve Board does not, and in fact cannot, alter interest rates directly; only indirectly through changes in the money supply.

49.   C   An increase in the monetary base at a rate faster than that of the GNP will lead to a temporary fall in interest rates and a temporary stimulation of economic growth.

50.   C   Failure of the government to balance its budget will likely lead to higher interest rates and also to a recession.

Investing in Real Estate

Chapter 23

1. Monetary benefits of investing in real estate come from
   A. cash flow.   C. mortgage reduction.
   B. tax shelter.   D. All of the above.

2. A positive cash flow occurs when a property generates income in excess of
   A. mortgage payments.
   B. depreciation and operating expenses.
   C. appreciation and mortgage payments.
   D. operating expenses and mortgage payments.

3. ABZ Realty offers you a four-unit residential building in which each unit rents for $500 per month. Given a 5 per cent vacancy rate, operating expenses of $700 per month, and mortgage payments of $1,500 per month, you can anticipate a monthly
   A. net spendable of $200.   C. negative cash flow of $200.
   B. net spendable of $300.   D. negative cash flow of $300.

4. A negative cash flow may be offset by
   I. tax shelter.
   II. appreciation.
   A. I only   B. II only   C. Both I and II   D. Neither I nor II

5. Same facts as in question 3, plus these facts: the monthly mortgage payment consists of $1,400 in interest and $100 in principal reduction and depreciation is $1,000 per month. How much is the monthly taxable income generated by this property?
   A. ($1,200)   C. ($1,300)
   B. ($300)   D. $1,000

Note: This chapter corresponds to Chapter 21 in <u>Real Estate: An Introduction to the Profession</u> and you may delete questions 21-37, 40-42, 45-50, 52, 55-58, 60 and 61.

6. What is the cash-on-cash ratio for a property which has a cash flow of
    $16,900 and could be purchased with a down payment of $130,000?
    A. 7.69%   C. .12
    B. .219   D. .13

7. Tax shelter in real estate
    I.   refers to the income tax savings that an investor can realize.
    II. is possible because depreciation is deductible as a cost of doing
         business.
    A. I only   B. II only   C. Both I and II   D. Neither I nor II

8. Tax shelter from a property
    I.   may sometimes exceed that needed to shelter the income from the
         property itself.
    II. may not be used to offset gains from other investments.
    A. I only   B. II only   C. Both I and II   D. Neither I nor II

9. Mortgage balance reduction
    I.   is an out-of-pocket expense.
    II. is a deduction for tax purposes.
    A. I only   B. II only   C. Both I and II   D. Neither I nor II

10. Depreciation on a property
    I.   represents an out-of-pocket expense to an investor.
    II. is a deduction against income taxes.
    A. I only   B. II only   C. Both I and II   D. Neither I nor II

11. The value of depreciation on an investment property is
    A. inversely proportional to the investor's tax bracket.
    B. the same to all investors, regardless of their tax bracket.
    C. directly proportional to the investor's tax bracket.
    D. not a factor in the investment decision.

12. Depreciation allowances make real estate investments attractive because
    I.   buildings do not necessarily drop in value as they get older.
    II. tax laws allow depreciation to be claimed over periods of time
         less than the economic life of the building.
    A. I only   B. II only   C. Both I and II   D. Neither I nor II

13. If an investor is allowed by the tax laws to take 200 per cent accelera-
    ted depreciation on a building, this means that
    I.   the total depreciation allowed will be equal to twice the
         building's value.
    II. the depreciation may be taken twice as fast as straight line.
    A. I only   B. II only   C. Both I and II   D. Neither I nor II

14. Tax laws allow depreciation on a building to be
    I.   started over each time the property is sold.
    II. more than its value.
    A. I only   B. II only   C. Both I and II   D. Neither I nor II

15. For an investment property, all depreciation claimed in excess of actual loss in value comes back to be taxed upon
    I. selling the property.
    II. trading the proerty.
    A. I only   B. II only   C. Both I and II   D. Neither I nor II

16. Equity build-up in a property can be the result of
    I. mortgage reduction.
    II. appreciation.
    A. I only   B. II only   C. Both I and II   D. Neither I nor II

17. Chen bought a home for $100,000, paying $20,000 cash and taking an $80,000 mortgage loan. Now, several years later, the loan balance is $75,000 and the home is worth $120,000. Which of the following is/are true?
    I. Chen's equity at the time of purchase was $20,000.
    II. Chen's equity now is $45,000.
    III. Chen's equity buildup is $25,000.
    A. I only   B. II only   C. III only   D. I, II and III

18. Baker used $35,000 in cash to purchase a property which was valued at $140,000. The property produced cash flow in excess of operating costs and payments on borrowed funds. Which of the following statements is/are correct?
    I. The purchase represented a 25 per cent leverage.
    II. Baker enjoyed a positive leverage.
    A. I only   B. II only   C. Both I and II   D. Neither I nor II

19. Negative leverage occurs when
    I. borrowed funds cost more than they produce in benefits.
    II. an investment property depreciates in value.
    A. I only   B. II only   C. Both I and II   D. Neither I nor II

20. Catherine is contemplating the purchase of a $1,000,000 apartment building by paying $250,000 cash down and borrowing the balance with a non-recourse mortgage loan. If the land is worth $150,000 and the building is worth $850,000 and Congress applies the "at risk" rule to investment real estate, will she be able to depreciate the entire $850,000?
    I. Yes, if she sees the change coming and buys before the rule takes effect.
    II. Yes, because ACRS overrides any "at risk" rules.
    III. No, because "at risk" would limit her depreciation to $250,000 plus loan reduction.
    IV. No, because she has no basis in the property.
    A. I and II only   C. III only
    B. III and IV only   D. I and III only

21. When one holds land as an investment, expenses such as taxes and interest are
    A. not deductible for income tax purposes.
    B. deductible in the year in which the expenses were incurred.
    C. deductible the following year.
    D. deductible only when the property is sold.

22. Houses and condominiums are attractive investments to a small investor during periods when
    I. the rate of appreciation exceeds the cost of borrowing money.
    II. mortgage loans are available on favorable terms.
    A. I only   B. II only   C. Both I and II   D. Neither I nor II

23. In relation to the monthly income produced, which of the properties listed below tend to be overpriced?
    I. Houses.   III. Condominiums.
    II. Apartment houses.   IV. Office buildings.
    A. I, II and III only   C. IV only
    B. I and III only   D. II and IV only

24. Houses and condominiums are attractive to some investors because
    I. they can generate a negative cash flow.
    II. when they are sold, they often sell at a higher price than would be justified by rents alone.
    A. I only   B. II only   C. Both I and II   D. Neither I nor II

25. To be considered a good investment, when a property which generates a negative cash flow is sold,
    A. there must be a substantial increase in property value.
    B. there need be little increase in property value.
    C. the investor is best off if the property has decreased in value.

26. Small apartment buildings are often attractive investments because
    I. returns from rental income can be more reliably forecast than changes in price.
    II. they can usually be managed by the owner without the expense of professional management.
    A. I only   B. II only   C. Both I and II   D. Neither I nor II

27. Lucky Lady is buying a 15-unit apartment building. The building will require
    A. two full-time managers.
    B. one full-time manager.
    C. a part-time manager who lives on the property.
    D. no on-site manager, just a couple of hours a week of her spare time.

28. An apartment building is usually considered large enough to support a full-time manager who lives on the property if it contains at least
    A. 25 units.   C. 75 units.
    B. 60 units.   D. 100 units.

29. Management costs per unit of an apartment building
    I. do not change as the number of units increases.
    II. rise in proportion to the number of units.
    A. I only   B. II only   C. Both I and II   D. Neither I nor II

30. Manny G'ment is looking for a job as a manager for a 20 to 30 unit apartment building. If hired, he will be expected to
    I.   interview prospective tenants.
    II. show vacant units.
    III. take rental applications.
    IV. perform maintenance tasks.
    A. I, II and IV only   C. II, III and IV only
    B. I, II and III only   D. I, II, III and IV

31. Butler's investment objective is to produce the highest possible cash flow per invested dollar. Should he choose an investment in an office building in preference to a similar investment in an apartment building?
    A. Yes, because office buildings cost less to build than apartments.
    B. Yes, because office buildings usually return a greater yield on investment.
    C. No, because apartments usually can demand a higher rent per square foot.
    D. No, because operating costs on apartment buildings are less than on office buildings.

32. Which of the following tends to produce the highest cash flow per dollar of investments?
    A. A single-family residence.   C. A large office building.
    B. A two-to-four unit apartment.   D. Vacant land.

33. Generally, the cost of providing amenities is greatest in
    A. office buildings.   C. small apartment buildings.
    B. single-family dwellings.   D. large apartment complexes.

34. Construction and operating costs per square foot tend to be greater in office buildings than in
    I.   garden apartment buildings.
    II. high-rise apartment buildings.
    A. I only   B. II only   C. Both I and II   D. Neither I nor II

35. The expenses of tenant turnover is greatest in which of the following types of property?
    A. Office buildings.   C. Large apartment buildings.
    B. Small apartment buildings.   D. Single family residences.

36. In giving a tenant a long-term lease, the owner takes the risk(s) that
    I.   the lease will make the building difficult to sell.
    II. operating costs may increase without an increase in rent.
    A. I only   B. II only   C. Both I and II   D. Neither I nor II

37. The risk in locating an office building is
    A. greater than with residential properties.
    B. less than with residential properties.
    C. about the same as with residential properties.
    D. no different than with residential properties.

38. Generally, the earlier in its development that an investor enters a real estate investment,
    I. the lower the risk he undertakes.
    II. the less the potential reward he expects to receive.
    A. I only   B. II only   C. Both I and II   D. Neither I nor II

39. The developer's profit on a new real estate development is taxable
    I. upon completion of the project.
    II. when the property is finally sold.
    A. I only   B. II only   C. Both I and II   D. Neither I nor II

40. After a new development is completed and estimates are replaced with actual operating expenses an investor
    I. would expect to receive lower returns per dollar of investment.
    II. is more certain of his return than if he had invested earlier in the development.
    A. I only   B. II only   C. Both I and II   D. Neither I nor II

41. Upon completion of a new development, tax benefits are
    A. no longer available.
    B. equal to those available during the development stages.
    C. higher than those available during the development stages.
    D. lower than during the development stages.

42. After its first year of life, a building begins to face competition from newer buildings. To some extent this competition may be offset because
    I. newer buildings cost more to build and require higher rents.
    II. newer buildings may be forced to use less desirable sites.
    A. I only   B. II only   C. Both I and II   D. Neither I nor II

43. Which of the following would expect to receive a higher return per investment dollar? An investor who purchased during the
    A. first decade of building life.
    B. second decade of building life.
    C. third or fourth decade of building life.
    D. All would expect the same return.

44. When an investor makes a decision to purchase a structure with the intent of demolishing it,
    I. he expects to receive a high return, because the risks are high.
    II. he is counting on the land being worth more in another use.
    A. I only   B. II only   C. Both I and II   D. Neither I nor II

45. Generally, a person's consumption exceeds income
    I. during the first 20 years of life.
    II. between age 35 and 55.
    A. I only   B. II only   C. Both I and II   D. Neither I nor II

46. For most people, when is the best time in life to undertake high-risk investments?
    A. Under age 25.   C. Age 55 to 65.
    B. Age 25 to 45.   D. Over age 65.

47. Mr. and Mrs. Wyse are in their late twenties and thinking about their lifetime investment strategy. In what order should the following occur?
    I. Emphasis on low risk investments and liquidation of assets.
    II. Emphasis on high return, risk-taking and tax shelter.
    III. Emphasis on moderate return, moderate risks and tax shelter.
    A. I, II, III   C. II, III, I
    B. II, I, III   D. III, II, I

48. A strategy to minimize taxes calls for sound investments that emphasize tax shelter during
    I. peak income years.
    II. post-retirement years.
    A. I only   B. II only   C. Both I and II   D. Neither I nor II

49. When looking at investment properties,
    I. an appraiser solves for value.
    II. an investor solves for return.
    A. I only   B. II only   C. Both I and II   D. Neither I nor II

50. Mrs. Ross invested in real estate by investing in a limited partnership which purchased two shopping centers. As a limited partner, she will enjoy
    I. management of the properties by the general partner.
    II. limited financial liability.
    III. diversification into two properties.
    IV. the same tax benefits as she would enjoy as a sole owner.
    A. I, II, III and IV   C. I and III only
    B. I, II and III only   D. I, III and IV only

51. In a typical limited partnership, the
    I. organizers are the limited partners.
    II. investors are the general partners.
    A. I only   B. II only   C. Both I and II   D. Neither I nor II

52. Property acquired by a limited partnership may be purchased by the
    I. specific property method.
    II. blind pool method.
    A. I only   B. II only   C. Both I and II   D. Neither I nor II

53. In a limited partnership, which cannot lose more than the amount they have invested?
    I. General partners.
    II. Limited partners.
    A. I only   B. II only   C. Both I and II   D. Neither I nor II

54. As an investment vehicle, limited partnerships offer which of the following advantages?
    I. The opportunity to diversify one's holdings and thus spread the risks undertaken.
    II. Taxation as if one were the sole owner of the property.
    A. I only   B. II only   C. Both I and II   D. Neither I nor II

55. From the investor's point of view, it is better to compensate the
     organizers by means of
     A. a fixed fee.
     B. a share of the partnership's profits.
     C. a brokerage fee on properties purchased.
     D. a brokerage fee on properties sold.

56. The risk of an investor losing his money is known as
     A. downside risk.   C. upside risk.
     B. backside risk.   D. limited risk.

57. To receive maximum benefits from a partnership, a person considering
     such an investment should
        I. be prepared to stay with the partnership until the properties are
            refinanced or sold.
       II. remember that limited partnerships are difficult to sell for the
            proportional worth of the investor's interest.
     A. I only   B. II only   C. Both I and II   D. Neither I nor II

58. Federal laws regulating limited partnerships are administered by the
        I. Federal Trade Commission.
       II. Securities and Exchange Commission.
     A. I only   B. II only   C. Both I and II   D. Neither I nor II

59. A disclosure statement given to prospective investors in a limited part-
     nership, outlining the plans and proposals for the partnership, is
     called a
        I. prospectus.
       II. forecast statement.
     A. I only   B. II only   C. Both I and II   D. Neither I nor II

60. Which of the following would require a more complete disclosure
     statement?
     A. A large undertaking offered to investors across state lines.
     B. A group of business associates forming a limited partnership among
         themselves.

61. Laws that permit a state government to halt the sale of an investment
     opportunity (such as limited partnership) are called
        I. disclosure laws.
       II. blue-sky laws.
     A. I only   B. II only   C. Both I and II   D. Neither I nor II

62. Successful real estate investing requires
        I. effort.
       II. luck.
      III. courage.
     A. I only   B. II only   C. I and III only   D. I, II and III

Investment Problems

Study the investment properties described below, then match them up with the investors which are described immediately following. It is possible that more than one property would be suitable for any investor, or vice-versa. After you have made your selection, give a brief summary of your reasons for the selection.

I. A condominium apartment in a new high-rise building, just completed. All amenities, good location on major bus routes, shopping and all other service facilities nearby, 80% conventional financing available. After mortgage amortization, association dues and taxes, you estimate that rental income will generate a small negative cash flow. Prospects for appreciation are good. Present and future indicators signify a strong rental market for this type of unit over the foreseeable future. Professional management is available.

II. A small apartment building containing five units, ten years old. New refrigerators installed in each unit within the past year. Located in a stable middle class neighborhood, convenient to shopping and on a bus route. Tenants pay their own utilities, except for heat and air conditioning. Presently managed by the owners, a married couple who live in one unit. Husband is ill and has been advised to move to another climate. All apartments are presently rented on one-year leases which have from six to ten months to run. Present rent schedule indicates a modest positive cash flow.

III. A garden apartment development containing 48 units, 12 in each of four buildings. The development is 12 years old, has been well maintained, and is managed by a professional management firm. Operating statements for the past several years indicate a good cash flow, but this is based on an existing mortgage loan on which the balance is low in relation to present value, and is at a rate of interest which you estimate to be at least 2% per annum below present rates for similar mortgages.

Note: If you are reading Real Estate: An Introduction to the Profession you may omit the questions above and the remaining questions in this chapter.

The existing mortgage cannot be assumed. Existing market conditions in the community indicate that if refinanced on available terms, the operating statements would reflect a strong negative cash flow. Location, construction, and market conditions indicate a probable appreciation of 30% over the next ten years.

IV.   A syndicate is being formed to construct an office building in a prime downtown location. Syndicators have been in business for 15 years, and have considerable experience in the field. Several prior enterprises have all been successful. Syndicate will be organized as a limited partnership. Property will be managed by the organizers upon completion. Firm commitments for leases from strong tenants have been secured for nearly 50% of the space. Market conditions indicate a need for modern office space in the community. Syndicators have set minimum individual participation in the syndicate at $50,000. Projections indicate a strong cash flow upon completion plus excellent investment tax credits.

V.   A single family house, two years old, in a suburban tract development. Three bedrooms, two baths, air conditioned and well maintained. Present owner is being transferred. VA loan representing 90% of present appraised value may be assumed. Estimated rent, based upon rents presently being received for similar homes in the development, would generate a small negative cash flow after deductions for mortgage amortization, taxes, insurance and reasonable allowances for maintenance and vacancy. Value of the house has appreciated 6% per year since it was built, and projections are for it to continue at this rate for the foreseeable future. Strong rental market indicates excellent possibilities for immediate rental to responsible tenants.

Match the investors described below to the properties previously described. You may assume that in each case the price is agreeable, and that adequate financing can be obtained. Remember, it is possible that more than one property may be suitable for each investor, and vice-versa.

1. A corporate executive whose income is entirely from salary and bonuses. Earnings place him in a tax bracket in excess of 50%. Employment requires long hours at work and considerable travel out of the city for days at a time. Has considerable funds available in the form of savings and investments in securities. Prospects for increased earnings are good, and present scale of living allows for continued savings. Age 42 years.

    Recommended investment: No. I II III IV V

    Reasons for recommendation: _____

    _____

    _____

2. Married couple, husband 57 years old, wife 55 years old. Wife does not work. Husband employed as a machinist in local manufacturing plant. Both in good health. Own present home, worth estimated $55,000, free and clear. Plans are for husband to retire in three years, and would like to make investment that would provide additional income to supplement retirement income. Have several thousand dollars in savings in company credit union, plus a few thousand cash value in life insurance. Wife finds present home too large for present needs.

    Recommended investment: No. I II III IV V

    Reasons for recommendation: _____

    _____

    _____

3. Young married couple, husband 30 years old, wife 28, no children. Both employed, he as a junior executive and she as an airline stewardess. All income is from salaries and husband's annual bonus. Several thousand dollars equity in home, plus cash in savings and mutual fund investments. Investment objective is to shelter some income from taxes and to build estate. Husband does some traveling in his work.

    Recommended investment: No. I   II   III   IV   V

    Reasons for recommendation: _____

    _____

    _____

4. A group of doctors organized as a corporation. All work long hours at their practice. The corporation has accumulated over $150,000 in undisbursed profits. Individual investment objectives are to build estates and secure any possible immediate tax shelter against personal income.

    Recommended investment: No. I   II   III   IV   V

    Reasons for recommendation: _____

    _____

    _____

5. Bachelor, 38 years old, no plans to marry. Above average income from employment as accountant in civil service position. Modest savings. No need for additional income, but desires to shelter some income from taxation, and to provide guard against inflation through investment with potential for greater appreciation than available through savings.

    Recommended investment: No. I   II   III   IV   V

    Reasons for recommendation: _____

    _____

    _____

Answers—Chapter 23

Multiple Choice Questions

1. D   Monetary benefits come from cash flow, tax shelter, mortgage reduction and appreciation.

2. D   Cash flow refers to the income generated by a property in excess of operating expenses and mortgage payments.

3. D   4 units x $500 rent/unit - 5% vacancy rate - $700 operating expenses - $1,500 mortgage payment = ($300) = $300/month negative cash flow.

4. C   A negative cash flow may be offset by tax shelter and/or appreciation.

5. A   4 units x $500 rent/unit - 5% vacancy rate - $700 operating expenses - $1,400 interest payment - $1,000 depreciation = ($1,200) = $1,200/month taxable loss.

6. D $16,900 cash flow divided by $130,000 down payment = .13

7. C   In real estate, tax shelter refers to the income tax savings that an investor can realize, and is made possible because depreciation is deductible as a cost of doing business.

8. A   Tax shelter from a property may exceed that needed to shelter the income from the property and the excess may be used to offset gains from other investments.

9. A   Mortgage balance reduction is an out-of-pocket expense but not a deduction for tax purposes.

10. B   Depreciation on a property is a deduction against income tax but is not an out-of-pocket expense to the investor.

11. C   The higher an investor's tax bracket, the more valuable the depreciation on a property in terms of tax shelter.

12. C   Because buildings do not necessarily drop in value as they get older, and because tax laws allow a building to be depreciated faster than its economic life, depreciation allowances make real estate investments attractive.

13. B   A 200 per cent accelerated depreciation allows depreciation to be taken twice as fast as straight line, but does not allow depreciation to exceed the building's value.

14. A   Tax laws permit depreciation to be started over each time the property is sold, but do not allow depreciation in excess of a building's value.

15. A   Depreciation claimed in excess of actual loss in value is taxed upon sale of the property but may be deferred if the property is traded.

16. C   Equity build-up can result from mortgage reduction or appreciation in the value of a property.

17. D   Current property value is $120,000 - $75,000 loan balance = $45,000 current equity. Original equity was $20,000 down payment. Equity build-up is $25,000 ($45,000 current equity - $20,000 original equity).

18. B   The purchase represented a 75% leverage ($105,000 indebtedness divided by $140,000 value = .75 or 75%). This represents a positive leverage because the cash flow and other benefits exceeded the operating costs and payments on borrowed funds.

19. A   Negative leverage occurs when borrowed funds cost more than they produce in benefits.

20. D   If the building were purchased before the "at risk" rule is applied, the entire value of the building may be depreciated. In contrast, an "at risk" rule would limit depreciation to the original investment plus loan reduction.

21. B   Taxes and interest are deductible in the year in which these expenses are incurred.

22. C   When mortgage loans are available on favorable terms so that net operating income and appreciation exceeds the cost of borrowing, houses and condominiums are attractive to small investors because of the relatively low initial investment and the tax shelter benefits.

23. B   Houses and condominiums tend to be overpriced in relation to the rent they produce because their prices are influenced by the amenity value of home ownership.

24. B   Because houses and condominiums can usually be resold for higher prices than would be justified by rents alone, they appeal to some investors.

25. A   To be a good investment, when a property which generates a negative cash flow is sold, there must be a substantial appreciation to offset the negative cash flow.

26. C   Small apartment buildings are often attractive investments because returns from rental income can be more reliably forecast than price changes, and they do not usually require professional management.

27. C   A 15-unit building usually will require a part-time resident manager. It cannot be managed on a couple of hours of spare time a week.

28. A   A minimum of 25 units is usually required to support a full-time resident manager.

29. D   Management costs per unit drop as the number of units in an apartment building increases.

30. D   The manager of a 20 to 30 unit apartment building may expect to interview prospective tenants, show vacant units, take rental applications and perform maintenance tasks.

31. B   Office buildings usually yield a higher return on investment than apartment buildings because although they cost more to build, they bring a higher rent per square foot.

32. C   Office buildings bring higher rents per dollar of investment than do one- to four-family buildings or vacant land.

33. A   Tenants in office buildings demand more services and other amenities than do residential tenants.

34. C   Office buildings must meet higher construction standards and provide more tenant amenities, so are more expensive to build than residential structures.

35. A   A change in office tenants can often result in a major vacancy loss and usually requires extensive remodeling. Therefore, tenant turnover is more costly than in residential properties.

36. C   A long-term lease exposes the owner to possible difficulties in selling the building and exposes the owner to the possibility that operating costs may increase without an increase in rent.

37. A   Location is more important to office tenants than to residential tenants, so there is greater risk in locating an office building.

38. D   Risks are greatest early in a building's development, so the earlier an investor enters an investment, the greater the profit he expects to receive.

39. B   Taxes on profits from a new real estate development are due when the property is sold.

40. C   Because the expectations are replaced with experience, the return is more certain after completion than during the development period and the investor would expect to receive lower returns per invested dollar.

41. D   Tax benefits are slightly less rewarding after completion than in the early stages of development.

42. C   Higher construction costs and less desirable locations may offset the competition from newer office buildings.

43. C   Because of the building's reduced economic life, the older the building, the higher the return per invested dollar demanded by investors.

44. C   The investor is counting on the land having more value in another use and expects a higher return because risks are high.

45. A   Consumption usually exceeds income during the first 20 years of life.

46. B   Income outpaces consumption during the period from 25 to 45 years, and there is time to recover from mistakes, so this is the best time to undertake high risk investments.

47. C   High risks should be taken during the 25-45 year-old period, followed by emphasis on moderate returns, moderate risks and tax shelters, followed by low risks and liquidation of assets in later years.

48. A   Tax shelters have their greatest value during peak income years.

49. C   When looking at investment properties, an appraiser solves for value and an investor solves for return.

50. A   Benefits of participation in a limited partnership include freedom from management decisions, limited financial liability, opportunity to diversify and tax benefits equal to sole ownership.

51. D   Typically, in a limited partnership the organizers are the general partners and investors are limited partners.

52. C   A limited partnership may acquire properties by either the specific property method or the blind pool method.

53. B   The liability of a limited partner for the partnership's obligations is limited to the amount of the limited partner's investment in the partnership.

54. C   Diversification of risk and taxation as if one were a sole owner are both advantages of investing in a limited partnership.

55. B   By giving the organizers a percentage of the profits instead of a fixed fee, the organizers have a direct stake in the partnership's success.

56. A   The risk of an investor losing his money is known as downside risk.

57. C   An investor in a partnership should be prepared to stay with the partnership until the properties are refinanced or sold, and should be aware of the difficulties of selling shares for the proportional worth of the investor's interest.

58. B   The Securities and Exchange Commission administers the federal laws which regulate limited partnerships.

59. A   The disclosure statement given to prospective investors in a limited partnership is known as a prospectus.

60. A   A large undertaking offered to investors across state lines will require a more complete disclosure statement than will a group forming a limited partnership among themselves.

61. B   Blue-sky laws permit state governments to halt the sale of an investment opportunity.

62. C   Successful real estate investing requires effort and courage. Luck has surprisingly little to do with success.

Investment Match-up
(Suggested Solutions)

1. Corporate executive: III, IV
Reasons: high tax bracket, substantial money available for investment, must have professional management.

2. Married couple 57 and 55 years old: II
Reasons: This would comfortably fit their available assets, not be too risky, and offer them part-time work as live-in managers.

3. Young couple: I, V
Reasons: This couple does not appear to have enough money for a larger purchase. Also, they need professional management. With regard to V, a local real estate agent might be engaged to manage it. Both I and V provide tax shelter benefits.

4. Group of doctors: III, IV
Reasons: large down payment available, need for tax shelter, need for professional management.

5. Bachelor, age 38: I, II, V
Reasons: limited down payment (number II may require junior financing), probably has some time to manage the property, tax shelter is needed.

Additional Math Questions

The following practice questions are typical of the calculations tested on real estate license examinations. Your ability to solve these quickly, easily and accurately will greatly aid you in passing real estate tests as well as when you buy and sell property for yourself and others.

Commission Problems

1. A house sells for $122,000 and the brokerage commission is 6.25% of the selling price. The commission is
   A. $6,250
   B. $7,320
   C. $7,625
   D. $9,375

2. A broker is to earn a fee of 6% of the sales price of a house. If the house is listed for $98,000 and is sold for $3,000 less than that, what will the broker earn?
   A. $5,700
   B. $5,880
   C. $6,000
   D. $6,060

3. A seller will pay a broker $1,000 for advertising plus 4% of the sales price. If the property sells for $250,000, how much does the broker get?
   A. $1,000
   B. $9,000
   C. $10,000
   D. $11,000

4. Last year, Sue Salesperson sold $1,000,000 worth of property. Half of it was from her own listings on which she received 4% of the sales price and the other half was from properties listed by others on which she earned 2% of the sales price. What was Sally's average rate of commission for the year?
   A. 2%
   B. 3%
   C. 4%
   D. 6%

5. Last year, Broker Boone earned 6% on $1,500,000 in property he listed and sold, 2% on $2,500,000 in property his sales staff listed and sold, 1% on $3,000,000 in property his sales staff listed that was sold by other brokers, and 1% on $2,700,000 in property listed by other brokers and sold by Boone's sales staff. All totalled, how much did Broker Boone earn last year?
   A. $50,000
   B. $57,000
   C. $90,000
   D. $197,000

6. Continuing the above problem: Broker Boone found that 50% of the commissions on property he listed and sold went to overhead, and 75% of his portion of commissions earned by his sales staff went to overhead. After paying overhead, how much did Broker Boone net last year?
   A. $26,750
   B. $71,750
   C. $80,250
   D. $125,250

7. What price should a house be sold for so a broker can receive a commission of 6% and a seller net $79,500. (Round to the nearest one hundred dollars.)
   A. $84,600
   B. $84,300
   C. $84,200
   D. $79,500

8. Homeowner Harry wants $90,000 for his house after closing costs of $975 and the broker wants a 6% commission. At what price must the property be sold to achieve these results? Round up to the nearest whole dollar.
   A. $90,975
   B. $95,800
   C. $96,720
   D. $96,782

9. When selling an apartment building, a broker charges 5% on the first $100,000, 4% on the next $200,000, 3% on the next $1,000,000, and 2% above that. On a property sold for $6,500,000, how much will the commission be?
   A. $104,000
   B. $134,000
   C. $147,000
   D. $152,000

10. Salesperson Fran just received a $3,300 commission check from her broker for her part in a sale. If Fran received 75% of what the broker received, and the broker received 50% of the commission generated by the sale, and the property was listed and sold at a 5.5% commission, how much did the property sell for?
    A. $48,400
    B. $80,000
    C. $90,000
    D. $160,000

11. Salesperson Silly lists a house worth $100,000 for 50% over that amount. Getting no buyers, the price is reduced by $30,000. Still there are no buyers and the price is reduced 20% and the property sells. At what price did the property sell?
    A. $96,000
    B. $100,000
    C. $130,000
    D. $150,000

12. Broker Billy's commission policy for managing rental property is one-quarter of the first month's rent to find a tenant plus 5% of each month's rent. Owner Ozzie has a fully-occupied five-unit building where each unit rents for $400 per month. If, in a typical year, two units become vacant and are rented, how much can Ozzie expect to pay Billy per year to manage this property?
    A. $200
    B. $1,200
    C. $1,400
    D. $2,000

Distance, Area and Land Description Problems

13. A 12' x 15' room will cost $400 to carpet. How much is this per square yard?
    A. $2,22
    B. $20.00
    C. $22.22
    D. $180.00

14. A man with a square lot that is 190 feet on each side wants to fence it in completely. Fencing costs $6.00 per lineal foot installed. How much will the fence cost?
    A. $1,140
    B. $2,280
    C. $4,560
    D. $9,120

15. A lot owner purchased a strip of land adjacent to his lot for $2,000. The strip of land was 8'3" wide and 75'6" long. How much did he pay per square foot?
   A. $3.18
   B. $3.19
   C. $3.20
   D. $3.21

16. Farmer Fred buys the NE 1/4 and the E 1/2 of the SE 1/4 for $360,000. How many acres and how much per acre is this?
   A.   160 acres at $2,250 per acre
   B.   320 acres at $1,125 per acre
   C.   240 acres at $1,500 per acre
   D.   360 acres at $1,000 per acre

17. How many square feet are in the lot shown here?
   A.   4,000
   B.   5,000
   C.   5,200
   D.   6,500

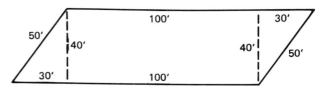

18. How many square feet are in Lot G?
   A.   7,875.0
   B.   9,060.2
   C.   10,093.5
   D.   10,800.0

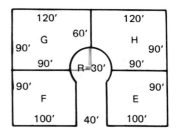

19. An L-shaped house has the dimensions shown plus a 15' x 25' patio and a 20' x 20' garage. If construction costs are $52 per square foot for the house, $3 per square foot for the patio, and $15 per square foot for the garage, what is the total of these costs?
   A. $27,925
   B. $59,125
   C. $72,800
   D. $79,925

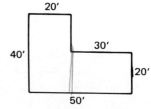

20. Because local zoning laws allow a greater density of apartment units on parcels of land over 15,000 square feet in size, they sell for $6.00 per square foot while smaller lots sell for $4.00 per square foot. Investor Iris owns a 6,000 sqft lot she just bought for $24,000 and can buy the 5,000 sqft lot next door for $20,000. Also contiguous to her is a 6,000 sqft lot that is not yet for sale. If she offered $5.00 per square foot for it and got it, how much plottage (increased) value will she have created?
    A. $28,000
    B. $34,000
    C. $68,000
    D. $102,000

21. Based on the section of land shown here, all of the following are correct EXCEPT:
    A. A is the SE 1/4 and contains 160 acres
    B. B is the W 1/2 of the SW 1/4 and contains 80 acres
    C. C is the NE 1/4 of the SW 1/4 and contains 20 acres
    D. D is the N 1/2 and contains 320 acres.

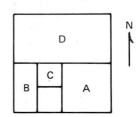

22. An industrial site of 2.6 acres is offered for sale for $250,000. On a square foot basis, how much is this?
    A. $0.45
    B. $1.04
    C. $1.13
    D. $2.21

23. The land description, "Due South 400 feet, thence due West 300 feet, thence Northeasterly 500 feet back to the point of beginning" describes a
    A. rectangle containing 200,000 sqft.
    B. rectangle containing 120,000 sqft.
    C. triangle containing 100,000 sqft.
    D. triangle containing 60,000 sqft.

24. The basement for a new home requires an excavation that is 45 feet by 27 feet by 9 feet deep. At a cost of $6.00 per cubic yard to dig, what will be the cost of this excavation?
    A. $405.00
    B. $1,481.48
    C. $1,822.50
    D. $2,430.00

25. How many posts are necessary to make a fence around a 36 ft. by 36 ft. corral if the posts are centered 4 feet apart?
    A. 35
    B. 36
    C. 37
    D. 324

26. An office building is 42 feet wide and 60 feet long. The entire building has a concrete sidewalk around it 6 feet wide and 3 inches deep. How many cubic yards of concrete is this?
    A.   6.33
    B.   8.00
    C.   12.67
    D.   93.33

27. If bricks sell for 25 cents each and are 8 inches long, what will it cost to encircle a circular flower garden that has a radius of 6 feet? Assume the bricks are laid end-to-end and they touch.
    A. $7.07
    B. $7.25
    C. $14.13
    D. $14.25

Taxes, Insurance and Proration Problems

28. The assessed value of a house is $90,000 and the tax rate is 8 mills. What is the tax?
    A. $72.00
    B. $720.00
    C. $112.50
    D. $1,125.00

29. The property taxes on a house are $1,000 per year and the house is assessed at 82.5% of its $120,000 market value. The tax rate on this house is nearest
    A.   10.1 mills
    B. $10.10 per hundred
    C.   9.9 mills
    D. $99.00 per thousand

30. Property insurance is offered for 25 cents per $100 of coverage on struc-tures. A house has a market value of $250,000 of which 30% is the land. A policy to fully protect the structure will cost
    A. $175.00
    B. $437.50
    C. $625.00
    D. $1,750

31. A property that cost $360 to insure last year, now costs $378 to insure. What percent increase is this?
    A.   1.80%
    B.   3.78%
    C.   4.76%
    D.   5.00%

32. Because a policy has been cancelled part way through the year by the insured, the insurance company will refund 44% of the premium. If the insured paid $250 for the policy, what will the refund be?
    A. $110
    B. $140
    C. $250
    D. $568

33. A one-year property insurance policy will be passed along to the buyer at closing. The policy covers April 1 through March 31 and cost the seller $180. The closing is on June 10th with the day of closing going to the seller. What proration is made?
    A. Charge buyer $35
    B. Charge buyer $145
    C. Charge seller $145
    D. Charge seller $35

34. The property tax year is the calendar year. The closing is January 10th and the annual tax bill of $720 has not been paid. At closing
    A. charge buyer $720
    B. charge seller $700
    C. charge buyer $20
    D. charge seller $20

35. A conveyance tax of $0.55 per $500, or fraction thereof, on the full amount of the transaction is charged plus $5 to record the deed. On a property sold for $97,750, the total of these two fees would be
    A. $53,76
    B. $107.53
    C. $107.80
    D. $112.80

36. The City of Ralston obtains 14.2% of its revenue from sales taxes, 20.1% from state revenue sharing, 5.7% from licenses and permits, and the balance from property taxes. If the city must raise $50,000,000, how much of that will come from property taxes?
    A. $20 million
    B. $30 million
    C. $40 million
    D. $50 million

37. Darryl owns a duplex where he lives in one unit and rents out the other unit. Darryl sells the duplex and it will settle on September 20th. If the monthly rent of $450 was paid on the first of September, and the day of closing belongs to the seller, what is the proration?
    A. Charge seller $150
    B. Charge buyer $150
    C. Charge buyer $300
    D. Charge seller $300

38. Smith sold for cash a small house which was unencumbered. Smith's closing expenses amounted to $450 plus a broker's commission of 7% of the selling price. At the closing, Smith received a check for $36,750. What was the selling price?
    A. $36,750
    B. $37,200
    C. $40,000
    D. $42,800

39. At closing, the abstract fee was $85, the title insurance $150, the closing agent $200 and miscellaneous charges of $45. If the seller paid 65% of these costs, and the buyer paid the remaining 35%, how much more did the seller pay than the buyer?
    A. $480
    B. $312
    C. $168
    D. $144

40. Zahn is looking at a home that would require monthly interest payments of $1,200 and annual property taxes of $1,200. If he is in a 30% income tax bracket and both interest and property taxes are fully deductible for him, how much less will his annual income taxes be as a result of this deduction?
    A. $360
    B. $390
    C. $4,320
    D. $4,680

Financing and Appraisal Problems

41. What is the interest on a $123,000 loan for one month if the annual rate
    of interest is 11 1/4%?
    A. $1,383.75
    B. $1,153.13
    C. $1,125.00
    D. $937.50

42. A loan is made for 80% loan-to-value on a $100,000 house. If the
    interest rate on the loan is 9.6% per annum, what is the first month's
    interest?
    A. $640
    B. $800
    C. $1,000
    D. $1,200

43. A $100,000, 30-year, fully-amortized, fixed-rate loan is made for 9.5%
    annual interest. The monthly principal and interest payment is $840.87.
    Calculate the principal balance owing after the second monthly payment
    has been made.
    A. $98,318.26
    B. $98,416.66
    C. $99,901.21
    D. $99,950.80

44. A buyer and seller agree to share in the ratio of 3 to 2, respectively,
    the 5 loan points on a new $60,000 FHA loan. How much more does this
    cost the buyer than the seller?
    A. $600
    B. $1,200
    C. $1,800
    D. $3,000

45. A lender offers fixed rate, 30-year, 80% loan-to-value loans at a monthly
    payment of $8.78 per $1,000 of loan amount on homes selling for between
    $90,000 and $100,000. How much more are the monthly payments for a
    $98,000 house than for a $93,000 house?
    A. $35.12
    B. $43.90
    C. $660.26
    D. $869.22

46. A $90,000 loan agreement with a bank calls for a builder to borrow
    $30,000 for 9 months, $30,000 for 6 months, and $30,000 for 3 months.
    The interest rate is 12% per year and interest is charged by the month
    on the money borrowed. How much interest will the builder pay?
    A. $1,800
    B. $2,700
    C. $5,400
    D. $8,100

47. Brown borrowed $10,000 on an interest-only note secured by a mortgage. Interest was payable monthly, and over the 12-month term of the note interest totalled $1,000. What was the rate of interest on the loan?
    A. 8.00%
    B. 8.33%
    C. 10.0%
    D. 12.0%

48. The Crane Company just made the first monthly payment on a new loan. The interest amounted to $2,400, the loan carries a 10% annual interest rate, and the loan-to-value ratio is 75%. For how much did the property appraise?
    A. $240,000
    B. $288,000
    C. $384,000
    D. $2,400,000

49. A buyer wants an FHA 203(b) loan to buy a $65,000 house. The FHA will insure a loan for 97% of the first $50,000 of the purchase price and 95% of the remaining $15,000. There is also a mortgage insurance premium (MIP) of 3.8% of the loan amount to be added to the loan amount. With the MIP included, the loan will be for
    A. $62,750.00
    B. $65,000.00
    C. $65,134.50
    D. $66,950.00

50. Continuing the previous problem: to make the loan, the lender will charge 2 points which the buyer will pay at closing. In order to close, how much cash will the buyer need for the down payment and points combined?
    A. $1,300.00
    B. $1,302.69
    C. $2,250.00
    D. $3,552.69

Answers for Additional Math Questions

Commission Problems

1. C $122,000 x .0625 = $7,625

2. A   ($98,000 - $3,000) x .06 = $5,700

3. D $250,000 x .04 + $1,000 = $11,000

4. B   50% x 4% + 50% x 2% = .02 + .01 = .03 = 3%

5. D $1,500,000 x .06 = $ 90,000
       $2,500,000 x .02 = $ 50,000
       $3,000,000 x .01 = $ 30,000
       $2,700,000 x .01 = $ 27,000
              Total   = $197,000 answer

6. B $90,000 x .50 = $ 45,000 for overhead
       $107,000 x .75 = $ 80,250 for overhead
              Total   = $125,250 for overhead
       $197,000 - $125,250 = $71,750 net to Boone, answer

7. A $79,500 ÷ .94 = $84,574.47 round to $84,600

8. D   ($90,000 + $975) ÷ .94 = $96,782

9. C $100,000 x .05   = $ 5,000 on first $100,000
       $200,000 x .04   = $ 8,000 on next $200,000
       $1,000,000 x .03 = $ 30,000 on next $1,000,000
       $5,200,000 x .02 = $104,000 on last $5,200,000
              Total   = $147,000 answer

10. D $3,300 ÷ .75 = $4,400 what her broker received
        $4,400 ÷ .50 = $8,800 total commission on the sale
        $8,800 ÷ .055 = $160,000 selling price of the property

11. A $100,000 x 1.50 = $150,000 listing price
        $150,000 - $30,000 = $120,000 new listing price
        $120,000 x .80 = $96,000 selling price after 20% reduction

12. C   5 units x $400 x 12 months x 5% = $1,200 ongoing 5% commission
        2 units x $400 x .25 = $200 for two vacancies
        $1,200 + $200 = $1,400 total, answer

Distance, Area and Land Description Problems

13. B   12' x 15' ÷ 9 sqft/yd = 20 square yards
        $400 ÷ 20 = $20 per sqyd, answer

14.   C   190' x 4 sides x $6.00/ft = $4,560

15.   D   8'3" = 8.25'   75'6" = 75.5'
          8.25' x 75.5' = 622.875 sqft
          $2,000 ÷ 622.875 = $3.21 per sqft, answer

16.   C   1/4 x 640 + 1/2 x 1/4 x 640 = 240 acres, answer
          $360,000 ÷ 240 = $1,500 per acre, answer

17.   C   (130' + 130') ÷ 2 x 40' = 5,200 sqft

18.   C   120' x 90'   = 10,800.0 sqft area of Lot G not counting street
          3.14 x 30'^{2} ÷ 4 =   706.5 sqft area street takes off of lot
                    Equals   10,093.5 sqft area of Lot G, answer

19.   D   (40' x 20' + 30' x 20') x $52 = $72,800 for house
                       15' x 25' x $3 = $ 1,125 for patio
                       20' x 20' x $15 = $ 6,000 for garage
                             Total   = $79,925 answer

20.   A   Lot #1 6,000 sqft at $4 = $24,000 lot now owned
          Lot #2 5,000 sqft at $4 = $20,000 lot next door
          Lot #3 6,000 sqft at $5 = $30,000 proposed offer
          Totals 17,000 sqft $74,000 amount invested
          Value of 17,000 sqft at $6 = $102,000
          $102,000 - $74,000 = $28,000 answer

21.   C   Parcel C is the NE 1/4 of the SW 1/4.
          It contains 1/4 x 1/4 x 640 acres = 40 acres

22.   D   2.6 acres x 43,560 sqft per acre = 113,256 sqft
          $250,000 ÷ 113,256 = $2.21 per sqft, answer

23.   D   1/2 x b x h = area
          1/2 x 300' x 400' = 60,000 sqft

24.   D   45' x 27' x 9' ÷ 27 cuft/yd x $6 = $2,430

25.   B   36' x 4 sides ÷ 4 feet per post = 36 posts
          (Note that if the fence did not return to its point of beginning,
          an extra post would be necessary. Drawing a picture will help you
          see this.)

26.   C   (54' x 6' x 2 sides) + (60' x 6' x 2 sides) x .25' ÷ 27 = 12.67 cuyds
          (Note that the best way to solve this is to draw a picture of the
          building and its sidewalks. This will show that increasing 42' to
          54' will account for the corners.)

27.   D π x d = circumference   (Note that d (diameter) = 2 x r (radius))
          3.14 x 2 x 6 = 37.68 ft circumference
          37.68' x 12" ÷ 8" per brick = 56.52 bricks
          But only whole bricks can be purchased, therefore:
          57 bricks x $.25 each = $14.25 answer
          (Note that drawing a picture first will help you solve this.)

28. B $90,000 x .008 = $720

29. A $1,000 ÷ $120,000 ÷ .825 = 10.1 mills

30. B $250,000 x .70 x $.25 ÷ $100 = $437.50
          (Note that .70 is the percentage attributable to the structure.)

31. D   ($378 - $360) ÷ $360 = 5.00%

32. A $250 x .44 = $110 refund

33. B   The buyer will have the benefit of the policy for 20 days in June
          plus the following nine months. For this, the buyer owes the seller
          $145 computed as follows:
          $180 ÷ 12 = $15 per month x 9 months = $135
          $15 ÷ 30 = $.50 per day   x 20 days = $ 10
                                        Total   = $145

34. D $720 ÷ 12 months in a year = $60 per month
          $60 ÷ 30 days in a month   = $ 2 per day
          The 10 days which the seller has occupied the property but not yet
          paid the tax result in a 10 x $2 = $20 charge to the seller.

35. D $97,750 ÷ $500 = 195.5
          However, the rate is $.55 per $500 or fraction thereof; therefore,
          round up to 196 before multiplying: $196 x $.55 = $107.80
          To this add $5 for recording the deed for a total of:
          $107.80 + $5 = $112.80 answer

36. B   All other sources total 14.2% + 20.1% + 5.7% = 40%.
          This leaves 100% - 40% = 60% to come from property taxes.
          $50,000,000 x .60 = $30,000,000 answer

37. A   Of the $450 collected by the seller for September, $450 ÷ 30 x 10
          = $150 belongs to the buyer and is charged to the seller.

38. C   ($36,750 + $450) ÷ .93 = $40,000

39. D   ($85 + $150 + $200 + $45) x .65 = $312 seller paid
          ($85 + $150 + $200 + $45) x .35 = $168 buyer paid
                              Difference = $144 answer

40. D   ($1,200 x 12 months + $1,200) x .30 = $4,680

41. B $123,000 x .1125 ÷ 12 = $1,153.13

42. A $100,000 x .80 x .096 ÷ 12 = $640

43. C $100,000 x .095 ÷ 12   = $791.67 interest first month
        $840.87 - $791.67   = $49.20 principal reduction first month
        $100,000 - $49.20   = $99,950.80 loan balance after one monthly
                                  payment has been made
        $99,950.80 x .095 ÷ 12 = $791.28 interest second month
        $840.87 - $791.28   = $49.59 principal reduction second month
        $99,950.80 - $49.59   = $99,901.21 loan balance after second monthly
                                  payment has been made, answer

44. A   A ratio of 3 to 2 means
        three-fifths or 3 ÷ 5 = 60% to the buyer and
        two-fifths or 2 ÷ 5 = 40% to the seller.
        Five loan points on a $60,000 loan is .05 x $60,000 = $3,000
        $3,000 x .60 = $1,800 for the buyer
        $3,000 x .40 = $1,200 for the seller
            Difference = $ 600 answer

45. A $98,000 x .80 x $8.78 ÷ $1,000 = $688.35
        $93,000 x .80 x $8.78 ÷ $1,000 = $653.23
          Difference in monthly payment = $ 35.12 answer

46. C $30,000 x .12 ÷ 12 x 9 months = $2,700
        $30,000 x .12 ÷ 12 x 6 months = $1,800
        $30,000 x .12 ÷ 12 x 3 months = $ 900
                              Total = $5,400 answer

47. C $1,000 interest ÷ $10,000 = 10.0% rate of interest

48. C $2,400 x 12 months = $28,800 interest per year
        $28,800 ÷ 10% interest = $288,000 amount of loan
        $288,000 ÷ .75 L/V ratio = $384,000 property value, answer

49. C $50,000 x .97 = $48,500
        $15,000 x .95 = $14,250
            Total   = $62,750 basic loan amount
        $62,750 x .038 = $2,384.50 MIP
        Total loan = $62,750 + $2,384.50 = $65,134.50 answer

50. D $65,000 - $62,750 = $2,250.00 down payment
        $65,134.50 x .02 = $1,302.69 points on loan
                    Total = $3,552.69 answer